Tennyson Laureate

VALERIE PITT

TENNYSON LAUREATE

UNIVERSITY OF TORONTO PRESS

For
Austin and Katherine Farrer

Contents

Preface

WHEN I was young my father entertained his children with a variety of songs and poems learnt in the Army and at school. Some of them were simply popular and folk ballads, but his repertoire included a good deal of Tennyson, *The Revenge*, *The Charge of the Light Brigade*, and the *Morte d'Arthur*. I remember now the fresh splendour of the sound:

> So all day long the noise of battle roll'd
> Among the mountains, by the winter sea;
> Until King Arthur's table, man by man,
> Had fallen in Lyonnesse about their Lord,
> King Arthur.

But children do not write books about poetry: given the chance, they simply enjoy it, as they enjoy ice cream and fire-works and the other uncovenanted pleasures of growing up. Dons and critics have lost this innocence: they discriminate, despise and dispute, and the origin of this book was a donnish dispute, an argument I carried on for years with my colleague, the late S. L. Bethell. Dr Bethell, like many of his generation, was nostalgic for the Victorian era, for a solidity, a religion, a tradition, which I am convinced it never really possessed, or rather, which, with certain exceptions, its intelligentsia did not share. I see Leslie now, looking, not Victorian, but Elizabethan, like a miniature by Nicholas Hilliard grown superbly stout, standing in his Victorian drawing-room passionately (and perversely) defending the funeral lines of *Enoch Arden*. He was at that time making a collection of Tennysoniana, for he intended, some time, to write a defence of Tennyson. He never lived to do so. And I wish he had.

This is not a substitute for Dr Bethell's book. I suppose we disagreed on all subjects of importance—except one. He had brought from Cambridge the conviction, which Dr and Mrs Leavis preached to a

reluctant English school, that the study of literature is not the mild
amusement of cultured gentlemen, but a discipline vital to a sound and
healthy culture. I had the oral tradition, and a resentment of that
clerkish treason which, so to speak, withdrew itself fastidiously from
my father's songs and stories, and made 'literature' the preserve of the
connoisseur. Both of us believed that the exclusiveness of aesthetic
coteries, *the art for the connoisseur's sake* movement, was a betrayal of
English culture. And there is no doubt that the critical treatment of
Tennyson is a type case of this betrayal. Here is a poet who was
undoubtedly a popular, almost a mass poet, whose work, like Shakespeare's and Milton's, added a stratum to our verbal tradition, and this
is precisely the poet whom the critics of the twenties and thirties drew,
or attempted to draw, into the gardens of a private sensibility. We felt,
in spite of disagreements, that a judgment which praised *The Lady of
Shalott* because of its private and psychological symbolism, but
dismissed *The Charge of the Light Brigade* because of its public sentiment
was distorted from the beginning. And both of us had an anxiety to
recover Tennyson from the errors of this judgment. Had Dr Bethell
not died prematurely I would have left it to him: as it was, I felt free to
write this book.

Now since I do not feel that the study of literature ought to be the
preserve of the erudite, it was not written, primarily, for critics, or for
scholars, and, with one exception, all the quotations are from the most
easily accessible source. All the quotations from Tennyson, except
those from his juvenilia and early poems, are from the Oxford
Standard Tennyson, and no references are given. The references to
Carlyle are given not by page numbers, but by chapters because of the
variety of the editions of his work, and the fact that there is no standard
modern edition which is easily available to the common reader. The
quotations from Maurice's *Theological Essays* are from the modern, not
the Victorian edition of this work and, wherever possible, I have
referred to the most recent edition of any book I have quoted. I have
made an exception for Sir Charles Lyell's *Principles of Geology*. After
the publication of *The Origin of Species*, Lyell, very honourably,
modified his opposition to Lamarck's theories, and, as a result, all
editions of *The Principles* after 1859 differ radically from that which
Tennyson studied in the late thirties. My quotations are therefore taken
from the first edition of *The Principles*.

The great reward of studying Tennyson is that it is a 'common
pursuit': help comes from all sides. I am especially indebted to

Professor Willey, and Mr A. L. Munby of King's College for the loan of books, and to Sir Charles Tennyson and the Librarian of the Harvard Library for information about Tennyson manuscripts. I have examined the manuscripts themselves in the Library of Trinity College, Cambridge, in the Fitzwilliam Museum, Cambridge, and in the Usher Art Gallery in Lincoln, and am grateful not only for the assistance of these institutions, but for the kindness of their librarians and curators.

All my friends have put up with this book for some time now, have read, discussed and listened to it, but none of them has endured more of the throes of its composition than Dr and Mrs Farrer to whom I owe the pleasures of gratitude, not only for reading and correcting the manuscript, and for help in scanning Tennyson's more difficult poems, but for an endless encouragement and affection without which I should never have finished the work.

V. P.

Chapter I

The Status of Tennyson in Criticism

IT is the curious fate of literary criticism, Arnold's 'fresh and free play' of the mind unhampered by dogma or definition, to create the orthodoxy it strives to avoid. A single book, a single article, even, if the critic is persuasive or eminent enough, a single sentence will control the thinking of a whole generation. Opinions, and, what is more important, the questions asked about writers or literary movements will for thirty years remain within the limits of an innovating criticism. Indeed, between the first plaudits of an 'in group' and the last dreary flattery of the G.C.E. paper, critical theories have a very long and active life. From these literary conformities Tennyson has suffered more than most, and especially from the dogmas formulated in the twenties. In the forties Auden turned the accepted orthodoxy into neat epigrams. Tennyson, he said,

> Had the finest ear of any English Poet; he was also undoubtedly the stupidest; there was little about melancholia that he didn't know; there was little else that he did.[1]

His discussion of Tennyson begins from, and is coloured by the assumption that Tennyson's great achievement as a poet was the mastery of mood, especially of morbid mood, and this was an assumption which the confidence of Sir Harold Nicolson's *Tennyson* made a shibboleth of literary opinion. Nicolson removed the portrait of the prophet poet from the gallery of literary portraits and replaced its Wattsian magnificence with a smaller piece of a brooding neurotic. He thought it a better picture. The ability to express states of the morbid mind was to him, if not the best, at least an excellent thing in poetry; the versifying of moral attitudes was not. Other critics found this romantic preoccupation with states of mind and sensation a vicious element in poetry. It was a disease, a verbal debility, which Tennyson passed on to his Victorian and Edwardian successors. In *New Bearings in English Poetry*, Dr Leavis consistently describes a certain sweetness in late Victorian writing as Tennysonian, and contrasts its melodious diffuseness with the stringency of Hopkins's writing. He places the responsibility for the unnatural aesthetic distinction between art and reality squarely on Tennyson's shoulders. Tennyson withdrew into a protected paradise of 'lyrical beauty', and, in consequence, his verse lacks the almost tangible quality of experience which we find in Hopkins or the later Yeats. Between these two opinions about Tennyson's mastery of 'metric and melancholy' the reading public was left with a Tennyson incurably dilettante, a poet who could not usefully write about anything but his own emotional states, but who, because he wrote about them, could not avoid unreality.

This 'metric and melancholy' doctrine was not the product of that healthy distaste which every new generation feels for the hackneyed virtues of its predecessors. Bradley, lecturing to the British Academy in 1916, on *The Reaction against Tennyson*, battles against an already established prejudice. Like W. P. Ker in an earlier lecture,[2] he defends Tennyson against the inevitable injustice of the new men who deprecated the didactic and admired lyrical perfection. They disliked Tennyson because so much of his later verse had an explicit moral meaning, and Bradley, like Nicolson, tries to persuade them that he also possessed the gifts they admired; that he was a 'lyricist'. But he is not concerned with the poet's personal neurosis, nor does he suggest that Tennyson was uncertain or timid in the convictions of his middle years. For between Bradley's audience and Nicolson's public there was a great gulf fixed. Bradley was analysing the literary opinions of a generation for whom literature was primarily *style*, and content a gross interference with the perfection of form, but Nicolson was writing after the First World War, for a generation whose poets had died a violent death. 'The poetry', they said, 'is in the pity', and their rejection of Tennyson's laureate didacticism was not aesthetic but fiercely moral. Hugh I'Anson Fausset, whose *Tennyson* was published in the same year as Nicolson's, regarded the Tennyson of the *Enoch Arden* period as something worse than a pedestrian poet. He was the embodiment of the smug, materialist, Victorian ethic. He fostered and encouraged, in such poems as *Enoch Arden, On the Jubilee* and the *Idylls of the King,* the complacency which produced the squalor of industrial civilisation. His flattery of the Queen-Empress, his outrageous glorification of military exploits made poetry the instrument of jingoism, and was in part responsible for the blind patriotism which whirled the British public into the holocaust of the Kaiser's war. Nicolson shared Fausset's views of the public Tennyson, and this 'reaction against Tennyson' was a far more serious business than the reaction of the aesthetes. It was part of the revolt against the 'old men', the philosophy of those who told with such high zest

> To children ardent for some desperate glory,
> The old Lie: Dulce et decorum est
> Pro patria mori.

Nicolson's contention, which is also Fausset's, is that Tennyson's real genius was falsified and betrayed by his yielding to the pressure of the Victorian ethic. They rediscovered the young Tennyson, the Tennyson before *In Memoriam,* and found in him a poet whose experience chimed with that of their own generation. The Kaiser's war was a traumatic experience, those who endured it and its aftermath of social change scarcely realised how deeply shaken they were,

> Moved from beneath with doubt and fear.

Tennyson's extraordinary insight into the darkened and disturbed mind was something which spoke to their condition, which was alive and precious to them. Nicolson's emphasis on the mood poetry was almost inevitable in the twenties. It was partly the product of a literary fashion, a fashion with a leaning towards the French symbolists, and the beginnings of a curiosity about psychology, but still more of the needs and tensions of an unlucky generation. *Tennyson: Aspects of his Life, Character and Poetry* is a gentlemanly book, carefully not sharp, not strident, easily at home with an unpedantic culture, but the vision behind it is not urbane, but uneasy, disturbed and distorted.

The natural history of the literary reaction is better illustrated by Dr Leavis's *New Bearings.* The aesthetes looked for beauty of form and despised Tennyson's didacticism: Dr Leavis and the critics associated with him in *Scrutiny* disliked and distrusted the literary attitudes represented by a reverential breathing of the word 'lyricism'. Leavis would agree with Bradley and with Nicolson that Tennyson's work displays lyrical

qualities, but he does not think them admirable. And it is just to say
that his judgment is, in every sense, more serious than Nicolson's
because, for him, criticism is a more serious activity. *New Bearings* is
the exploration of a state of literary culture and that, as always for Dr
Leavis, implies the imaginative life, the moral sensibility of a generation.
He sees Tennyson not so much as a bad poet but as a willing victim of a
false tradition whose influence vitiated that sensibility, and made it
difficult for his successors to discover a masculine use of language. There
is certainly a limp mildew, an unpleasant greenery yallery, about the
literary conventions which Dr Leavis describes, but it is permissible, at
this distance of time, to wonder if his excellent analysis of a contemporary need did not condition his view of a past achievement. But there
was a necessary stringency in his approach, for it is impossible to feel
that our understanding either of Tennyson, or of the functions of
literature are much assisted by this kind of thing:

> 'Poor fellow' thought I [the 'fellow' is Tennyson's gardener
> who had spoken of Tennyson's irregular attendance at
> Church] 'how little do you realise that the dead poet there, in
> the Aldworth sanctuary, has done more than any prophet of
> song, for this past forty years, to keep our land and people
> near to God. He needs not apology for non-attendance at
> Haslemere Church, who, a votary of the Temple's inner
> shrine, was always at Divine Worship.'[3]

The adulation of Tennyson, of which this is not too extreme an
example, substantiates Fausset's complaint and Nicolson's, and it tends
to fossilise a particular attitude to literature and to morals. If Tennyson
was to be read as a live poet the legend of the prophet of song had to be
shattered, and the poet's work subjected to a proper criticism.

Unfortunately the morbid Tennyson seems, in his turn, to have
acquired the privileges of a legend. Thirty, forty years after Nicolson's
book two full-length studies of Tennyson, both by American scholars,*
still present what is virtually Nicolson's Tennyson, the double creature,
the private poet uneasily united and for ever divided from the con-
scientious Laureate. Indeed, since the twenties, critics have confined
themselves to analysing, by means of the verbal techniques of practical
criticism and the interpretative methods of psychoanalysis, the various
expressions of Tennysonian melancholy. In Mr Killham's collection,

---

* P. F. Baum: *Tennyson Sixty Years After*, Chapel Hill, 1948. J. H. Buckley:
Tennyson, Oxford, 1960.

Critical Essays of the Poetry of Tennyson, there are three examinations of 'Tears, idle tears': this is almost symbolic. There are of course exceptions to this preoccupation. Sir Charles Tennyson's *Six Tennyson Essays* is written in the tradition of an older, more academic criticism. He is moved to discuss the content as well as the tone of his grandfather's poetry, and to commit himself in detail about those metrical techniques which, for forty years, we have praised and not examined. Sir Charles gives, too, a reasoned account of Tennyson's approach to social and political questions, and it is on the issue of the poet's social conscience that solid orthodoxy begins to crack. The gravamen of Nicolson's attack was that Tennyson, to use Mr Eliot's words, became the 'surface flatterer of his time', that he allowed his moral sensibility to be dulled by the routine conformities of his age. But in a sensitive and important essay W. W. Robson says:

> Tennyson was one of the most intelligent and morally concerned men of his time, and I cannot see why it should be so complacently granted that he could not, in the nature of the case, write poetry about these things.[4]

The things are the social questions which Tennyson treats in *Maud*, and *Locksley Hall Sixty Years After*. Mr Robson does not, I think, allow for the fatigue of mind, part age, part grief, which Tennyson was obviously suffering at the time when he wrote *Locksley Hall Sixty Years After*, but he does recognise that it and the rest of Tennyson's poetry were 'aimed at a whole moral community of which he is one member.'[5] This sentence may well be a turning point in our understanding of Tennyson. All the same Mr Robson still sees two Tennysons, 'the "committed" Victorian intellectual' and 'the most unstrenuous, lonely, and poignant of poets'.[6] We are still within the limits of the legend.

The substitution of a brooding boy for a monolithic sage, gave us, at first, a much more interesting poet and a more exciting poetry. Auden, for instance, writes about Tennyson's 'doubt', not as an intellectual phenomenon, a contribution to the 'thought of his age', but as something more fundamental:

> Two questions: Who am I? Why do I exist? and the panic fear of their remaining unanswered—doubt is too intellectual a term for such a vertigo of anxiety—seem to have obsessed him all his life.[7]

This emphasis on the emotional state, the 'vertigo of anxiety', rather than the rational difficulty, makes Tennyson's poetry about doubt at once more personal and more universal. Who now cares much for religious difficulties about the age of the earth or the nebular hypothesis? But the inner anxiety of a mind insecure in the conventions of its own culture, at once desiring and rejecting the complex of beliefs on which it depends, must remain interesting for this is a state which is common, or potentially common, to all civilised and sensitive intelligences. The personal opens on the universal, for Tennyson's apprehensions of his own state clothe and express themselves in common symbols. Working on the assumption that Tennyson withdrew from reality to art, scholars are able to show how poems like *Tithonus* and *The Hesperides*, which appeared to an earlier generation as merely rhapsodic, possess an inner and significant coherence.[8] Moreover a tradition of criticism which considers Tennyson as an emotional, not as a philosophic or moral poet, also sees him as sharing in the movement of European culture, a movement of which he was, explicitly, deeply suspicious. Dr Leavis reminded us of Yeats's Tennysonian phase, and we may also recall Mallarmé's[9] interest in him, and Eliot's. For there was a current of influence from Tennyson to Poe, from Poe to Baudelaire, from Baudelaire to the Symbolists and outwards, which was alive for more than fifty years. In technique, in atmosphere, sometimes even in content, Tennyson's work has surprising affinities, and it is a gain to literature when such relationships are recognised.

But Tennyson is not, though Nicolson would sometimes like to think so, a *poète maudit*. The limitations of viewing him purely as a 'morbid mystic' without the courage of his insight appear as soon as this is suggested. When Nicolson says that Tennyson might have been a greater Swinburne if he had not spoiled himself, we are aware that it was not an imposed sense of duty but something in the man's character which kept Tennyson both from Swinburne's variety of failure and Baudelaire's kind of achievement. Even favourite 'morbid' poems, like *The Two Voices*, assert the stringently normal:

> Whatever crazy sorrow saith,
> No life that breathes with human breath
> Has ever truly long'd for death.
>
> 'Tis life, whereof our nerves are scant,
> Oh life, not death, for which we pant;
> More life, and fuller, that I want.

These passages are sometimes said to represent not what Tennyson felt, but what he felt he ought to feel, and because of this they are supposed to lack the imaginative intensity of the passages of despair. Even so they represent a struggle with the dominating mood, an attempt by the will to impose order and sanity on inchoate emotion, a struggle not without its own passion. There was never, even in the young Tennyson, any kind of *nostalgie de la boue*, he is not enamoured of the perverse but struggles to escape it.

It would be easier if he *were* a decadent struggling in moments of repentance for then the critic would be spared the burden of 'saving the phenomena'. It is not only the expression of moral sentiment which defies the theory. No stretch of the imagination can turn the Ballad of *The Revenge* into a poem of personal mood, or *Northern Farmer* into a glorification of Imperialism. The orthodox critic can only manage the sober and settled element in Tennyson either by ignoring it or by refusing to allow that his imagination is at all engaged with it. It is regarded as a deviation from the line of his special genius, forced on him, first by the insistence of his Cambridge friends that a poet must have a mission, and afterwards as a means of retaining public favour. He can be allowed to be a good poet in his youth only by being both a fool and a hypocrite in his middle years. For it is axiomatic in this doctrine that when Tennyson writes as a civic poet, in the period of the *Idylls of the King* and the *Idylls of the Hearth*, he was pandering to the prejudices of his generation, and betraying his gifts. Another version of the doctrine holds, not that Tennyson is too moral, but that he is not moral enough. He never integrated his imaginative insight and his moral fervour, so that he is moral without conviction. Sometimes this statement of the case comes near to declaring that Tennyson was not a good moral poet because he was not an orthodox Christian: a view which condemns itself.[10] But all schools agree that Tennyson's real development stopped in 1842: after that his poetry is either unworthy of consideration, or repeats the content and technique of earlier work.

This opinion of 'the later Tennyson' depends on two unstated presuppositions. One is an assumption about the contemporary response to his work, the second, and more important, is the curious belief that to be a good moral and civic poet one must be an intellectual. 'Of English poets', Auden says, 'Tennyson was undoubtedly the stupidest; there was little about melancholia that he didn't know; there was little else that he did.' This is just not true. Tennyson was, for instance, as an amateur in the biological sciences, rather better informed than a good many of his contemporaries. He appears to have inspired the respect of men as eminent in their own fields as Gladstone, Jowett, Maurice and Huxley. They thought he possessed a wisdom deeper than the mechanical knowledge of scientist or scholar. This respect for the poet is part of the Victorian *Weltanschauung*, and perhaps a Victorian definition of wisdom would not quite correspond with Auden's. His meaning is more apparent when he describes Tennyson as 'easy to psycho-analyse' . . . 'knowing nothing' would almost seem to equal 'limited in emotional experience', and 'stupid', one surmises, 'simple, naïve, uncomplicated in his response to things'. 'Stupid' has other overtones as well: it is the opposite of 'clever', and is the adjective most easily applied by a mind perpetually analysing and defining, everlastingly making epigrams about its state and everyone else's, to a mind which is intensely intuitive and slow in movement. In some ways Tennyson's understanding of things *is* what Auden would call 'stupid'—that is, it is an understanding in which the discursive intellect is largely passive, in which the mind comes to know by groping for the shape and feeling of things rather than by striving for exact verbal definition. Tennyson's was a mind not easily led to explain things to itself in terms of rational analysis: he thinks, it would be reasonable to say, in the arrangement of sounds, in symbols and in pictures. His interpretation of experience was slow in forming itself, moving not by the arrangement of neat conceptual counters, but in a long organic growth. His mental life was, if the distinction be admitted, feminine, not masculine, contemplative, not active. Auden, and some other critics, in describing Tennyson as 'knowing nothing', have forgotten that human experience differs in its effect on different natures. The brooding mind makes more of a limited experience than the minds of brisker, less introspective men. Emotion, especially strong emotion, is rarely understood in the moment of feeling; its quality, and its place in the rhythm of experience is revealed only after the event. Such reflective minds as Tennyson's are always attempting to find in their emotions a coherence, a continuity which as it were makes sense of them:

> I see in part
> That all, as in some piece of art,
> Is toil co-operant to an end.

It is because his mind was of this kind that Tennyson's major poems were not works planned in advance. In most of them an immediate expression of feeling is later reconsidered and subordinated to a more or less coherent theme. Tennyson discovered and created the underlying themes of *In Memoriam*, *Maud* and the *Idylls of the King* while he was working on them. The unity and meaning of the poems grew under his shaping mind. *Maud* is perhaps the most interesting example of this retrospective shaping. The poem was built outwards from the core of a single beautiful lyric, 'O that 'twere possible', written in the period after Hallam's death. Fifteen or so years later Sir John Simeon suggested that it might be used as the basis of a longer poem and, working under this stimulus, Tennyson's imagination drew out the dramatic possibilities of the poem. He moved from it to the distracted and disturbed mind which would and could speak it, and from thence to the full narrative of *Maud*. But that narrative carries with it a considerable understanding both of the neurotic personality, and of those conditions in society which produce neurosis. The explorations made within the framework of the *Maud* narrative have to be discussed later; the important thing is that they are the work of a feeling mind. The word 'mind' is as significant here as the word 'feeling', for in rational beings insight does not cease to be rational when it ceases to be analytic. This 'feeling mind' is at work in other poems, but, where *Maud*, though it began with a lyric of earlier inspiration, was comparatively swift in composition, the shaping of *In Memoriam* from 'short swallow flights of song', to a sustained and serious comment on the experience of bereavement took more than ten years, and the *Idylls of the King* was even longer in the making. Tennyson was engaged, especially in *In Memoriam*, in an interpretation of experience through experience. The mind that knows 'everything about melancholia', cannot be entirely ignorant of everything else; for amongst the things to be known about an emotional state is its relations with other states, and its quality as contrasted with theirs. Little is known about an experience until it is known as part of an order of things.

If the reflective quality of Tennyson's mind had been recognised, a great many difficulties would have been avoided. For if Tennyson is to be fitted into the critical theory, he must never be successfully moral. A good deal of Tennyson's moral poetry does, of course, seem tailor-made to fit with this doctrine. The additions to *The May Queen* in the 1842 volume illustrate it perfectly, so does the remodelling of *Œnone* which destroys the explanatory context of Pallas Athene's axiom:

'Self-reverence, self-knowledge, self-control,
These three alone lead life to sovereign power.'[11]

Everything of Tennyson's, or nearly everything, in which he chooses to state his moral with clumsy explicitness, bears out the theory. But other poems, *Ulysses, Tithonus, Merlin and the Gleam, The Vision of Sin,* and so on, carry a moral content without the burden, or the betrayal of explicit moral sentiment, and these are not only recognisably Tennyson's best work, but are also remarkable for that 'mastery of mood' which is labelled as the Tennysonian talent. There are two ways of handling these poems, one is to ignore, the other to deny their moral content. *Ulysses* and *The Vision of Sin* are test cases. *Ulysses* is sometimes seen as Tennyson's most considerable achievement, but it is on the face of it impossible to see Ulysses as a neurotic. He is perhaps an escapist, but his escape is by means of endeavour.

> One equal temper of heroic hearts,
> Made weak by time and fate, but strong in will
> To strive, to seek, to find, and not to yield.

Ingenious analysis traces in the unstrenuous movement of these lines, the almost forced pressure on 'strive', and 'seek', falling away to 'not to yield', a division between Tennyson's declared and his real mind, but it would perhaps be fair to suggest that we are faced, in this curious movement of the lines, with the common psychological phenomenon of a determination of will matched with a failing energy—a situation of which the journey of the aged Ulysses is not an unsuitable representation. In any case these lines represent the 'moral' Tennyson, but the moral Tennyson pursues, unfortunately, a goal belonging to his aesthetic twin:

> Yet all experience is an arch wherethro'
> Gleams that untravell'd world, whose margin fades
> For ever and for ever when I move.

Looking back on his own life Tennyson was to pick up this theme again in *Merlin and the Gleam*, but that was in his 'complacent' period. Puzzled critics dealing with Tennyson as a schizophrenic, half the prophet of endeavour and domesticity, half the aesthete, are surprised to find that the heroic Ulysses has the quality of moral determination without its expected complement, a worthy acceptance of practical duties:

> It little profits that an idle king,
> By this still hearth, among these barren crags,
> Match'd with an aged wife, I mete and dole
> Unequal laws unto a savage race,
> That hoard, and sleep, and feed, and know not me.

At the same time the values represented by practical virtues are not rejected but recognised in the person of Telemachus:

> Most blameless is he, centred in the sphere
> Of common duties, decent not to fail
> In offices of tenderness, and pay
> Meet adoration to my household gods,
> When I am gone. *He works his work, I mine.*

This contradiction, or ambiguity, in *Ulysses* is increased by the contrast between it and its companion-piece *Tithonus* with its rebuke to human presumption:

> Why should a man desire in any way
> To vary from the kindly race of men,
> Or pass beyond the goal of ordinance.

This would seem to make nonsense of a search for 'that untravell'd world'. Critics faced with all this are obliged to find fault with the construction of *Ulysses*, or rather to find psychological contradictions in it which destroy its unity as a symbol, or failing this, and in order to show Tennyson as thoroughly approving of the domestic, to attempt to demonstrate that he is mocking at, and entirely disapproving of his hero.[12] *The Vision of Sin* provokes a different kind of selective interpretation. It is treated as a splendid example of the morbid Tennyson at work, almost melodramatic in his imagination of evil and decay. A momentary comparison of it with *Les Fleurs du Mal* would reveal at once that the genre is different. *The Vision of Sin* is, in the first place, really about sin, not about evil; it is not concerned with spectacular vices but with breach of order, the mere inordinate use of permitted goods and its inevitable results: its subject is the moral act, not the perverted state. In the second place it is macabre. The macabre is simply the invocation of a hidden laughter, a mockery of the morbid for not being quite real; a plain man's attempt to keep a grip on his imagination by making the horrible appear funny. In later life Tennyson read this poem to his friends as a comic performance. Merely this then, the attempt to keep a grip on his imagination, and the attempt to balance in *Ulysses* and *Tithonus* opposing perceptions of value, would indicate not a neurotic wallowing in his own state, nor a melancholic escaping to the comfort of cliché, but a man attempting to make sense even of neurotic, or morbid states of mind, and somehow bring them into line with normal experience.

The poems we have discussed belong to the 1842 volume. It is argued that the fading of the morbid mood into an attitude of moral determination is a characteristic of that volume, and that here we find the limit of Tennyson's development. Already, in *Dora*, in the revised version of *The May Queen*, and in other poems we can see the fatal surrender to Victorian taste. It only needs the Laureateship for Tennyson to adopt his task of exhorting the public to the Sunday School virtues. This is an accusation of cowardice: Tennyson is supposed to be escaping the terrors and conflicts of a sensitive temperament, and the responsibility of his own insight, by running into the shelter of standard Victorian morality. This view of his Laureateship is as much a reaction against the Victorians as against Tennyson, and no one will deny to him what he held in common with his contemporaries, reverence for chastity, and its intellectual counterpart, integrity, an affection for the domestic charities, a passionate response to physical or spiritual courage, and an intense, insular, and irritable attachment to the order and values of the society of which he was a member. It cannot be denied that these preoccupations often made him insensitive to the non-moral, or even the moral aspects of a situation. The man who, born in the Regency period, could write forty years later of England's 'Loyal passion for her temperate kings', may at the least be said to be without historical sense, and the poet who puts into the mouth of King Arthur a lecture on the evils of tolerating adultery is certainly sacrificing aesthetic to moral considerations, and may have lost his sense of humour. This admitted blindness in particular cases does not, on the other hand, necessarily mean that chastity, patriotism or a respect for order are unfit matter for poetry, or have an inevitably deleterious effect on it. Nor need we suppose that respect for these things is, by definition, a frightened love for the safety of conformity.

It is worth pausing to consider this question of conformity and Tennyson's position as Laureate, which, I said earlier, depends on certain assumptions about the public response to his poetry. That assumption is roughly this: that the Victorians liked a certain moral uplift in their verse and Tennyson gave it to them; they liked domestic poems and Tennyson gave them to them; they disliked passion, intellectual disturbance, and any questioning of the established order; Tennyson refrained from these. It is true enough that Tennyson possessed a capacity not ultimately for his own good, an innocent capacity for turning moral experience into convenient apothegms:

'Tis better to have loved and lost
Than never to have loved at all.

More things are wrought by prayer
Than this world dreams of.

He was fated to be quotable, and the Victorian use of his poetry for potted morality does not commend him to later generations. But when his generation turned to him for moral strength it was not these axioms, nor the work of the middle years that they turned to, but the poems admired by the later generation which 'discovered' them, *Ulysses, The Two Voices, In Memoriam*. The show-pieces of Tennyson as moral guide to his age were the expression of his private grief. The Victorians missed a good deal of the moral point of the *Idylls of the King*: they saw, of course, that it was wicked of Guinevere to be so sinful, but the abstruser allegory had to be explained to them in innumerable 'keys'. Their liking for these, as for other Tennysonian poems, was often as much aesthetic as moral: they enjoyed the near Pre-Raphaelite accumulation of beautiful detail. They pursued him with enquiries about the exactness of his detail, and though they did sometimes write to him for serious accounts of the meaning of things, many of their letters were occupied with questions about the exact species of the 'sea-blue bird of March', or some other detail of natural history. In fact when Tennyson did take it upon himself to be moral the public was not always sure what he was at, and not always in agreement with him. Sometimes this is his own fault. A real distaste for certain kinds of social behaviour in *Lady Clara Vere de Vere* is lost beneath a slickness of expression which turns the poem into proverbs. It is pleasant to rattle off as accepted sentiment:

Kind hearts are more than coronets,
And simple faith than Norman blood.

But in the reign of William IV, when this was written, coronets retained their market value and Norman blood had distinct advantages over simple faith. What Tennyson is saying in this little ballad is thoroughly subversive of accepted social order. If this can be missed in *Lady Clara Vere de Vere*, it cannot and ought not to be missed in *Maud* or *Aylmer's Field*. It is not surprising that *Maud* found so little favour when it was first published[13] for it presents both a near-explicit account of passionate, unauthorised love (nearly all Tennyson's lovers have clandestine affairs) and a full-scale attack on commercial values. As late as the period of *Hilda Lessways*, *Maud* was regarded in some social groups as a 'naughty and forbidden book'. The picture of an entirely respectable Tennyson adored by an entirely respectable public is exaggerated. It is worth setting against the critic's Tennyson a picture of a distressed publisher refusing to handle an unexpurgated *Lucretius*, or of the disturbed and venerable Gladstone rebuking the author of *Locksley Hall Sixty Years After* for upsetting the rejoicing at Victoria's Jubilee.

That Tennyson the Laureate can justly be regarded as the voice of the Victorian public does not mean that his Laureate poems are full of Victorian platitudes, but that they are startlingly impersonal. In them Tennyson is not, really, so much concerned with moral sentiment, as with the formal expression of public emotion. Only the familiarity of much repetition disguises from us that Tennyson's official poetry is very good of its kind. The mere technical achievement of, say, the *Ode on the Death of the Duke of Wellington* is considerable enough: what is perhaps more important is Tennyson's capacity for discovering under the individual personality, or the single event, with all its extraneous and irrelevant detail, the shape of a legend or a public symbol. *The Charge of the Light Brigade*, hackneyed as it is, reveals this more than anything else. The poem is as near to impersonality as a poem well can be. Lines like

> Their's not to make reply,
> Their's not to reason why,
> Their's but to do and die:
> Into the valley of Death
>   Rode the six hundred.

or even,

> Some one had blunder'd:

do not express personal impressions or judgments, but straight facts, and the total effect of this poem on the Victorian public was not to rouse it against Lord Raglan or Lord Lucan, but to quicken and express its realisation of a heroic action. In a sense, the poem has crystallised for later generations not merely the memory of a particular and comparatively unimportant military action, but the muddle and achievement of the Crimean War. Similarly, in a much less well-known poem, *A Welcome to Alexandra*, Tennyson by-passes the tangle of dynastic marriages, and the domestic politics of the royal house, and fixes on the symbolic character of Alexandra:

> Sea-Kings' daughter from over the sea,
> Alexandra!
> Saxon and Norman and Dane are we,
> But all of us Danes in our welcome of thee,
> Alexandra!

In so addressing a nervous young woman in a crinoline about to enter the stuffy domestic circle of the Widow of Windsor, Tennyson draws on that wealth of simplifications to which the common mind reduces history. This simplification may be, and is normally considered to be, politically dangerous, since the tendency to simplify and to create symbols lays the popular mind open to exploitation and abuse. But what is politically dangerous may be poetically fruitful as the splendid formalities of the Wellington Ode and the excitement of the Ballad of *The Revenge* show. The really interesting problem in the study of Tennyson becomes, then, not 'Why did his poetic power flag and fail after he became Laureate?' but 'How did the poet of a purely private emotion become the poet of a public order?' In a sense it is not a question of his 'becoming' anything: the formal, impersonal elements of the Laureate verse were always to be found in Tennyson, and are recognised by that class of criticism which speaks of him as 'classical'. The recognition of this 'classicism' should lead us to the real dialectic of Tennyson's mind. There is in it certainly the morbidity, the melancholia, the extraordinary sensitivity of the neurotic but there is also, if only in the form of the verse, an awareness of order and formality, the imposition, if only in a pattern of words, of an objective shape on a subjective feeling. The mastery *both* of metric *and* melancholia implies a tension and balance in his work:

> For he tames it who fetters it in verse.

He is, besides, classical in more than his verse-forms: what gives him his sympathy with Virgil, what is the really Virgilian element in his verse, is that element in his consciousness which needs the satisfaction of public order:

> A land of just and old renown,
> Where Freedom slowly broadens down
> From precedent to precedent:

The poetic mind, because of this passion for order, constantly imposes on itself, or attempts to discover, in romantic mood, law, purpose and reason:

> It may be we shall touch the Happy Isles,
> And see the great Achilles, whom we knew.

But if this Virgilian element in Tennyson's mind counterbalances and
controls personal neurosis, there is another element in classicism, the
Horatian element, which answers and balances the enamelled artificiality of late romanticism. This shows itself, partly, in technique. The
dying fall of Tennyson's romantic verse,

> And after many a summer dies the swan,

can, if too often repeated, seem no more than a trick with lilt. On the
other hand if he opens a poem

> I waited for the train at Coventry;

the newspaper flatness of the line destroys the reader's interest. The
great achievement of his later verse is the combination of the subtle
incantatory rhythms of his early period with the rhythms of the living
voice:

> Here will I lie, while these long branches sway,
> And you fair stars that crown a happy day
> Go in and out as if at merry play,
> Who am no more so all forlorn,
> As when it seem'd far better to be born
> To labour and the mattock-harden'd hand,
> Than nursed at ease and brought to understand
> A sad astrology, the boundless plan
> That makes you tyrants in your iron skies,
> Innumerable, pitiless, passionless eyes,
> Cold fires, yet with power to burn and brand
> His nothingness into man.

This is a combination which, in Tennyson's verse and for Tennyson's
purposes, serves some of the functions of colloquial rhythms in later
writing. This technical achievement reveals something more interesting
than itself. The civilised mind presents in Horace a different aspect
from that which it presents in Virgil. Order, the Imperial legend, the
Augustan myth remain, but in Horace the sentiments of Imperialism
are not thrust upon us. Except in particular poems the Imperial order
is taken for granted. What is important in Horace is the detail, the
intimacies of a complex social order operating against the background
of the Pax Romana. In his poems it is the individual not, that is, the

eccentric, but the conforming individual, whose minor moments, personal friendship, private comforts, and private griefs, take their place within the great formal movements of *Res Publica*. Tennyson, like all major poets, has a sharp awareness of minor moments:

> No more in soldier fashion will he greet
> With lifted hand the gazer in the street.

In unfortunate experiments like *The May Queen* his mistake was to confuse the minor moments of human life with its essentials. The girl's remorse and death are cluttered with domestic detail. Immaturity, Wordsworth, and the advice of his high-minded friends led him to identify this instinctive feeling for the social with a concern for simple rural life, and even to confuse it with this interest in the merely domestic. But something of this sense of human beings in friendship, in normal light-hearted activity, is always present in his verse, in *Will Waterproof's Monologue*, in *The Goose* and in the comic scenes which take the sugar out of *The Day-Dream*. It is also a constant background to the personal grief of *In Memoriam*, for the sense of bereavement there includes, not only the pain of personal loss, but the want of something expected in a social group, the loss of pleasant conversation and friendly gatherings. Consequently, the anguish of Arthur's death is played against the record of many social and friendly occasions:

> O bliss, when all in circle drawn
> About him, heart and ear were fed
> To hear him, as he lay and read
> The Tuscan poets on the lawn:

> Or in the all-golden afternoon
> A guest, or happy sister, sung,
> Or here she brought the harp and flung
> A ballad to the brightening moon.

This continued awareness of a sanity in human relations is, as we shall see, an important element in Tennyson's moral synthesis, but it finds its real flowering later, in Tennyson's occasional poetry, where he celebrates the urbane friendships of his middle and later life.

All this is by no means to discount the criticism which presents Tennyson as a melancholic, and emphasises the continuance of the melancholic strain in his verse: the morbidity of his temperament is a matter of fact, not of opinion. What must be denied is that melancholy is the only important element in his poetic development, and that he was as escapist as he has been represented to be. There is in his work a true dialectic, a tension between the insight of the solitary and the sense of the common and the social. An awareness of the romantic wastes, the fluent and unshaped, appears through, and sometimes is imposed upon, an intense realisation of normal activity and order.

> There where the long street roars, hath been
> The stillness of the central sea.

It is this tension and its effect on Tennyson's poetry which needs investigating.

Chapter II

Tennyson's Sensibility

THE history of Tennyson's temperament is the history of a delicate sensibility disturbed by emotional insecurity, and controlled, if at all, not by reason but by moral determination. No one disputes this: the influence of disturbed emotions is evident in the subject matter of his poetry. But we may as well be clear: Tennyson's difficulties with his father, the death of Hallam, and the postponement of his marriage did not make him a poet, did not, that is, give him a poet's vision of reality nor the verbal skills to express it. A poet is, like the rest of us, conditioned by what happens to him but his awareness of the world is determined not by the history but the kind of his sensibility. A tougher, more optimistic temperament might have thrown off the influence of a shadowed childhood, but a natural optimist would never have created the Tennysonian world reflected in *The Merman*, *Maud* and *The Ancient Sage*. The question for the critic is not, primarily, 'How did Tennyson become neurotic?' but 'What is it in the quality of Tennyson's feeling and imagination which modifies the stuff of common experience?'

The Tennyson family temperament was not bright and sunny. His grandfather's grandmother was a member of the elder branch of the Earl of Chatham's family, the Pitts of Strathfieldsaye.[1] That taint of melancholy which drove the elder Pitt mad, and produced the fantastic imagination of the creator of *Vathek*, was transmitted to the Tennyson family. Two of Tennyson's brothers, Edward and Septimus, gave their family acute cause for anxiety because in them this blackmindedness

reached the edge of derangement and beyond. And it darkened
Tennyson's own experience of the world. It is always the thinner, the
mistier, the more ancient elements in, say, landscape which fascinate
his mind, 'Tears, idle tears' are more natural to him than laughter. This
natural melancholy was deepened by his family's situation. Tennyson's
father, George Tennyson, was perhaps the most afflicted of them all.
He was violent, morbid and embittered and given to such frightening
fits of despondency that the young Alfred would run from him into
the churchyard and pray for death. Death, with its appurtenances, the
grave, the winding-sheet and the coffin worm, obsessed his boyish
imagination:

> My being is a vacant worthlessness,
> A carcass in the coffin of this flesh,
> Pierced through with loathly worms of utter death.

We have, of course, to allow for the influence of the Byronic and the
'horrid' on the adolescent mind in this period, but it was not the
reading of novels which sent Tennyson rushing into the churchyard
or blindly wandering by the bleak sea at Mablethorpe.

The first eighteen years of his life were spent at home, in the village
of Somersby, a place which even now is so remote that the bus from
Louth visits it only once a week. He was educated at home, principally
by his father, and in company with his brothers and sisters. It was a
narrow and highly coloured existence. The children had many
cousins, but as their father was on bad terms with his father and his
brother, their relationships with their kin were bedevilled by the
quarrel and they were cut off from this entry into the wider world.
Their early lives were characterised by an intimate, almost petty,
relationship with those nearest and dearest to them, and an almost complete want of contact with anyone outside the family circle. This insecurity in the outer world combined with an exceptionally tightly woven
relationship with his immediate family was a part of Tennyson's
youthful consciousness, and reinforced his natural melancholy. It is
worth remembering, especially when we talk of Tennyson's 'unreality',
or his unawareness of social questions, that in some ways the Somersby
remoteness persisted all through his life. The vast social movements of
his time did not encroach on his way of living for he had, apart from
short periods in London, no experience either of great cities or the life
of the new industrial communities. The Somersby life was not,
however, the prototype of his later life at Farringford or Aldworth, or of

any kind of gracious living. The Rectory was too small for the family, and, though the brothers and sisters were close and affectionate, the life of twelve sensitive, physically beautiful and emotionally unbalanced, youngsters thrown together in a confined space with a pious mother and a father given to despondency and dipsomania, would certainly be difficult. Indeed it promises an almost Brontëan intensity. Even without the Tennyson temperament, so narrow an existence would overcast the mind and encourage dreary imaginations foreign to normal experience.

Tennyson's isolation from the world was increased by a defect of sight. Sir James Knowles, in his *Personal Reminiscences* of Tennyson, tells us:

> The shortness of his sight, which was extreme, tormented him always. When he was looking at any object he seemed to be smelling it. He said that he had 'never seen the two pointers of the Great Bear except as two intersecting circles, like the first proposition in Euclid.'[2]

But this shortsightedness had compensations. Tennyson had at short range, so it is said, a vision so sharp that he could see the eye of a nightingale gleaming in a dark bush. Now we have an interesting description of the effects of this kind of sight not in any account of Tennyson, but in Dr Joan Evans's life of her half-brother, the archaeologist, Sir Arthur Evans:

> Evans was extremely shortsighted, and a reluctant wearer of glasses. Without them he could see small things held a few inches from his eyes in extraordinary detail, while everything else was a vague blur. Consequently the details he saw with microscopic exactitude, undistracted by the outer world, had a greater significance for him than for other men; it was this cloistered vision that fostered his power of seeing and interpreting details in coins and engraved gems.[3]

The phrase 'cloistered vision' exactly describes the quality of some of Tennyson's descriptions. He seems to move in a world of over-emphasised detail so precisely stated that it appears fantastic to a normal vision:

> The lizard, with his shadow on the stone,
> Rests like a shadow,

The artificiality of these descriptions is increased by Tennyson's sensitiveness to sharp light and bright colour, a sensitiveness which imparts to his poems an effect of glitter, or near glitter:

> All in the blue unclouded weather
> Thick-jewell'd shone the saddle-leather,
> The helmet and the helmet-feather
> Burn'd like one burning flame together,
>   As he rode down to Camelot.
> As often thro' the purple night,
> Below the starry clusters bright,
> Some bearded meteor, trailing light,
>   Moves over still Shalott.

We are told that Sir Lancelot's image 'flash'd into the crystal mirror'. The impact on the imagination of brightness laid like this on brightness is intolerable in brilliance, and yet the scene remains artificial to a normal sight. This artificiality is created by the isolation of certain visual details from the things with which they would be associated in a normal field of vision. The sharpness of detail belongs only to the foreground of Tennyson's descriptions, more distant objects appear with a kind of mysterious generality: landscape takes on a haziness like a landscape in the half light, and seems like the country of a dream or a fantasy. Such a combination of detail and generality appears, for instance, in *Mariana*, where it is deliberately used to create the emotional effect of isolation:

> About a stone-cast from the wall
>   A sluice with blacken'd waters slept,
> And o'er it many, round and small,
>   The cluster'd marish-mosses crept.
> Hard by a poplar shook alway,
>   All silver-green with gnarled bark:
> For leagues no other tree did mark
>   The level waste, the rounding gray.

Tennyson's short sight provides him in the physical world with a pattern of reality not unlike that which the Somersby life created in the world of human relationships. His world, physically and emotionally, is a world without middle distance where the near is detailed, intimate and striking, and the distant unreal, ungraspable, and vague.

This alternation of the sharply defined and the merely vague is closely related to a peculiarity of Tennyson's mental experience which he describes in an early poem called *Armageddon*:[4]

> Each failing sense,
> As with a momentary flash of light,
> Grew thrillingly distinct and keen. I saw

The smallest grain that dappled the dark earth,
The indistinctest atom in deep air.

This clear awareness of distinct identities is like the detailed vision of short sight which I have just described, but here it is a prelude to something else:

I wondered with deep wonder at myself:
My mind seem'd wing'd with knowledge and the strength
Of holy musings and immense ideas
Even to Infinitude. All sense of Time
And Being and Place were swallowed up and lost
Within a victory of boundless thought.
I was a part of the unchangeable
A scintillation of the Eternal Mind,
Remix'd and burning with its parent fire.

This, though it is explicable in terms of the Idealist speculation which colours a good deal of Tennyson's early writing, has the note of personal experience. Tennyson seems to have been susceptible to states of mind in which the consciousness of the self as a distinct identity dissolved away. He could, especially when young, induce in himself a state of trance, or semi-trance, by repeating to himself the formula 'far, far away', or even by repeating his own name.[5] And it is not surprising to discover that as the awareness of his own identity dissolved so did his sense of the solid identity of other things. He was acutely conscious of flux and change:

The varied earth, the moving heaven,
The rapid waste of roving sea,
The fountainpregnant mountains riven
To shapes of wildest anarchy,
By secret fire and midnight storms
That wander round their windy cones,
The subtle life, the countless forms
Of living things, the wondrous tones
Of man and beast are full of strange
Astonishment and boundless change.

A sense of the ever-changing nature of the external world is only one step from a sense of its unreality:

All sense of Time
And Being and Place were swallowed up and lost
Within a victory of boundless thought.

These earlier poems are remarkably similar in sentiment to poems like

The Voice and the Peak and *The Ancient Sage*, which Tennyson wrote in his old age, and which his generation took as the expression of his 'message'. A concern with ultimate reality and changing phenomena was a constant element in all his work, but it does not belong, as the Victorians supposed, to the realm of deliberate philosophy—Tennyson was never, after all, a *real* philosopher—but to the nature of his consciousness. It is perhaps the strongest element in his awareness of the world.

This sense of the instability of the external world, and even of his own identity, did not, at first, worry Tennyson. Auden says that his inability to establish identity produced a 'vertigo of anxiety', and so it did, but not invariably. The experience of being caught out of himself, away from the familiar bounds of distinct personality was a cause of great anguish to Tennyson, but also the occasion of a great rapture:

> So word by word, and line by line,
> > The dead man touch'd me from the past,
> > And all at once it seem'd at last
> The living soul was flash'd on mine,
>
> And mine in his was wound, and whirl'd
> > About empyreal heights of thought,
> > And came on that which is, and caught
> The deep pulsations of the world.

In later life this experience of the 'sum of things' was to lead him not to questions about his own nature but to a steady certainty about ultimate reality. The knowledge of reality lying under the thin veil of the phenomenal world, as it is described in this passage from *In Memoriam*, and in *The Ancient Sage*, and even in *Armageddon*, is the knowledge of a completed experience; the mind or soul leaves its own identity and discovers 'that which is'. But Tennyson's experiences of the dissolving of the self did not always reach the consummate intuition of another identity in which the self is contained as a spark in the parent fire. There was a period in which the dissolution of the barrier of consciousness appeared to him as a danger. The descriptions, in *The Princess*, of the weird seizures to which the Prince is subject resemble the description of mystical vision in *Armageddon* and, like it, appear to be based on Tennyson's personal experience:

> On a sudden in the midst of men and day,
> And while I walk'd and talk'd as heretofore,
> I seem'd to move among a world of ghosts,
> And feel myself the shadow of a dream.

These seizures affect the Prince's consciousness both of himself and of the world in which he lives:

> While I listen'd, came
> On a sudden the weird seizure and the doubt:
> I seem'd to move among a world of ghosts;
> The Princess with her monstrous woman-guard,
> The jest and earnest working side by side,
> The cataract and the tumult and the kings
> Were shadows; and the long fantastic night
> With all its doings had and had not been,
> And all things were and were not.

These states of the Prince's are constantly spoken of as 'seizures' and are described as a variety of catalepsis. The Prince 'swoons', speaks of his 'sickness' and so often considers his trances as the symptoms of an illness that we could conjecture that experiences of this kind troubled Tennyson in the nervous illness from which he suffered in the early eighteen-forties. Tennyson does not regard them as altogether physical in origin. The trances fall on the protagonists of the *Idylls of the King* and especially upon Sir Percivale and Arthur himself. In *The Holy Grail* Sir Percivale goes through adventures which derive from, and resemble the adventure of his original in *The High History of the Holy Grail*. But *The High History* recounts its marvels as matters of fact. The castles and the magic and the Grail exist solidly in a solid three-dimensional world. Sir Percivale in *The Holy Grail* travels through a world of illusion: like the Prince he suffers from a state in which common things seem like hallucinations, and fall into nothingness before him:

> 'And then behold a woman at a door
> Spinning; and fair the house whereby she sat,
> And kind the woman's eyes and innocent,
> And all her bearing gracious; and she rose
> Opening her arms to meet me, as who should say
> "Rest here;" but when I touch'd her, lo! she, too,
> Fell into dust and nothing, and the house
> Became no better than a broken shed,
> And in it a dead babe; and also this
> Fell into dust, and I was left alone.'

Percivale's phantoms are not the illusions of a physical but of a moral malady; he is, the hermit tells him, without true humility. The illusion spreads, however, to the entire Round Table. Even Arthur who

> Knew himself no vision to himself
> Nor the high God a vision,

finds that 'a blind haze' falls on him at the end of his life. In the mist that obscures the shape of the world at the end of the *Idylls of the King*, the mist in which enemy and friend are confounded, we can find a symbol of the unsureness of the soul which finds a known order dissolving into chaos. This melting away of the clear limits which define the identities of things is almost exactly the opposite of that sharp definition of detail which we have already noticed, and it is clear that Tennyson was in some way afraid of it. He is afraid of illusion, of the loss of self, as well as of the unreality of the experience. It may be that the careful observation, almost the cataloguing, of detail in his poetry became for him a prophylactic against the external world's refusal to hold its identity and its significance. In any case the experience of two sharply opposite states of consciousness impart a special, a Tennysonian, quality to his awareness of the world.

He sees external nature with a selective eye, and notices especially those things in landscape which confuse or do not permit definition: water, especially flowing water, brook, rill or river, and above all the sea. He observes things like wind changes, cloud effects, or the moods of light, which modify the character of scenery. Such things of course dominated the perceptions of his childhood: the brook ran by the Somersby garden, the sea of Arthur's 'last great battle in the west' was the sea at Mablethorpe where Tennyson spent his holidays, while the landscape of his native Lincolnshire is peculiarly susceptible to changes in the sky. It is indeed sometimes difficult to tell whether the sights and scenes of his boyhood conditioned his mind to the awareness of a continuing shift and flux, or whether, being to hand, they were integrated into, and used as the symbols of a particular state of consciousness. But in the long run it is the state of consciousness which imposes itself on the landscape and not the landscape on the state of consciousness. The sense of flux produces among other things a peculiar sadness which is transferred from the sufferer to the physical universe:

> For even and morn
> Ye will never see
> Thro' eternity.
> All things were born.
> Ye will come never more,
> For all things must die.

This is a sadness for what has been, a nostalgia for past splendours which Tennyson himself recognised as part of his psychological life. The curious home-sickness of 'Tears, idle tears', which he ascribed to the 'passion of the past',[6] conditions his consciousness of ordinary landscape, and in his youth this nostalgic sadness was more deeply shadowed by the melancholy peculiar to his temperament and circumstances. There is no detail, for instance, in the following description which does not belong to a commonplace scene:

> At eve the beetle boometh
>   Athwart the thicket lone:
> At noon the wild bee hummeth
>   About the moss'd headstone:
> At midnight the moon cometh,
>   And looketh down alone.
> Her song the lintwhite swelleth,
> The clear-voiced mavis dwelleth,
>   The callow throstle lispeth,
> The slumbrous wave outwelleth,
>   The babbling runnel crispeth,
> The hollow grot replieth
>   Where Claribel low-lieth.

The melancholy which pervades this scene is not a charnel house melancholy: that 'Claribel low-lieth' gives the clue to all this sadness but does not create it. What makes for the sense of sadness in the poem is the selection of detail. Everything from the bird song to the 'babbling runnel' flows away and moves, the only static object is the 'moss'd headstone'. This in itself suggests and evokes sadness, but, in describing the scene, Tennyson has intensified his effect by the use of sounds and associations which deepen melancholy. The sound of the words 'lone,' 'alone', 'slumbrous', 'hollow', imparts a quality to the scene which they describe. What Tennyson sets before us is not, in fact, landscape as it is, but landscape as it is seen through the medium of a particular kind of sensibility.

A vivid awareness of flux and change does not of course mean that Tennyson's landscape is always gloomy. Before the state of trance described in *Armageddon*,

> Each failing sense,
> As with a momentary flash of light
> Grew thrillingly distinct and keen.

Often and often the clarity of a beautiful thing poised on the edge of change promises something beyond itself—it is bright and sharp in 'a light that never was on sea or land', and the fact that the phenomena of the external world often seemed to Tennyson a mere veil hiding something not yet seen or known imparts a special beauty to his world:

> Yet all experience is an arch wherethro'
> Gleams that untravell'd world, whose margin fades
> For ever and for ever when I move.

In Tennyson's boyhood this sense of the unseen, but desirable, translated itself into a healthy enthusiasm for strange names, travellers' tales, and the fantastic world of the Orient which characterises *Poems by Two Brothers*. The Tennyson Boys fixed their eyes on mountains more exotic than the conventionally sublime Mont Blanc:

> Thy snow clad peaks, stupendous Gungotree!
>   Whence springs the hallow'd Jumna's echoing tide,
> Hoar Cotopaxi's cloud-capt majesty,
>   Enormous Chimborazo's naked pride.[7]

This passion for the strange and the distant is united, in the youthful Tennyson, with the passion of the past, and is again reflected back on the experience of commonplace realities. The finest flower of Tennyson's early exoticism is the *Recollections of the Arabian Nights* which first appeared in *Poems, Chiefly Lyrical*. In an attempt to produce the emotional effect of *The Arabian Nights* Tennyson described the gardens of Haroun Alraschid:

> Black the garden-bowers and grots
> Slumber'd: the solemn palms were ranged
> Above, unwoo'd of summer wind:
> A sudden splendour from behind
> Flush'd all the leaves with rich gold-green,
> And, flowing rapidly between
> Their interspaces, counterchanged
> The level lake with diamond-plots
>   Of dark and bright. A lovely time,
>   For it was in the golden prime
> Of good Haroun Alraschid

Ostensibly this is a description of palm trees in an eastern garden, in fact all its detail is derived from the observation of English landscape. This is the way that light falls through the leaves of trees by the

Somersby or any other English brook. The picture is given an exotic atmosphere partly by the sensuous effect of the epithets 'rich, gold-green' (though the words realise certain aspects of English rather than of oriental gardens), partly by associations of 'gold' and 'diamond', and partly by the context. A sense of costly artificiality is imparted to the familiar scenes of a journey along a river, by calling the boat a 'shallop', describing the waterfalls as 'diamond rillets' and by playing against the Englishness of the 'clear canal', the 'cool turf on the bank' and the 'summer wind', the oriental suggestions of cedars and tamarisks, shrines of fretted gold, and bulbuls in lemon groves.

This treatment of the commonplace as exotic is observed and sometimes laughed at in Tennyson's major poems. How odd that the island of the Lotos-Eaters should be the apotheosis of Torquay, that *Crossing the Bar* should be created during a crossing from Yarmouth to Lymington. A more serious criticism is that this transformation of commonplace reality destroys the texture of normal experience. 'This', it could be said of the half-English, half-fantastic garden of Haroun Alraschid, 'is exactly what we mean—this colouring of landscape by mere mood, passion for the past, or desire for the exotic—it matters little which—this avoidance of reality by transforming it into an artificial Paradise represents for us the literature of escape. It is a refusal to engage with real life, a non-acceptance of things as they are.' Given the present orthodoxy about what should be the concern of literature this criticism is hard to meet. But there is perhaps another way of considering these transformations of the world. A mind in love with the exotic need not travel to the orient for inspiration. The elements of the strange and fantastic are a part of his normal life. Nothing in a sense is more ordinary, more normal than the scene described in Tennyson's song 'A Spirit haunts the year's last hours'. The common experience of autumn is alive and almost tangible in it:

> the moist rich smell of the rotting leaves,
>   And the breath
> Of the fading edges of box beneath,
>   And the year's last rose.

Yet this common, almost banal description of an autumn garden threatens like coming thunder:

> Heavily hangs the broad sunflower
>   Over its grave i' the earth so chilly;
> Heavily hangs the hollyhock,
>   Heavily hangs the tiger-lily.

This threat, this strangeness is built up within the poem by the selection of details real enough in the scene and which, besides, express a real quality in autumnal gardens. It could be argued that Tennyson's poetry, however fantastic, achieves the aim which Wordsworth set himself, to impart the colours of the imagination to everyday scenes and incidents. The island of the Lotos-Eaters bears more resemblance to Torquay than might at first appear, at any rate the descriptions of it force on us a new attention to West Country landscape. The 'rich gold-green' of the palm trees in the gardens of Haroun Alraschid does not, in the poem, cease to be a quality of English landscape, and its association with the more glittering splendours of Arabia strengthens and exaggerates qualities which really exist in an English scene:

> By garden porches on the brim,
> The costly doors flung open wide,
> Gold glittering thro' lamplight dim,
> And broider'd sofas on each side:

This exaggeration has its value, and is often not so much an escape from reality as an entrance into it, an awareness of qualities in the commonplace which are often concealed in the routine of observation.

Tennyson's capacity for creating a fantasy world from the elements of and with the solidity of real experience is especially shown in his descriptions of dreams and dream states. The American scholar, E. D. H. Johnson, in drawing attention to Tennyson's use of dream, suggests that in his dream descriptions Tennyson is reacting against the *mores* of his age, that he is able in the poetic dreams to defy the conventions by which the rest of his poetry is controlled.[8] There is more to it perhaps than this. Dream and trance, the trance-like states which we have been discussing, have a great deal in common. In both the barriers and definitions of normal consciousness are dissolved, and the mind seems to enter on a world which promises and threatens more than normal experience. In many of the dream poems, *Sea Dreams*, for example, or the dream poems in *In Memoriam*, this strange new world is represented by the sea, but sometimes, as in *A Dream of Fair Women*, the dream world is a wood. Even outside the dream poem the sea, from *The Mermaid* to *Crossing the Bar*, is a persistent symbol in Tennyson's poetry, and its recurrence is significant. For it is the peculiarity of the water worlds which Tennyson describes to have no limits; in water everything is, more than ever, flowing away from its real identity. Under the sea everything is mysteriously unlike the normal world.

But if the sea world is a world without sharp definitions it is also a world without restrictions and characterised by irresponsibility. In *The Merman* Tennyson seems to shed, vicariously, the responsibilities of an adult and to delight in mere formlessness:

> There would be neither moon nor star;
> But the wave would make music above us afar—
> Low thunder and light in the magic night—
>   Neither moon nor star.
> We would call aloud in the dreamy dells,
> Call to each other and whoop and cry
>   All night, merrily, merrily;
> They would pelt me with starry spangles and shells,
> Laughing and clapping their hands between,
>   All night, merrily, merrily:

This irresponsibility is a characteristic of a dream state, for sleep is the state in which common awareness of the world is lost, and in which the mind finds itself free from normal restraints. Tennyson himself knew this. *A Dream of Fair Women* displays him entering the wood of vision as one with a special command of it. In the dream wood he is delivered from care and guilt:

> I knew the flowers, I knew the leaves, I knew
>   The tearful glimmer of the languid dawn
> Of those long, rank, dark wood-walks, drench'd in dew,
>   Leading from lawn to lawn.
>
> The smell of violets, hidden in the green,
>   Pour'd back into my empty soul and frame
> The times when I remember to have been
>   Joyful and free from blame.
>
> And from within me a clear under-tone
>   Thrill'd thro' mine ears in that unblissful clime,
> 'Pass freely thro': the wood is all thine own,
>   Until the end of time.'

Freudian psychologists might see in the wood and the sea symbols of Tennyson's unconscious mind, and discover in the poems which describe them a suppressed desire to return to a state of being before moral imperatives were thrust upon the personality. But these early verses sometimes seem to demand the interpretation not of Freudian but of Jungian psychologists. In them Tennyson seems to be using not private but common symbols:

And I should look like a fountain of gold
　　　Springing alone
With a shrill inner sound,
　　　Over the throne
In the midst of the hall;
Till that great sea-snake under the sea
From his coiled sleeps in the central deeps
Would slowly trail himself sevenfold
Round the hall where I sate, and look in at the gate
With his large calm eyes for the love of me.

Fountains and serpents are the common furniture of folk tales and myths, and it looks as if Tennyson's capacity to lose identity in the 'great all' carries with it a capacity to dive below the depths of his own normal consciousness, and perhaps even an uncanny sensitiveness to race memory. The experience was not altogether delightful. The wood of *A Dream of Fair Women* is a menacing place:

There was no motion in the dumb dead air,
　　　Not any song of bird or sound of rill;
Gross darkness of the inner sepulchre
　　　Is not so deadly still

As that wide forest.

The sea of the Sea Fairies and the Merman is also the dwelling of the Kraken, and of the Sea Snake. Tennyson's attitude to this underworld of the mind, and the world of sleep and dream is ambivalent. Sleep in *In Memoriam* delivers from the awful reality of present bereavement, and reunites Tennyson with Hallam. At the same time the escape from normal restraints which it promises can, Tennyson sees, become a drift into nothingness, taking a man too far from his control of himself:

To Sleep I give my powers away;
　　　My will is bondsman to the dark;
　　　I sit within a helmless bark,
And with my heart I muse and say:
O heart, how fares it with thee now,
　　　That thou should'st fail from thy desire,
　　　Who scarcely darest to inquire,
'What is it makes me beat so low?'

Something it is which thou hast lost,
Some pleasure from thine early years.
Break, thou deep vase of chilling tears,
That grief hath shaken into frost!
Such clouds of nameless trouble cross
All night below the darken'd eyes;
With morning wakes the will, and cries,
'Thou shalt not be the fool of loss.'

This ambivalence is clear enough in *In Memoriam* where indeed it is part of the theme. Elsewhere, as in *A Dream of Fair Women*, when the wood both repels and attracts, it is implicit only. The desire to escape, and the desire to hold on to the self, to achieve the clear definiteness of conscious existence are in constant tension one with another.

Tennyson's sensibility appears then to have a double quality. The world of trance, the world of sleep and dream, in which the identities of things are lost, shares his vision with a world which is sharply defined, clear, and even minute in detail. His imagination is always slipping from the real to the fantastical, but his careful observation of real things imparts solidity to the very fantasy. In entering Tennyson's mind we are entering a world in which reality does not repel, as it so often does, the fantastic; on the contrary it is often the fantasy which interprets or symbolises something discerned in the real.

II

The question we are bound to consider now is the effect of the sensibility which we have just described on the style and texture of Tennyson's poetry. Tennyson is one of the group of English poets who *made* a style; it has its antecedents, in Virgil, in Milton, even in Pope, but it is not an imitation or even a derivative. It is Tennysonian. It is certainly distinctive enough to suggest a relation between it and the temperament of its inventor. Indeed the relationship is in one way obvious: the loving and elaborate, sometimes the pedantic attention to detail in Tennyson's verse proceeds from the minuteness of his 'cloistered vision', and it is this attention to detail which gives his poetry its characteristically tapestried quality. Of course it was this quality which, in part, made Tennyson so popular with his contemporaries: the Victorians delighted in the close observation of nature in a way which their descendants do not.

But is is a mistake to think of the Tennysonian style as uniform. The enamelled elaboration of *The Gardener's Daughter* or of *Morte d'Arthur* is abandoned in the meditative allegory of 'Of old sat Freedom on the heights', and in parts of *In Memoriam*. It is altogether forgotten in the verve and vigour of the Ballad of *The Revenge*. Tennyson was the last of the professional poets, the last to be interested in form as form, and he has many styles of writing. The earliest of them was not what we should call Tennysonian. For although he was young during the creative period of the great Romantic poets, Tennyson seems to have had no real acquaintance with any of them, except Byron, until his brother went to Cambridge and Byron, brilliant and startling as he was, continued the traditions with which Tennyson was already familiar. The models for *Poems by Two Brothers*, Tennyson's earliest publication, were the poets of the mid-eighteenth century, Thomson and Collins, Gray and Cowper.[9] All these writers are, in spite of their romantic subject matter, notably rhetorical and conceptual in style. They are not, that is, concerned to recreate experience but to say things about it, and they present conceptions of feelings, of scenes and of situations in terms of general and already accepted conventions. This is true even of their allegorical poetry; the allegory of Gray, for instance, is no more than the translation of concepts into capital letters. In the long run the eighteenth-century convention of allegory, allegorical progress, and personification is only a more elaborate common idiom, a means of statement and argument rather than of the realisation and communication of quality. Tennyson inherits this rhetorical method: it is not, certainly, a product of his sensibility, but a habit of mind derived from his early reading. Although in some of the early poems it leads him to an empty oratory, which, like a great deal of youthful verse, has no real referent in the world of sense or of the imagination, it does provide him with a technique of argument, the capacity to state a case through personification and analogy:

> Of old sat Freedom on the heights,
>   The thunders breaking at her feet:
> Above her shook the starry lights:
>   She heard the torrents meet.
>
> Then in her place she did rejoice,
>   Self gather'd in her prophet-mind,
> But fragments of her mighty voice
>   Came rolling on the wind.

This capacity for metaphorical statement persists and modifies nearly all Tennyson's later verse, but, as we shall see, it is not native to his sensibility. Indeed the combination of this kind of writing with what, for the moment, we may call Tennyson's 'moody' writing, shows very clearly the interaction of personal sensibility and a poetic tradition.

It is possible to watch the young Tennyson developing, or rather breaking away from the poetic tradition of his youth. His early work, that is the work of his early adolescence, is noticeably mature, and in some ways very un-Tennysonian:

STEPHANO: I tell thee, fellow, I'm half drown'd in love.
ANTONIO: I'faith! I see that thou art half seas over.
STEPH.: How! you landlubber, do you banter me?
My senses are all founder'd in deep love
My cables rotted and my timbers beaten
In by the force of love!
ANT.: And wilt thou place
Thy claim in opposition to mine?
Oyer and terminer! What misdemeanour
Wilt thou be guilty off?
STEPH.: And who art thou?
Thou cockboat—thou poor cockboat—thou mere shallop
Varnished and painted, whose weak delicate planks
Would shrink beneath a capfull o' wind.[10]

This dialogue, in *The Devil and the Lady*, between a lawyer and a sailor, in which both employ the jargon of their professions and draw their metaphors from them, shows Tennyson at fifteen with a good deal more dramatic sense than Tennyson at sixty, and with a feeling for the meaning and play of words. This sense of the conceptual value of words is not what we should normally expect of Tennyson; not four years later he has ceased to experiment with the meanings of words and has turned his attention to their metrical and musical value. He is, in *Poems by Two Brothers* and *Poems, Chiefly Lyrical*, experimenting with noises:

Low-flowing breezes are roaming the broad valley dimm'd in the
gloaming:
Thoro' the black-stemm'd pines only the far river shines.
Creeping thro' blossomy rushes and bowers of rose-blowing bushes,
Down by the poplar tall rivulets babble and fall.
Barketh the shepherd dog cheerly; the grasshopper carolleth clearly;
Deeply the wood-dove coos; shrilly the owlet halloos;
Winds creep; dews fall chilly; in her first sleep earth breathes stilly:
Over the pools in the burn water-gnats murmur and mourn.

Except, perhaps, for some of Coleridge's metrical experiments which the young Tennyson could not have seen, there is no real precedent for this kind of writing in English. In the four years between the writing of *The Devil and the Lady*, and the writing of *Leonine Elegiacs* Tennyson had discovered his mode and it was something entirely new.

The merely novel of course has nothing to recommend it: the value of these experiments lies in the use Tennyson made of the technique which he developed through them. The experimental poems of the immediately pre-Cambridge period, *Leonine Elegiacs*, *Ilion*, *Claribel* and others, are like incantations: Tennyson seems, in them, to be emptying words of their conceptual meanings. At least he is trying to direct the reader's mind away from meaning, and to produce in him the trance-like state which he himself experienced on the repetition of the words 'Far, far away'. This effect is maintained by a technique which is purely verbal and metrical. The use of labials and sibilants, of hollow vowels, and of feminine and repetitive endings, together with an unemphatic beat, produces a characteristically Tennysonian cadence:

> Her song the lint-white swelleth,
> The clear-voiced mavis dwelleth,
> The callow throstle lispeth,
> The slumbrous wave outwelleth,
> The babbling runnel crispeth,
> The hollow grot replieth
> Where Claribel low-lieth.

The cadence itself is not unrelated to the equally characteristic Tennysonian melancholy. In the merging together of these liquid sounds, their flow and fall in the rhythm of the poem, definition seems to melt away in a haze of luxurious sadness. But I do not think that at this stage in Tennyson's development this metrical melancholy arises from a deliberate attempt to create a state of mind or a mood. *Supposed Confessions of a Second-rate Sensitive Mind*, the poem in which, at this early period, we should most expect to find Tennyson adapting sound to state of mind, is comparatively unsubtle in verbal and metrical method, and makes its point rather by talking about and describing the poet's state of distress than by evoking it in the reader's own mind. The really experimental poems of this period are not concerned with Tennyson's feelings at all. It is clear, for instance, that in *Leonine Elegiacs* Tennyson's real intention was to reproduce by means of word-sounds the various noises of the countryside; and in the twin poems *Nothing will Die* and

All Things will Die, he is deliberately playing with and modifying aural and sense impressions to suit different themes. Yet the flow of sound in these poems, and the haziness and unreality which it casts on the world are exactly what we would expect of a mind whose view of things was conditioned by its sense of perpetual change. *All Things will Die* does not merely state a theme, it expresses it, and the mode of its expression is directly related to Tennyson's sensibility:

> Clearly the blue river chimes in its flowing
> > Under my eye;
> Warmly and broadly the south winds are blowing
> > Over the sky.
> One after another the white clouds are fleeting;
> Every heart this May morning in joyance is beating
> > Full merrily;
> > Yet all things must die.
> The stream will cease to flow;
> The winds will cease to blow;
> The clouds will cease to fleet;
> The heart will cease to beat;
> > For all things must die.
> > All things must die.

In this description even the things which promise joy are presented as moving; nothing in the poem suggests permanence except the abrupt check in the rhythm in the second part of the verse:

> The stream will cease to flow;

Both eye and ear suggest transience, passing away, death.

In the experiments of this period Tennyson discovers not merely the power of musical incantation but also that of emotional evocation. It is this discovery which is largely responsible for his success as a 'poet of mood'. *Leonine Elegiacs* looks at first like a poem of simple description:

> Low flowing breezes are roaming the broad valley dimm'd in the
> > gloaming;
> Thoro' the black-stemm'd pines only the far river shines.
> Creeping thro' blossomy rushes and bowers of rose-blowing bushes,
> Down by the poplar tall rivulets babble and fall.

This appears to be descriptive but it is in fact evocative. The twilight word 'gloaming', and the mention of the far river 'shining' through the 'black-stemm'd pines' create a visual impression, but it is a very vague impression, and the emotional effect of the passage is very much stronger. This is because twilight and distant water create certain associations in the mind, associations which are recalled by the words 'gloaming' and 'far river'. Tennyson has selected precisely those elements in the landscape, the distant shine, the black trunked trees, and precisely those words 'dimm'd', 'far', 'fall' which most vividly convey the associations of mystery and nostalgia and gentle melancholy. These associations are under the domination of sound: Certain consonants *m* and *s* in particular, produce an emotional onomatopoeia, a sense of languor and peace. Keats's musk rose is 'the *murmurous* haunt of flies on *summer*-eves', so here 'the water-gnats *murmur* and *mourn*'. *Leonine Elegiacs* is not a major poem, but it is a remarkable poetic achievement for a boy, and it indicates the development of Tennyson's art; the art which is peculiarly his, but which he passed into the main stream of English poetry, that of building the effect, and later the meaning, of a poem upon visual and aural associations.

This art is the product of the special sensibility described earlier in this chapter, for in part it depends on the thinness of the barrier between the object seen and the state of the seer. The observer or the listener receives, so to speak, and incorporates with his mental state, the objects of sense, so that at future moments the thing seen or heard, or touched or smelt, evokes and stands for the mood in which it was first sensed. The mind colours its objects, endows them with a peculiar quality and later receives back from them the quality which it has itself imparted to them. The Romantic poets understood this relationship between the mind and the world very well; indeed Tennyson's predecessor in the art of creating emotional states by means of visual and aural detail was Coleridge. But Tennyson never had, and certainly not at nineteen, Coleridge's phenomenal power of psychological analysis. There is nothing in these first poems of his to compare with a work like *Dejection: an Ode* in which Coleridge expresses his understanding of his own state by describing effects in landscape. Tennyson is not even in these poems concerned with his own state of mind, but is caught up in the first pleasure of the young poet, the sheer delight in the resources of his own art, and the knowledge of his own capacities. It is, in part, the lack of self-analysis in the really juvenile poems which leads one to question the conception of Tennyson's always seeking and finding his subject matter in his own moods. What we receive from his early work is not the awareness of a poet's brooding on his own problems, but the recreation of perception. The world we see takes on in Tennyson's early poems a particular quality, certain features of the landscape stand out more clearly than others, and we realise that this in fact is how the poet saw what he presents.

At this stage in his development that state of Tennyson's perception is not especially interesting. He sees a world which is faintly morbid, faintly theatrical, an adolescent world in which the prevailing note is gloom. The technical achievement of poems like *The Kraken* and 'A spirit haunt the year's last hours,' in which this mood is enshrined, is very remarkable, but their substance belongs to a passing phase of adolescent nostalgia and nightmare which it would be a pity to confuse with the very real problems of Tennyson's later life. But it is idle to suppose that a young man capable of so much technical virtuosity, and so well aware of his own gifts would not wish to apply them to more effective subjects. The tedious album verses which he wrote on the characters of various ladies show him as engaged, rather clumsily, in widening the range of his technique. Each young lady has her own characteristic; Lilian is 'airy fairy', Margaret 'sweet and pale' and Adeline 'shadowy, dreaming'. These poems I believe were meant to reproduce the emotional impression made by the personalities of these various misses, and to communicate their quality by means of the things associated with them:

> The quick lark's closest-caroll'd strains,
> The shadow rushing up the sea,
> The lightning flash atween the rains,
> The sunlight driving down the lea,
> The leaping stream, the very wind,
> That will not stay, upon his way,
> To stoop the cowslip to the plains,
> Is not so clear and bold and free
> As you, my falcon Rosalind.

Tennyson takes an obvious pleasure here in recording the sunlight on the lea and all the rest of the catalogue, but this aesthetic savouring of things is subordinate to the theme of the poem. He wishes to emphasise Rosalind's quality of openness and he does so by evoking the associations of sun and sea and wind. Other ladies are represented by other types. The most highly finished and the most interesting poem of this group is *Mariana* for here the attempt to make a fanciful portrait of the heroine has receded into the background, and what is important is the evocation of her psychological state. This is perhaps the first poem of Tennyson's in which he sets out deliberately to recreate a particular and personal emotional state, and yet it is something more than a poem of mood. Tennyson is not, as in *Leonine Elegiacs*, luxuriating in pleasant melancholy, he is exploring and examining someone else's state of mind in particular conditions. In the poem Tennyson uses all the evocative devices which we have noticed elsewhere. He deliberately associates physical environment with sadness and grief:

> About a stone-cast from the wall
>   A sluice with blacken'd waters slept,
> And o'er it many, round and small,
>   The cluster'd marish-mosses crept.

The gloom of Mariana's physical surroundings and their effect on us are emphasised by verbal and metrical devices:

> She only said, 'My life is dreary,
>   He cometh not', she said;
> She said, 'I am aweary, aweary,
>   I would that I were dead!'

In no other poem of Tennyson's is the physical detail which evokes the mood so closely integrated with the mental state it evokes.

The lady of the poem is not like Adeline or Lilian one of a bevy of Victorian young ladies, she is Shakespeare's Mariana, Mariana of the Moated Grange, who as we know had been jilted by Angelo and is the perfect type of hopeless, deserted, but faithful love. Tennyson's lady suffers the disconsolate despair of her prototype, but it seems, as we read the poem, that 'he', and even the sense of being deserted, are remoter and less real than the lady's strange curious inertia. She is imprisoned in her own mental condition like someone locked up in a prison house. The 'moated grange' is the prison house and stands for the imprisoning power of her mood. In consequence there seems to be very little distinction between the house itself and the mood. Mr Eliot remarks on the brilliance of one descriptive passage:

> All day within the dreamy house,
>   The doors upon their hinges creak'd;
> The blue fly sung in the pane; the mouse
>   Behind the mouldering wainscot shriek'd,
> Or from the crevice peer'd about.
>   Old faces glimmer'd thro' the doors,
>   Old footsteps trod the upper floors,
> Old voices called her from without.

This evokes with great skill and conviction the brooding atmosphere of an old and lonely house; an atmosphere which, if long endured, would certainly create the inertia from which Mariana suffers. Yet our attention is not directed to the house just as a house. The old voices and old footsteps resound through it but they belong not to the house itself but to the brooding imagination which discovers them in the creaks and sighings of ancient wood. The physical state and the mental condition are indivisible; each colours the other. In the integration of the two realities we have passed from the evocation of mental states through images to their representation by symbols.

This can be said with more certainty because in many of Tennyson's poems a house, or some other form of dwelling-place such as a castle or a tower is deliberately made to stand for the body itself, or else for some condition, spell, or mood, or obsession, in which the personality is fettered. In the early poem *The Deserted House* the house is clearly a metaphor for the body of a dead man:

I

Life and Thought have gone away
   Side by side,
   Leaving door and windows wide:
Careless tenants they!

II

All within is dark as night:
   In the windows is no light;
   And no murmur at the door,
So frequent on its hinge before.

III

Close the door, the shutters close,
   Or thro' the windows we shall see
   The nakedness and vacancy
Of the dark deserted house.

Later on, in *The Lady of Shalott* and in *The Palace of Art* the tower and the palace are both symbols of the soul's withdrawal into certain states of pleasure and isolation. Their relationship to what they stand for is however formal and arbitrary. The palace and the tower are simply the terms which are for the moment assigned to the state of isolation and in which it is discussed: Mariana's grange is more interesting. The symbol of the grange is not arbitrarily assigned to Mariana's state of mind; on the contrary the grange is a real house and its power to represent a mental state is built up within the poem itself by the same means as those used by Tennyson to evoke Mariana's state of mind. The impression of the house in decay is created for us so that we may enter into the mood of its inhabitant, and because of this the emotional and sensuous links between the house and Mariana's mood are so strong that, little by little, the house comes to stand for the mood.

This use of evocative imagery for symbolic purposes is the foundation of Tennyson's distinctive poetic technique, but it is developed in conjunction with the method of rhetorical and allegorical statement which he had inherited from his predecessors. There seems perhaps to be nothing in common between the method of *Mariana* and that of the long reflective passages in *In Memoriam*, but they are capable of a union the fruits of which begin to be visible even in Tennyson's early work. He showed all through his life a very real fondness for allegorical argument of the kind represented by *The Deserted House*. It is a conceptual argument.

Life and Thought are gone away.

'Life' and 'Thought' are still abstract nouns even though they are given capital letters, and the Deserted House of the poem is not a real house like Mariana's grange, but a synonym for body. Still, allegory is at least representative; is stands for something other than itself. The difference between the allegorical symbol of the house in one poem and the image symbol of the grange in the other is that one is arbitrarily selected to stand for something else, and operates within a clearly defined area of formal meaning, and the other comes to represent something else because there is a real affinity between the thing represented and its symbol; the symbol represents the feeling and imagination of a situation rather than an idea about it or a definition of it. It is so far from operating within a clearly defined area of meaning that, not infrequently, it carries meanings of which the poet himself is not fully aware. The affinity between Mariana's mood and the grange is emotional: it arises from certain similarities between the emotions of desolation felt by a deserted mistress, and those aroused by a half-ruined house in a lonely countryside.

It is possible by evoking the emotional connotations of formal allegorical symbols to endow them with emotional as well as intellectual significance. By the manipulation of sounds and images the poet can awake the associations of dead symbols and bring them into active life. In this passage, for instance, from Tennyson's youthful poem *The Poet*, the well-worn metaphor of the arrows of wit is endowed with imaginative power, partly by the re-imagination of the arrow as an Indian reed, partly by the complex of associations wakened by 'Calpe unto Causasus', and by 'flame', 'light', 'silver' and 'flower all gold':

> with echoing feet he threaded
> The secretest walks of fame:
> The viewless arrows of his thoughts were headed
> And wing'd with flame,
>
> Like Indian reeds blown from his silver tongue,
> And of so fierce a flight,
> From Calpe unto Caucasus they sung,
> Filling with light
>
> And vagrant melodies the winds which bore
> Them earthward till they lit;
> Then, like the arrow-seeds of the field flower,
> The fruitful wit
>
> Cleaving, took root, and springing forth anew
> Where'er they fell, behold,
> Like to the mother plant in semblance, grew
> A flower all gold.

Now this is not a good poem. The thought is confused by a plethora of metaphors; vagrant melodies, and arrows, and plants do not fit with each other. Yet underneath the rhapsody we can perceive the imagination really at work on its images, moving from the conventional arrows of thought, to the Indian reeds of the blow-pipe, and then to the arrow-shaped seeds of the field flower by means of which the sharpness of the poet's thought is associated with its fruitfulness. It is this re-imagination of the arbitrary, sometimes even of the stock symbol, which revivifies Tennyson's use of his predecessors' rhetoric. On the other hand his own device, the image symbol which has been built up on a complex of affinities can become, like the allegorical symbol, a means of presenting an argument. The many evocations of spring in *In Memoriam* are made, for instance, to argue out Tennyson's reflections on the experience of sorrow:

Dip down upon the northern shore,
  O sweet new-year delaying long;
  Thou doest expectant nature wrong;
Delaying long, delay no more.

What stays thee from the clouded noons,
  Thy sweetness from its proper place?
  Can trouble live with April days,
Or sadness in the summer moons?

Bring orchis, bring the foxglove spire,
  The little speedwell's darling blue,
  Deep tulips dash'd with fiery dew,
Laburnums, dropping-wells of fire.

O thou, new-year, delaying long,
  Delayest the sorrow in my blood,
  That longs to burst a frozen bud
And flood a fresher throat with song.

This development in his use of evocation belongs to Tennyson's maturity. We can, however, observe the fusion of the two methods of writing poetry in the companion-poem to *Mariana*, *Isabel*. This poem, though less perfect in itself than *Mariana*, is in some ways more interesting because it promises more. It is for the most part in Tennyson's reflective vein, he is not so much trying to evoke the quality of Isabel as to say in so many words what kind of a person she is:

Eyes not down-dropt nor over-bright, but fed
  With the clear-pointed flame of chastity,
  Clear, without heat, undying, tended by
    Pure vestal thoughts in the translucent fane
Of her still spirit; locks not wide-dispread
Madonna-wise on either side her head.

We are told that she is chaste, wise, humble, a perfect wife. In the last verse of the poem, however, Tennyson ceases to say what Isabel is like, and tries rather to suggest her quality by means of certain images:

The mellow'd reflex of a winter moon;
A clear stream flowing with a muddy one,
  Till in its onward current it absorbs
    With swifter movement and in purer light
      The vexed eddies of its wayward brother;
      A leaning and upbearing parasite,

Clothing the stem, which else had fallen quite
With cluster'd flower bells and ambrosial orbs
Of rich fruit-bunches leaning on each other—
Shadow forth thee:—the world hath not another
(Tho' all her fairest forms are types of thee,
And thou of God in thy great charity)
Of such a finish'd chasten'd purity.

We have already been told that Isabel is peculiarly chaste: the moon and
especially the winter moon evoke the sense of coldness and serenity
which belong to the chaste woman. But, and this is most interesting,
the sense of cold and barrenness is not allowed to dominate the
reader's imagination. The image of the moon is modified by the word
'mellow', and contrasted with the image of the clinging and upbearing
vine: that is, the associations of harvest and fruitfulness are brought in to
qualify the normal response to the coldness of chastity. Yet, although
these associations are certainly present in the images, the images are not
used primarily to excite an emotional effect. The moon and the fruit-
bearing parasite, Tennyson says, 'shadow forth' Isabel, that is give some
idea of, stand for Isabel, just as Isabel's charity is a type of God's.
Tennyson is using these images quasi-intellectually, as representing
ideas present and already recognised in the reader's mind. The images
he chooses, the moon, the clear stream, the ambrosial fruit, belong to
the common stock of symbols and, by accepted tradition, they stand
for chastity, fruitfulness and the other characteristics he discerns in
Isabel. They have, indeed, almost ceased to be symbols and have
become synonyms, conceptual counters by means of which he tells us
the lady's history. For the heroine of this poem is his mother, and when
he speaks of the 'clear stream flowing with a muddy one' and of the
'upbearing parasite' he is almost certainly thinking of the difficulties
created for her by his father's temperament, and his later illness. Here
certainly he combines the poetry of statement with a new kind of
evocative and symbolic poetry.

There remains one interesting fact about this building of images into
types and symbols. In some phases of literary history a common stock
of types and symbols is available to poets. Over centuries of use the
symbols have accumulated associations and meanings and it is possible
for poets to use them almost casually, building up their poems by a
manipulation of accepted types. So Shakespeare can write:

For nothing, this wide universe, I call
Save thou, my Rose, in it thou art my all.

and Burns,

> My love is like a red, red rose
> That's newly sprung in June,

and neither of them need elaborate further on the image of the rose. This possibility is not open to later poets, and many of them are obliged to create their own common symbols; that is to use certain images with such frequency that, after a while, the reader learns to recognise and attach significance to them. A good deal of the meaning of Tennyson's poetry depends on dominating symbols of this kind, such for instance as the house or castle, the sea, and later on, the cycle of the seasons. The significance of these symbols is modified by the varying contexts of emotions and sense associations in which they are found. There is a constant play between Tennyson's apprehensions of the shifting world of sense, and the symbols in which he has defined and crystallised his meditations on that world. It is as we shall see a play which continues through the best part of his poetic life.

Chapter III

'Tennyson, we cannot live in Art'

THE young Tennyson, the Tennyson of *Poems, Chiefly Lyrical* and the 1832 *Poems,* had not as yet developed the full potentialities of his manner. He had of course very little to say: there is in these verses nothing which requires a special struggle with the means of expression, or the strengthening and modification of a technique. The content of the volume was more or less what was to be expected of a sensitive, gifted and neurotic young man. The lyrics are mostly what used to be called 'pure poetry', a poetry, that is, of a purely sensuous kind, fantastical, beautiful, and devoid of explicit purpose. The manner of these early poems, however, is the complement and the expression of Tennyson's peculiar vision. To say this is to invite rather than to allay the accusations of morbidity and self-indulgence made against his poetry: indeed both the psychologist and the literary critic may well have doubts about a poetry in which the concrete realities of the world dissolve in a mist of modulation, and which dwells so continually on symbols of escape from normal responsibility. But no one asserts that Tennyson's state of mind would not be alarming to a careful and responsible parent, or that his early poetry does not remain too long or too lovingly within a very narrow range of sense experience. All that is suggested for the moment is that the volumes were the work of a very young man whose vision and technique suggest possibilities not seen before in English poetry.

Tennyson's vision was certainly eccentric in the proper sense of the word, but its eccentricity is in the long run of minor importance. The question is: Does the abnormality of his vision throw light on normal experience? He might, with greater truth than Wordsworth, say 'I was the dreamer, they the dream', and this does not, psychologically speaking, represent a very happy way of seeing the world and one's fellows, yet the demolition and reassembling of the elements of normal reality in the dreamer's mind can be a revelation, for it shows us what is hidden under the irrelevant sequences of moment to moment experience. The principle of association is at work in the new and significant fantasies of the dream order, and it is by means of the principle of association that Tennyson inducts the reader into his consciousness of reality. The very lingering of the mind upon isolated sense perceptions intensifies sensation until it reveals more than itself, as, for instance, in *Mariana in the South*, when Tennyson's concentration on the sensations of drought and heat brings us to the realisation of an emotional situation. Indeed in certain respects it becomes a comment on that situation, for the barrenness and heat suggest perhaps a certain barrenness in Mariana's indulgence in grief. Although these early poems are certainly free from any explicit moral it would be wrong to suggest that they are entirely without moral meaning.

But a technique of writing so ideally suited to a young man's vision may well be a handicap to a man of more experience. 'I was the dreamer, they the dream': the sentence describes a state of perception so intensely tranced that all the elements of reality are drawn into the dreamer's field of influence, they exist only in obedience to his perceptions, and are under his power. His selective vision dismisses the uncomfortable or the insubordinate, so that, however significant the dream's distortions of the normal world, they lack the dynamic quality of real things. In the dream, as in Tennyson's *The Day-Dream*, the normal functions of life, time and movement, physical and moral law, and the interaction of person and person are suspended. The undersea country of the Merman and the Mermaid, and the gardens of Haroun Alraschid are territories without sorrow or responsibility, like the day-dreaming worlds of children, and they are not less so for being, as they are, recreations of the waking world. But one aspect of reality can never really be drawn into the dream's orbit, and it cannot be dreamt out of existence. Other people and that system of relationships between other people which we call the social order remain obstinately objective, obstinately independent of the manner in which we perceive them. Their active reality will, from time to time, impose itself on the order which we had supposed obedient to our vision. Awareness of a world subject to the idiosyncrasies of other minds and personalities is not an epistemological but a psycho-philosophical problem. It is not a matter of how I see, or how I understand its relationship to myself in my act of perception, but how I manage its painful or pleasant invasion of my own private world.

Because the circumstances of Tennyson's early life were so unusual this inevitable invasion was especially violent and confusing. Within the closeness and isolation of the Somersby circle he was able to sustain, for much longer than is usual, the enclosed protected world of childhood. The temptation to escape into the inner and inviolable castles of this fantasy world would, of course, have been increased by the tensions and troubles of his home life and it became, or so it seems from *The Merman*, a haven of refuge. It was unfortunate that these family tensions reached their crisis at about, and during the time of Tennyson's undergraduate career. A young man going up to college begins to accept adult responsibilities. The standards and conventions of his home circle are bound to suffer the shock of encounter with other people's standards and conventions. There are new experiences to be assimilated, moral and metaphysical questions to be settled in discussion with other young men, decisions to be made about the future. The outer world of society invades the private world, invites the dreamer to step out of the dream. For Tennyson all this was complicated by family circumstances. Even the business of choosing a career was bedevilled by dynastic policy. Tennyson's grandfather did not consider his elder son, Tennyson's father, a suitable head for the family, so he arranged to leave the family estates to his second son, and settled the elder boy's future by forcing him into the Church. He made the same plans for his grandsons; Frederick, Charles and Alfred were all to take orders. Frederick and Alfred were both averse to and totally unsuited to the clerical profession, and their opposition to the old man's designs caused a good deal of family friction. In the meantime George Tennyson's malady laid fast hold on him: melancholy, bitterness and dipsomania undermined his constitution and at last he died. In the underwater halls of *The Merman* no one is responsible for anything. In real life responsibility and duty now pressed hard on Tennyson, for though he was not the eldest son he came down from Cambridge on George Tennyson's death to be with and to help his mother. Grandfather Tennyson's hold on the purse strings made him the ultimate arbiter in family affairs, but Tennyson himself seems to have assumed the burden of day to day problems in the Somersby household. It was no light burden: the guidance of a large family of brothers and sisters, all difficult in temperament, all with some problem of career or marriage or nervous illness, is no sinecure for a young man.

This domestic responsibility was probably less important in itself than the sense of a duty to society which his high-minded Cambridge friends fostered among themselves. Tennyson was an undergraduate at the end of the eighteen-twenties and the beginning of the thirties, just when the breath of liberalism was blowing one of its periodic gales. This is the period of Catholic emancipation, of Reform Bill agitations and the 'Year of Revolutions' in Europe. New ideas were about: young men took them seriously and felt themselves to be important, the *avant garde*, no less, of a new age. Tennyson's friends nearly all belonged to, or were associated with the *Cambridge Conversazione Society* nicknamed, because of its pretensions, *The Apostles*.[1] One of its earliest members, F. D. Maurice,[2] implanted in the members of the society a strong sense of their heavy responsibility to the community. They were to be the bearers of new ideas in literature, politics and religion. What is surprising is not that they should have felt this sense of mission but that they were so active in fulfilling it. While they were still undergraduates, or very young graduates, the Apostles, under the leadership of John Sterling,[3] made themselves responsible for a disastrous intervention in the Spanish rebellion of 1830.[4] In the less dangerous field of literature they conducted a campaign to further the reputation of Keats and Shelley, and in the enthusiasm for these maligned poets Arthur Hallam[5] had Shelley's *Adonaïs* printed in England for the first time.[6] When they went down Maurice and Sterling between them edited the *Athenaeum* and filled it with Apostolic reflections. The Society lacked neither energy, nor confidence in its own purposes, and its atmosphere, in spite of the lightheartedness of its members, must have been heavy with an intense awareness of their special powers and duties. Behind all, though obscured in some accounts by the brighter personality of Arthur Hallam, was the figure of Maurice, always a worrying, scrupulous man, never at rest about his own duty and doomed for the rest of his life to be a weighty moral influence on his friends.

The seriousness of the Apostles is recognised as an influence in Tennyson's mental history. They had firm ideas about the function of the poet and his moral duty to society which they urged on Tennyson. Here we must clear our minds of cant. These young men were not, as they are sometimes represented, Victorian moralists turning up their noses at aestheticism. Victoria was not yet on her throne, and the

Apostles, so far from representing solidity and smugness in the arts, were connoisseurs, the highbrow revolutionaries of their own time and champions of the new poetry of Wordsworth, Keats and Shelley which the organs of established opinion, the *Edinburgh Review*, the *Quarterly*, and *Blackwood's*, rejected and despised. What they urged on Tennyson was the exalted role given to the poet in the ethos of liberalism, the role which is assigned to him both in Wordsworth's *Preface to Lyrical Ballads*, and in Shelley's *Defence of Poetry*. They saw the poet as having a prophetic function in society; he helps the regeneration of mankind by rousing men with song. But the means by which he is to rouse them is clearly indicated by Wordsworth. 'A poet', he says in the *Preface*, 'is a man speaking to men.' The poet, that is, deals with the great common emotions displayed in the common activities of men. It was Tennyson's apparent withdrawal from the commonplace in human life, his escape into fantasy, which distressed his friends as it disturbed the first reviewers of his poetry. 'Tennyson', said Trench, who was later an Archbishop, 'we cannot live in Art'.[7] The Apostles wanted him to converse 'with things that really are', to make his field 'man, the heart of man, and human life'. He was, after all, *their* poet, the mouthpiece of the new spirit of which they were the bearers. He must not waste his talents in the composition of beautiful but private verse.

Tennyson was not particularly rebellious about their high sense of his duty; his view of his vocation was as exalted as anyone else's and he certainly intended to fulfil it. *The Poet*, an early poem, takes the high romantic view of the poet as a herald of Freedom:

> Her words did gather thunder as they ran,
>   And as the lightning to the thunder
> Which follows it, riving the spirit of man,
>   Making earth wonder,
>
> So was their meaning to her words. No sword
>   Of wrath her right hand whirl'd,
> But one poor poet's scroll, and with *his* word
>   She shook the world.

Tennyson had no qualms about his friends' feeling that he was to deliver some message to the nations. But what to say? that was the question. Tennyson's experience had not yet established itself sufficiently for him to understand and interpret reality through it. Except for the conventionally liberal sentiments of the sonnets on Bonaparte and

Poland he had, in the early Cambridge period, nothing to present to the world but the picture of a mind in confusion. The real danger of the Apostles' advice to him was not that they urged on him the unsuitable role of a moral poet, but that they urged on him, as on themselves, the duty of leading and guiding the world before he had really got over the young man's work of understanding himself.

It says much for Tennyson's moral character that he was able to take the strain of so many demands at once. But we are not so much concerned with his moral character as with the effect of these new strains and new experiences on his poetry. The immediate effect is plainest in his subject matter: much of the poetry of the Cambridge period is devoted to an exploration of his own position. But the poems in which he confronts himself with his own problem clearly show that it cannot be stated, as it has been, in the simple terms of an Art/Life, Beauty/Duty antithesis. Indeed the manner in which he was to exercise his poetic abilities concerned him much less at first than the much more commonplace problem which he sets out in an unpublished poem called *Sense and Conscience*.[8] This is an allegory in which Reason and Conscience are represented as betrayed and drugged by Sense. Conscience is carried off to a dark wood in which he is laid asleep:

> His awful brows
> Pillow'd on violet woven mosses deep.

Pain and Memory awake the sleeping giant, but the poem is unfinished and stops with this awakening. We do not know, though we can very well conjecture, what will happen next. The situation is, of course, classic. Conscience is lulled to rest by Sense, and Sense here does not signify the cultivation of an exclusively aesthetic pleasure but laziness, gluttony and sensuality. The position represented is that of an earnest young man caught between the temptations of pleasure and the demands of the moral law. *Œnone* develops the same subject. Paris is not offered a choice between Art and Reality. Three possibilities are set before him. Hera offers the temptation of power and riches, Pallas a life of strenuous endeavour and Aphrodite 'the fairest and most loving wife in Greece'. What he chooses is not an Aphrodite who represents the charms of the aesthetic life, but the bait she holds out to him, the wanton Helen. The presence of Œnone, the discarded mistress, defines the status of his choice; it is not a noble worship of beauty but an illicit love. The overtones of sensual self-indulgence in the description of Aphrodite are transferred to his choice:

Idalian Aphrodite oceanborn
Fresh as the foam, new-bathed in Paphian wells,
With rosy slender fingers upward drew
From her warm brow and bosom her dark hair
Fragrant and thick, and on her head upbound
In a purple band: below her lucid neck
Shone ivory like, and from the ground her foot
Gleam'd rosywhite, and o'er her rounded form
Between the shadows of the vine-bunches
Floated the glowing sunlights as she moved.[9]

This description of the goddess is in deliberate contrast to that of her rival:

> Pallas, where she stood
> Somewhat apart, her clear and baréd limbs
> O'erthwarted with the brazen-headed spear
> Upon her pearly shoulder leaning cold.[10]

The tone of the Pallas passage is determined by 'clear and baréd' 'brazen-headed' and 'pearly', that of the description of Aphrodite by 'Paphian', 'rosy', 'rounded form' and the 'shadows of the vine-bunches'. The shadow of Pallas's brazen-headed spear and Aphrodite's vine-bunches alter the quality of their bodies, the bronze of the spear is hard and chaste, but the vine, particularly in association with the epithets 'rosy' and 'rounded', promises other things:

> Braid your locks with rosy twine,
> Dropping odours, dropping wine.

The choice offered to Paris is effectively between the offer of Aphrodite and that of Pallas, who, it must be remembered, is the Goddess both of reason and of war. Paris refuses her offer of the life of self-achievement, for the sake of Helen, a choice which is ultimately to destroy both him and Ilion. There is nothing peculiarly Apostolic about Tennyson's meaning in this poem, nor is it particularly Victorian. His theme is the theme of the Bower of Bliss passages in Spenser's *Faerie Queene*, of Milton's *Comus*, of *The Idle and the Industrious Apprentice* and other works of morality too numerous to be mentioned. The only peculiarity in the poem is that Tennyson is able, for a moment, to make virtue sensuously attractive:

> Pallas, where she stood
> Somewhat apart, her clear and baréd limbs
> O'erthwarted with the brazen-headed spear.

There are those who might find this clarity more pleasing than the faintly Hollywood femininity of Aphrodite.

There is an interesting variation in Tennyson's repetitions of this moral theme: Conscience, when drugged by Sense, is carried to a forest which in some ways recalls the gardens of Haroun Alraschid, but unlike these gardens, it has a beauty tainted with evil:

> The rose fell, the argent lily
> The dappled foxglove with its poisoned leaves
> And the tall poppy fell, whose eminent flower
> Hued with the crimson of a fierce sunrise,
> Like to the wild youth of an evil king,
> Is without sweetness.[11]

This evil and the drugged enervation of Conscience are linked together. This link between self-indulgence and the corruption of beauty in the imagination is again emphasised in *The Palace of Art*. The theme is even taken up in *Œnone*. Paris's choice menaces both Ilion and the Beauty of Ida (They came, They took away my tallest pines) but its immediate effect is on Œnone herself. She is more or less in the same position as Mariana and her state of mind is the same:

> My heart is breaking, and my eyes are dim,
> And I am all aweary of my life.

It is significant that the scene for her lament is set in the intense hot stillness of noon:

> The lizard, with his shadow on the stone,
> Rests like a shadow.

and it recalls the scenery of *Mariana in the South* a poem with which *Œnone* has many affinities.[12] It would appear from these poems that what Tennyson fears in sensuous self-indulgence is Accidia, not merely lethargy and sloth, but the terrible motionlessness of the mind and the poisoning of good which arises from a want of activity. His perpetual emphasis on the need to nerve the pulses and act, and his perpetual return in these early poems to the souring of the beautiful which is so vividly described in *The Palace of Art*, suggest that Tennyson was feeling, perhaps indulging, a sense of guilt about a natural shrinking from practical responsibility. The psychological accuracy of his description of the morbid mind should free us from the mistake of thinking that he is ascribing these feelings to breaches of conventional morality merely to please his friends. This corrupted enervation was a mental state which he knew something about, and which, even as late as *The Vision of Sin*, he associated with self-indulgence and the refusal of moral responsibility. The Tennyson of the Cambridge period was really discovering the dangers of withdrawal. The Gardens of Haroun Alraschid had to be left behind, not so much for moral as for psychological reasons.

The choice dramatised in these poems, and its consequences, is something very much more in the normal run of moral choices than the artist's highly specialised choice of his genre. Tennyson himself had to make such an ordinary choice: to exchange the delights of an idyllic existence in Cambridge for the family duties of Somersby, and the situation explored in the poems is perhaps a more deliberate and conscious version of the undergraduate's inevitable recognition that life is not one long series of parties and philosophical discussions. But if life is not all honey and roses, neither, it follows, is poetry. Consideration of the seriousness of life may have led Tennyson to consider the seriousness of poetry and even to conclude that to recollect Arabian Nights is not entirely to fulfil the poet's vocation. Certainly, at this period, he begins to handle subjects like that of *The May Queen* and of *The Miller's Daughter* which represent, at this stage, a Tennysonian version of 'man, the heart of man and human life'. Despite this, his acceptance, in writing *The Palace of Art*, of Trench's antithesis between Art and Life has, I think, been misinterpreted. In this poem Tennyson describes the Soul as having chosen to build itself a palace of aesthestic pleasure, but in the end,

> She howl'd aloud, 'I am on fire within.
>   There comes no murmur of reply.
> What is it that will take away my sin,
>   And save me lest I die?'
>
> So when four years were wholly finished,
>   She threw her royal robes away.
> 'Make me a cottage in the vale,' she said,
>   'Where I may mourn and pray'.

These lines come with a shock to readers of post-aesthetic times. A sense of guilt about aesthetic pleasures, the suggestion that there might be sin in the enjoyment of the pictures, sculptures and landscapes with which the Soul had furnished her Palace, has, to the modern mind, a flavour of immorality. Besides, Tennyson's capacity for the enjoyment and the expression of sensuous beauty is so great that his choice of Pallas rather than of Aphrodite, endeavour rather than indulgence, looks like a betrayal. Many critics see this choice as the abandonment of his genuine talent for lyric, and to them it seems a violence against the bent both of his genius and of his desires. This view is, I think, based on a genuine misunderstanding. It is true that in making decisions about the right values in life Tennyson would also be making decisions about the right values in poetry. Neither in life nor literature could he approve an idle indulgence, and there is no doubt that the decision to abandon the Palace of Art for the lowly cottage extended to the choice of subjects in poetry. But the original choice was between two courses of action, and it cannot be entirely stated in the strict terms of aesthetic dalliance versus duty. The Soul is not rejecting the beautiful, nor does Tennyson suppose that beauty is an evil in itself: it would be logical, on that supposition, to stop writing poetry. But the Soul says:

> 'Yet pull not down my palace towers, that are
> So lightly, beautifully built:
> Perchance I may return with others there
> When I have purged my guilt.'

The guilt of which she speaks is certainly not centred in the enjoyment of art but in more orthodox vices:

> Back on herself her serpent *pride* had curl'd.

> ★　　★　　★

> Inwrapt tenfold in *slothful* shame.

These are vices which invite their own punishment: Art provides only the medium of their indulgence. Tennyson has reduced Trench's antithesis not to the statement of an absolute opposition between aesthetics and morals, but to a view of things in which for the moment 'Art' equals self-indulgence of a particular kind, and 'live' means 'live in contact with one's fellows'. The temptation which he perceived before him was not beauty as beauty, but beauty as a means of withdrawal, as the medium of a fantasy world.

The evil of the Soul's position is clearly stated in the poem. It ends with hope:

> 'Perchance I may return *with others* there
> When I have purged my guilt.'

There is no danger in the Palace when its pleasures are shared. Something of the problem which really troubles Tennyson in this poem may be seen if we turn for a moment to an analogous problem, that of

Tennyson's famous 'doubt'. 'Doubt' of course was the occupational disease of the Victorian, and 'doubt' means the intellectual questioning of dogmas of the Christian faith. Ostensibly this is what *Supposed Confessions of a Second-rate Sensitive Mind* is about, but no one could suppose from reading it that Tennyson's objections to Christianity were rational. He is not like George Eliot, engaged in weighing the evidence for and against specific dogmas, and indeed a poem would not be a proper place for any such examination of belief. What troubles him is not a considered scepticism but a mood of unbelief:

> I am too forlorn,
> Too shaken: my own weakness fools
> My judgment, and my spirit whirls,
> Moved from beneath with doubt and fear.

The poem does not on a closer examination reveal any traces of a genuine unbelief or even of agnosticism. On the contrary it expresses a good deal of involuntary belief, a certainty about existence of the supernatural felt at levels of the mind which rational discussion of evidence and dogma cannot touch. Tennyson expresses by implication here what he explicitly asserts in *In Memoriam*:

> If e'er when faith had fall'n asleep,
> I heard a voice 'believe no more'
> And heard an ever-breaking shore
> That tumbled in the Godless deep;
>
> A warmth within the breast would melt
> The freezing reason's colder part,
> And like a man in wrath the heart
> Stood up and answer'd 'I have felt.'

This inner, inexplicable and sometimes irritating conviction of the inward mind belongs to people subject, as Tennyson was, to states called 'mystical'.

> The soul
> Remembering how she felt, but what she felt
> Remembering not, retains an obscure sense
> Of possible sublimity.

The conviction of possible sublimity is not without its difficulties. *Supposed Confessions* is concerned with precisely that awkward condition of mind in which the clear certainties of the rational intellect are opposed to the cloudy certainties of the intuition: the poet calls on a God, whom his intellect has taught him to doubt, to deliver him from the formless horrors of doubt. Faith and form are indeed 'sunder'd in the night of fear'. But the real centre of Tennyson's emotional disturbance is not in this conflict of certainties; the context in which the suicide states his problem makes this clear. He continually sees it in terms of his relationship with other people, especially with his mother:

> How sweet to have a common faith!
> To hold a common scorn of death!

His involuntary belief in God is not framed in the common formulas in which most men accept their faith: it is individual, it separates the speaker from other men. It cuts him off from that security expressed in the image of the child praying at its mother's knee:

> Would that my gloomed fancy were
> As thine, my mother, when with brows
> Propt on thy knees, my hands upheld
> In thine, I listen'd to thy vows,
> For me outpour'd in holiest prayer—
> For me unworthy!—and beheld
> Thy mild deep eyes upraised, that knew
> The beauty and repose of faith.

This desire to return to security we have already discussed, and there can be little doubt that the confusion of *Supposed Confessions* was produced by Tennyson's emergence into a wider world than that of Somersby. The beliefs of the home circle no longer satisfy the enquiring mind, and yet the sheet-anchor represented by those beliefs, and the practices which go with them, is missed in the emotional life. The confusion is crystallised in the second part of the title, the sensitive mind is 'not at unity with itself'. There is a desire to advance from, and a desire to retire into the safety of a known world.

Mutatis Mutandis the aesthetic difficulty, the apparent conflict between life and art, presents the same pattern as the problem of religious doubt. There is in it the same persistent under-theme, the same burden of insecurity. The theme here is not, however, that of the security of the home world, but the much greater difficulty of reconciling the life of the inner and personal world with the demands of the social order. Only in a secure world can the poet find the identity which means so much to him. The conflict can be stated in this way:

the real centre of personality can only be found by withdrawal into the self, but, on the upper levels of consciousness, identity is only established by a clear definition of relationship. Things are only known to be what they are by the delimiting qualities which mark them off and relate them to alien identities. Persons on the other hand do not know themselves in contact with, or by reflection from other beings, but in themselves. The problem is much more acute for a mystical temperament in which the need to retire from the pressure of daily life is imperative. Symbols of this withdrawal and the need for it are persistent not only in mystical theology, where they might be expected, but also in poetry. The garden, the island, the tower, fantastic oversea countries or cities like Sarras and Byzantium, the pleasure dome of Kubla Khan, are all versions of the same symbol. The theme of the secret garden is persistent, for instance, in Mr Eliot's work, just as Byzantium is persistent in that of Yeats. The fact that Mr Eliot singles out Tennyson's early poem, *The Hesperides*, indicates the affinity between poets in this mysterious need for withdrawal. For *The Hesperides* is a thoroughly integrated poem expressing, by means of symbol, the need to preserve untouched and inviolate an inner and mysterious world:

> The golden apple, the golden apple, the hallowed fruit,
> Guard it well, guard it warily,
> Singing airily,
> Standing about the charmèd root.
> Round about all is mute,
> As the snowfield on the mountain-peaks,
> As the sandfield at the mountain-foot.
> Crocodiles in briny creeks
> Sleep and stir not: all is mute.
> If ye sing not, if ye make false measure,
> We shall lose eternal pleasure,
> Worth eternal want of rest.
> Laugh not loudly: watch the treasure
> Of the wisdom of the west.

The Hesperian Paradise, notably paradisal in its want of stir and activity, is preserved by watchfulness and incantation. The poem is a confident one. The value of the Hesperian Tree, and of the Hesperian existence is never for a moment questioned; there is no sense that an eternity spent in guarding this symbolic apple could be a sin or a mistake. There is an uncanny fear in the poem; but this is a fear of possible attacks from the world beyond the sea:

Number, tell them over and number
How many the mystic fruittree holds,
Lest the redcombed dragon slumber
Rolled together in purple folds.
Look to him, father, lest he wink, and the golden apple be
                                                    stol'n away,
For his ancient heart is drunk with over-watchings night and day,
Round about the hallowed fruittree curled—
Sing away, sing aloud evermore in the wind, without stop,
Lest his scalèd eyelid drop,
For he is older than the world.

In this poem Tennyson seems serenely conscious of the necessity and value of a place of withdrawal. Indeed the symbols of withdrawal, the garden, the tower and the palace, appear again and again in poems of his period, and, for good measure, the Lady of Shalott's tower is 'On an island in the river'. But *The Hesperides* has a more positive symbol:

The golden apple, the golden apple, the hallowed fruit.

Perhaps the apple is, as some critics have suggested,[13] a symbol of poetic power; certainly it is described as 'the treasure of the wisdom of the West', and is infinitely precious, far more precious than the web of the Lady of Shalott. The perpetual incantation, the ritual, not only of the singing daughters of Hesperus, but of the poem itself suggests more than this, it suggests the creation and preservation of integrity, the making of an unstained and virgin world, a charmed province of being into which the outer world cannot break. No false note, no false step in the dance is possible; were the ritual order broken, the enemy would rush in and the island paradise be destroyed.

The Hesperides is, however, the only poem of the period in which Tennyson seems absolutely sure that there is a sovereign obligation to the island paradise and the symbolic apple. Elsewhere personal withdrawal is obtained at a cost. And yet there is no question, except in *The Palace of Art*, of a moral condemnation of this withdrawal. Neither *The Lotos-Eaters*, nor *The Lady of Shalott* are held up for censure. Yet the paradise of the Lotos-Eaters is subtly different from that of the daughters of Hesperus. The island of Hesperus is a place of absolute silence and slumber, and yet of incessant activity: the three sisters are perpetually weaving the spell which preserves the apple, and the peace. The island of the Lotos-Eaters is, on the other hand, a place where 'it is always afternoon', and so far from preserving anything, it is represented as giving rest only by the denial of natural affections:

> And sweet it was to dream of Fatherland,
> Of child, and wife, and slave; but ever-more
> Most weary seem'd the sea, weary the oar,
> Weary the wandering fields of barren foam.
> Then some one said, 'We will return no more;'
> And all at once they sang, 'Our island home
> Is far beyond the wave; we will no longer roam.'

The reality of normal relationships already appears pleasant to the poet, and, even given the promise to the mariners, of an end to strife and trouble, the island is only attractive to those rejecting life; there is a twilight, dying quality about it:

> Dark faces pale against that rosy flame,
> The mild-eyed melancholy Lotos-eaters came.

In *Mariana* the sense of dreariness is deepened; though the moated grange is an ideal place for withdrawal, its inhabitant wilts and fades for want of human companionship:

> She only said, 'My life is dreary,
> He cometh not,' she said.

On the other hand in *The Lady of Shalott* Tennyson is acutely aware that there is a danger in the encroachments of the outer world. The magical lady, watching her mirror, becomes aware of human relationship and its possibilities:

> Or when the moon was overhead,
> Came two young lovers lately wed;
> 'I am half sick of shadows,' said
> The Lady of Shalott.

The fact that these lovers are 'lately wed' has made Tennyson too much an object of derision; they are not, after all, types of a sentimental but of a recognised and permanent social relationship, just as the other figures seen in the mirror, the market girl, the knight, the squire, even the funeral cortège, represent the real order and the real happenings of human life. Still watching the mirror the Lady falls in love with Sir Lancelot,

> She left the web, she left the loom,
> She made three paces thro' the room,
> She saw the water-lily bloom,
> She saw the helmet and the plume,
> She look'd down to Camelot.

She attempts to leave the world of shadows, but in the attempt she destroys both her retreat and herself. Here the theme of *The Hesperides* is repeated. If the spell is broken by a disobedient or an erratic movement the precious thing is in danger. If the outer world exerts too great an attraction the inner world is shattered, and the soul dies. But in *The Lady of Shalott* the outer world is thought of as a real good.

This, then, is the dilemma. The soul only preserves its integrity and power when it is withdrawn, but while it is withdrawn, it is turned in on itself, misses the liveliness of common life and turns sour, corrupt and sluggish. I do not think that, in the poems we have been discussing, Tennyson is apprehending this dilemma as a moral problem. There is no suggestion that the Lady is guilty of a crime in isolating herself, and in *The Hesperides* the enchantment which keeps the island safe is clearly thought of as good, good, that is, not in a moral sense, but in the sense that the apple itself is 'good', golden, precious and desirable. Even in *The Lotos-Eaters* there is no explicit condemnation of the mariners; they obey the soul's deep need for rest and they pursue no forbidden pleasure. But there is a superficial resemblance between the wood of pleasure in *Sense and Conscience* and the islands of the Lotos-Eaters and the daughters of Hesperus; it is easy to see how one situation could be mistaken for the other, and how, under the pressure of Apostolic argument and Tennyson's own conscience, the dilemma presented in these poems could be turned into a moral issue, an issue, that is, which required judgment of values and deliberate choice.

Tennyson's awareness of his own needs was largely non-rational and in attempting to give to himself as well as to others a rational account of his own confusion he was apt to adopt the formula nearest to hand. Later on in life, in speaking of *Ulysses* he said that it expressed his need to go on more simply than anything in *In Memoriam*. Both *Ulysses* and *In Memoriam* represent an experience a great deal more complex than this simple moral predicate suggests, but the statement indicates if it does not sum up Tennyson's situation at the time of writing these poems. In the same way the Apostolic formula 'We cannot live in Art' indicates something of Tennyson's position when he was an undergraduate. The Apostolic discussions about their mission to society, and their strong sense of purpose, may well have brought his problem to the surface. For the deep psychological craving for relationship, the need to be at one with one's fellows, is neatly, too neatly, represented in the argument that individuals were made to be of service to the community, and the deliberate isolation of the soul very adequately symbolised by the self-cultivation of aestheticism. Tennyson apprehended Trench at a deeper level than Trench realised, but it is clear from the 1832 version of *The Palace of Art* that he was translating a spiritual problem into moral terminology:

> So that my soul beholding in her pride
>   All these, from room to room did pass;
> And all things that she saw, she multiplied,
>   A many-facèd glass.
>
> And, being both the sower and the seed,
>   Remaining in herself became
> All that she saw, Madonna, Ganymede,
>   Or the Asiatic dame—
>
> Still changing, as a lighthouse in the night
>   Changeth athwart the gleaming main,
> From red to yellow, yellow to pale white,
>   Then back to red again.[14]

These verses, omitted in the 1842 and later editions of the poem, make it clear that 'my soul', is one stage further from reality than the Lady of Shalott. She saw all things in the mirror of the mind, and wove them into a web of fantasy. The Soul draws everything into itself, it feeds on and nourishes itself. Even in the final version of *The Palace of Art* we are left with the impression that it is not the pursuit of 'Art', but the pride of isolation which has tainted and destroyed life in the Palace of Art; not that the poet has too much indulged his sense of beauty, but that he has withdrawn himself too much from his fellows. His state, even to the morbid corruptions of the beautiful things collected together, is not unlike that of the Ancient Mariner, 'Alone, alone and all alone/Alone on a wide sea.' where 'the very deep did rot.' This kind of image recurs in *The Palace of Art*:

> But in dark corners of her palace stood
>   Uncertain shapes; and unawares
> On white-eyed phantasms weeping tears of blood,
>   And horrible nightmares,
>
> And hollow shades enclosing hearts of flame,
>   And, with dim fretted foreheads all,
> On corpses three-months-old at noon she came,
>   That stood against the wall.

> A spot of dull stagnation, without light
>   Or power of movement, seem'd my soul,
> 'Mid onward-sloping motions infinite
>   Making for one sure goal.
>
> A still salt pool, lock'd in with bars of sand,
>   Left on the shore; that hears all night
> The plunging seas draw backward from the land
>   Their moon-led waters white.

Tennyson, like Coleridge tacked a moral explanation on to his poem, an explanation which, though accurate, is not adequate to what is expressed in the imagery. But, unlike *The Ancient Mariner*, *The Palace of Art* was first conceived of as an allegorisation of this superficial moral. That it also retains and conveys other meanings is due, partly, to the power of the imagination to resist the merely rational, partly to the fact that, on its own level, the Art/Life antithesis really does represent the deeper problem of Tennyson's kind of temperament. Art is, and can stand for a fantasy world, but, more than this, it presents a situation analogous to that in which Tennyson was involved. The need of such a temperament as his is for withdrawal, a withdrawal in which it remains passive, and contemplates rather than acts on reality. Aesthetic awareness also depends on this passiveness; contemplation and some kind of perceptive quiet is, and must be, a preliminary to creation. The Lady of Shalott contemplates in her mirror what she afterwards weaves into her tapestry. At the same time, just as nothing so much stultifies the contemplative mind as mere passivity, mere solitude, so nothing so much enervates the artist as a deliberate and exclusive cultivation of the 'artistic'. *The Palace of Art* and the other poems of this period are not exclusive in their allegorical significance, they can refer to more than one aspect of this problem. By the same token it is a mistake to suppose that any one of them presents a solution of, or delivers judgment about the situation described. Most of them are ambiguous. All of them are delicately balanced between two worlds.

It is easy, confronted with this problem in Tennyson's development, to speak of him as 'lacking the courage of his experience'. That is not the question. The man was faced with two possibilities, both good, both fundamental to his soul's health and to his vocation as a poet, and yet apparently mutually exclusive. The poetry he was writing at this time is an exploration of this question: How is the poet to find and establish himself? It is fairly easy to see this in the fantasy poems we have been discussing. The situation would have arisen even if the Apostles' club had never been invented, nor endowed by Maurice with moral earnestness. It is a perennial problem for the human mind. But the deliberations of the Apostles did give Tennyson's consideration of it a particular bias; and a bias, moreover, which affected the whole technique of his writing. The establishment of relationship, in the discussion of the Apostles, required an attention to one's fellow men, a duty conceived of in the liberalistic terms of the period, and inspired with the profound conviction of the value of the individual which had been common to all the Romantic poets. Everything human was valuable and therefore fit for poetry. The Wordsworthian tendency to base a theory of poetry upon doctrines about the 'primary laws of our nature', persisted throughout the century. The insistence on the social responsibility exercised by the poet in describing and moving 'the passions which built up our human soul' seems to have had Tennyson's approval; the poetry which he writes under the conviction of social duty is Wordsworthian, that is, it is about simple people, it is anecdotal, it is intended to point the moral of man's relationship to man in nature and in the common social order. Its model (one has to remember that *The Prelude* was not published until 1850) was the lyrical ballad. But the net result of Tennyson's attempt to do his duty as a poet was the transference of his own problem into the outer world. Lady Clara Vere de Vere is exhorted to take on the responsibilities of her station:

> Oh! teach the orphan-boy to read,
>   Or teach the orphan-girl to sew,
> Pray Heaven for a human heart,
>   And let the foolish yeoman go.

And she is described as, like the Soul in *The Palace of Art*, sickening of a vague disease of the mind. Practical activity instead of the contemplation of her own beauty and power is what is required of her. Even the unfortunate May Queen is guilty of a village self-indulgence, a concentration (to the detriment of one Robin) on her personal pride in being May Queen. Nor is it fanciful, I think, when we come to the 1842 volume to see poems like *Godiva* and *St. Simeon Stylites* in the same context as *Lady Clara Vere de Vere* and *The Lady of Shalott*. St Simeon Stylites is the representative of an unnatural withdrawal, of excessive self-cultivation, leading to the maceration of all that is natural and decent in human life, but Lady Godiva, in order to help the citizens of Coventry, comes naked from her sheltering castle, and puts aside her modesty as the poet has to put aside reticence about his inner life. I do not know whether Tennyson intended to express this meaning —his explicit moral is social and political: the fable illustrates the contention that care for the poor is a matter not only for reform agitations, but for personal sacrifice:

> Not only we, the latest seed of Time,
> New men, that in the flying of a wheel
> Cry down the past, not only we, that prate
> Of rights and wrongs, have loved the people well,
> And loathed to see them overtax'd; but she
> Did more, and underwent, and overcame.

But the choice of an illustration in which the sacrifice admired is one in which nakedness and integrity are linked together, and the persistence in the poem of the symbol of the Lady in the Tower, do suggest yet another image of the soul's encounter with the world. But here, as with *St. Simeon Stylites*, there is a note of moral judgment absent from earlier poems on this theme.

With these two poems we have moved on to a new phase of Tennyson's work, the phase after the death of Hallam in which his personal problem, if not solved, at any rate begins to be seen in the context of a rudimentary social philosophy. This we have to discuss in later chapters, and must for the moment return to Tennyson and the Apostles. If the conflict in Tennyson's personality really runs through such diverse poems as *The Lady of Shalott* and *The May Queen*, how is it that so many of these pastoral idylls arouse criticism, not only for their content but also for the remarkably smooth and polished surface of the verse itself? There is nothing technically wrong with Tennyson's poetry at this period, no horrid solecism like false rhyme or stumbling beat; the real trouble is that the polish is so high that it seems glittering and artificial. If we are to blame Hallam and the Apostles for anything, it is for this. Their original premise was sound enough—poetry *has* a social function, and the corollary drawn from this premise, that it exercises that function by moving the heart is, if controversial, not necessarily false. But they were urging on Tennyson a function which he was too inexperienced to fulfil. At twenty-one he had no knowledge at all 'of man, the heart of man and human life'. This would not have mattered if Tennyson had not already been so *technically* competent within his own range: normally, in dealing with subjects outside his range, a poet writes badly. He only finds an appropriate manner when

he gets the measure of his subject. Tennyson had evolved a style suited
to his own fantasies, and he transfers it, almost unaltered, to the domestic
and pastoral subjects urged on him by his friends and critics. The effect
is very much what it might be if Milton, say, or Keats, were to write
The Idiot Boy and *The Mad Mother* in the style of *Comus* or *Endymion*.
The extraordinary glitter, for instance, of *The Miller's Daughter*, in
which the heroine, poor girl, is decked out in metrical diamonds, softens
into pleasant lyric when the subject matter invites Tennyson's technical
gift:

> Remember you the clear moonlight
> That whitened all the eastern ridge,
> When o'er the water dancing white,
> I stepped upon the old mill-bridge.
> I heard you whisper from above
> A lute-toned whisper, 'I am here'
> I murmured, 'Speak again, my love,
> The stream is loud: I cannot hear.'
>
> I heard, as I have seemed to hear,
> When all the under-air was still,
> The low voice of the glad new year
> Call to the freshly-flowered hill.
> I heard, as I have often heard
> The nightingale in leavy woods
> Call to its mate, when nothing stirred
> To left and right but falling floods.

Even at its most pleasant there is more in this diction of Tennyson's
observation and sensibility than of his knowledge of the heart of man.

All this does not mean that Tennyson's manner of writing necessarily
forbids him the treatment of the 'primary laws of our nature'. All it
means is that his development had to be Tennysonian, not Wordsworthian. As we saw in the last chapter there is a direct relationship between
his incantatory style and the curious dream-like state of his sensibility.
We also saw that it is possible to use this dream-like awareness of the
world to express and explain reality. In *Mariana* and most of the poems
of *Poems, Chiefly Lyrical* Tennyson's concern was to create symbols for
the quality of experience, or of persons, but in the *Poems* of 1832 he
seems to be extending the range of symbols. No one can fail to see that
Tennyson's method of writing is mythological. In the poems we have
been discussing he has been exploring his own position, but he presents
his state, and the dilemmas which create it, in terms of significant

narrative, a narrative which is, ostensibly, remote from his particular situation. This has a curious effect. It cannot be said that the problems Tennyson expresses are altogether remote from 'man, the heart of man and human life'. He happens to be aware of these particular problems because they are his own, and his interest in them is primarily personal, but his choice of the indirect medium of expression, the story, as it were universalises his knowledge. It makes a personal poem the objective symbol of a human situation. This is a method of writing peculiarly congenial to the romantic mind, and by the romantic mind I mean a consciousness which, while apparently withdrawn into itself, away from the pressure of routine existence, is engaged in the continuous discovery of the strange, underlying rhythms of that routine existence. Its actual apprehension of significance is largely non-rational, that is, it is not the result of a train of argument, or the fierce activity of the discursive reason, but rather of the accumulation and contemplation of impressions. Such a mind presents its intuitions to itself in images and pictures, or in stories where the significance of human behaviour is revealed by the accentuation of a simple and striking context. In *The Ancient Mariner*, for instance, the narrative carries a moral and psychological meaning more important than the story, although the actual events of the Mariner's voyage do not themselves suggest, except in the crudest manner, any significance at all. The importance of what happens is revealed in the underlining of detail, the emphasis which brings particular events into prominence. The constant reference to the movement of sun and stars serves, in this poem, not a narrative, but an emotional purpose. But, *pace* Mr House, the emotional purpose is only served, the significant pattern is only revealed, because the human mind is accustomed to attach mysterious meanings to ordinary natural forces and to cause them to stand for something other than themselves. The Romantic poets, with a kind of obstinate unanimity, persistently return to symbols of this kind; to the sea, the desert, the mountain, the running stream which certainly in Shelley, and perhaps in Keats, comes to stand for life and thought united in the personality of the poet. Constant use of this common imagery serves a symbolic rather than a narrative purpose, that is it directs the reader's mind to the fact that the story told has a mysterious significance reflected in the images used. By the way in which they are handled, the images through which they are presented, events are mythologised, they stand not only for themselves, but for something, not always neatly definable, common and recognisable in the deeper life of human beings.

This is most obvious in Coleridge's best work, and the odd thing is that Coleridge does not seem to have been one of Tennyson's early masters. But Tennyson had fully grasped the use and value of Coleridge's method. We find him, almost unaware of what he was doing, struggling with it in *Sense and Conscience*. This poem was in intention a simple allegory; it presents a story in which the narrative is no more than a vehicle for a moral meaning, is unreal apart from that meaning. Even the characters are faculties of the mind personified. But when Conscience, drugged by the arts of Sense, is carried into a dark wood, the poem begins to suggest a significance beyond that which Tennyson intended. For the purposes both of story and moral the wood might as well have been a field, a drawing-room, or a dungeon, but it is described in a manner which gives it a sinister significance; it is a flowery land that becomes barren, and displays in its visible beauty the suggestion of corruption and doom. The same dark wood appears in *A Dream of Fair Women*:

> At last methought that I had wander'd far
>   In an old wood: fresh-wash'd in coolest dew
> The maiden splendours of the morning star
>   Shook in the steadfast blue.
>
> Enormous elm-tree-boles did stoop and lean
>   Upon the dusky brushwood underneath
> Their broad curved branches, fledged with clearest green,
>   New from its silken sheath.

* * *

> There was no motion in the dumb dead air,
>   Not any song of bird or sound of rill;
> Gross darkness of the inner sepulchre
>   Is not so deadly still
>
> As that wide forest. Growths of jasmine turn'd
>   Their humid arms festooning tree to tree,
> And at the root thro' lush green grasses burn'd
>   The red anemone.

The reader's mind is stirred with the memory of other dangerous woods, the memory, enshrined in fairy tales, of the great dark forests of Europe in the Middle Ages, or even the literary recollection of the woods in *Comus* and *A Midsummer Night's Dream*. Woods are known to be places of enchantment and danger, and Tennyson recreates the chill fear and attraction of them. The context in which he does so is significant. Conscience, the active moral power, is laid asleep there; in *A Dream of Fair Women* the poet enters the forest, where he meets the Enchantresses of the past, and all his fancies and half dreams, in the first drowse of sleep,

> Stream'd onward, lost their edges, and did creep
> Roll'd on each other, rounded, smooth'd and brought
> Into the gulfs of sleep.

If this were not enough, a voice reminds the poet that the wood, which he recognises, and where he remembers to have been 'joyful and free from blame' is all his own until the end of time. The poet has clearly passed into the underworld of sleep for which, in this poem, the mysterious wood stands. It is imperative to add that this symbolic relationship is not a static one: what is said about the wood must be understood as said of the subconscious mind for which it stands, so that when Conscience, awaking from sleep, casts down the beautiful flowers with which the forest of his prison is adorned, we are not surely at fault in supposing this to mean the blasting of flowery irresponsibility when conscious moral judgment takes over. This is the way in which myth is made, indeed it is its very substance.

In moving away from conscious allegory, Tennyson shows his awareness of this. In *The Palace of Art* he is still creating a mechanism for a moral, and this is to some extent true even of *Œnone* where the judgment of Paris is represented as a judgment between values, rather blatantly typified by the three goddesses; a judgment in which Tennyson was at that time especially interested. But the story of *Œnone* is not, like that of *The Palace of Art*, a story invented for Tennyson's purposes and therefore subordinated to them. It has a life and meaning of its own. The gods will not obey the dictates of a mere moral fable, and though Pallas, Hera and Aphrodite are the mouthpieces of Tennyson's debate they are still powers in their own right:

> Naked they came to that smooth-swarded bower,
> And at their feet the crocus brake like fire.

The implications of Paris's choice cannot be made merely moral or personal: the great tragedy of Troy, the pathos of the Prince's desertion of the nymph Œnone appear through and almost overwhelm the allegory:

Dear mother Ida, hearken ere I die.
They came, they cut away my tallest pines—
My dark tall pines, that plumed the craggy ledge
High over the blue gorge, or lower down
Filling greengulphèd Ida, all between
The snowy peak and snowwhite cataract
Fostered the callow eaglet—from beneath
Whose thick mysterious boughs in the dark morn
The panther's roar came muffled, while I sat
Low in the valley. Never, nevermore
Shall lone Œnone see the morning mist
Sweep thro' them.[15]

Tennyson does not achieve all the potentialities of his story, for the truth is that Œnone is a young man's poem and rather self-conscious. But it is unfair to suggest that he was ignorant that the story had possibilities beyond the deliberate moral of his allegory. His account of Paris's judgment is, after all, cast into the form of Œnone's lament; we are not dealing with an emblematic presentation of the case. It is true, however, that the stiffness and unsubtlety of the overt moral hinders the dramatic and narrative interest of the poem and prevents the other, the latent meanings of the story, from coming to the surface, except at odd moments in the descriptions when Ilion is contrasted with Ida, or Pallas with Aphrodite.

A good many of these early poems are not narrative poems in the fullest sense: they are what Tennyson called 'Idylls', that is, they combine the characteristics both of the narrative poem and the lyric. The poet selects some moment in a well known story, for dramatic or descriptive presentation, and builds his theme upon this narrow base. The narrative, descriptive, or psychological interest of the story is maintained. *The Lady of Shalott*, *The Hesperides*, *The Lotos-Eaters* all present a true dramatic interest, they are not simply the obvious vehicle of a theme. Sometimes these poems may seem to be no more than 'pure poetry', nothing but incantation. Their underlying meaning begins to appear only with the repetition of images and symbolic motifs. The persistence of such images impresses the reader with a sense of meaning: it is not that he is forced to translate and decode the poem's descriptions, but that the constant recurrence of towers, islands, enchantments awakens associations in his mind and communicates a sense of significance not apparent on the surface of the poem. That this is not a subjective process, something that readers imagine, is indicated by Tennyson's explanation, to Canon Ainger, of *The Lady of Shalott*:

> The new born love for something, for some one in the wide world, from which she has so long been excluded, takes her out of the region of shadows into that of realities.[16]

Hallam Tennyson speaks of the 'key to the tale of magic "symbolism" ' and says that it is to be found in the lines about the lovers,[17] a view which one supposes he derived from his father. Now no one ascribes mystical or symbolic meanings to his own poetry unless he had intended the meanings to be there. The interesting thing is that Tennyson uses symbols which are by no means exclusively personal; they belong to the myths and legends which he is using. The tower in which a lady is imprisoned is ubiquitous in fairy tale, it is the tower in which the fairy Princess is always imprisoned by the enchanter. The spells and enchantments which suspend the activity of the ordinary world for the Lady of Shalott appear again in the islands of Hesperus and the Lotos-Eaters and they are not Tennyson's inventions. No more is the golden apple of the Hesperian tree which, in *Œnone*, Paris gave to Aphrodite; it is the apple of discord which turned the course of Atalanta. And we remember that Eve plucked an apple from a tree in a garden. These are universal symbols. The question is, if Tennyson is trying to explore human reality by means of these symbols, how does he achieve this end, and why, of all the stories which were available to him did he choose those with these repetitive elements?

The first question, in a sense, answers the second, for it is the mode in which he explores human reality which determines Tennyson's choice of story. The use of narrative as symbol is the natural development of the poetic technique discussed in the last chapter. Where detail is used to evoke mood the detail itself appears to have a significance beyond its immediate context. This is especially true of a poem like *The Hesperides*. In many ways this poem has considerable affinities with *Leonine Elegiacs*, that is, the aesthetic pleasure which we derive from it appears to be largely dependent on modulation. It is unashamedly incantatory. But this incantation is used to preserve the 'treasure of the West'. In the repetition of the line,

The golden apple, the golden apple, the hallowed fruit,

the pleasure of which turns on the shift and balance of vowels, we become aware that the apple is infinitely mysterious and meaningful in itself. It is the very rhythm which suggests and defines its status as a symbol. In the same way we find Tennyson using those powers of emotional and sensuous association which we noted in the last chapter, to bring out the value of his symbol. In *The Lady of Shalott*, for instance, a change of weather marks the change of mood and the progress of the enchantment. When Sir Lancelot appears it is in the bright, clear light of the sun:

> A bow-shot from her bower-eaves,
> He rode between the barley-sheaves,
> The sun came dazzling thro' the leaves,
> And flamed upon the brazen greaves
>   Of bold Sir Lancelot.

But when the Lady attempts to go to the window, and breaks the enchantment

> In the stormy east-wind straining,
> The pale yellow woods were waning,
> The broad stream in his banks complaining,
> Heavily the low sky raining
>   Over tower'd Camelot;

All the way through the poem there is this contrast between the fruitful world, the world of the barley sheaves, the fields and the reapers, and the world of the Lady in the tower. Tennyson has used his peculiar art to build up a true contrast, emotional and imaginative as well as symbolic, between these two states. The associations of sun and harvest, the constant recalling of the bearded barley, the barley sheaves, the fields of barley and of rye, and the repeated detail of the harvest picture, bring the mind into a mood of tranquil content totally absent from the world of enchantment in which the Lady lives:

> Willows whiten, aspens quiver,
> Little breezes dusk and shiver
> Thro' the wave that runs for ever
> By the island in the river
>   Flowing down to Camelot.
> Four gray walls, and four gray towers,
> Overlook a space of flowers,
> And the silent isle imbowers
>   The Lady of Shalott.

The Lady's world, in descriptions which recall parts of *Mariana*, is presented as one of remoteness and stillness set in an environment of barren motion, for the emphasis of this description on the movement

of the willows and the wave colours our awareness of her unmoving
life in the tower, especially of her contemplations in the mirror:

> And moving thro' a mirror clear
> That hangs before her all the year,
> Shadows of the world appear.

The mirror is felt to have an affinity with the river, and the mood which
we associate with the Lady is created by Tennyson's description of the
waves and willows. The sense of barrenness is deepened again by the
description of the sky and the weather at her death. The mood of
melancholy associated with the sighing movement of willow trees and
water stands for the Lady in our minds. It fixes her significance in the
poem, and, in conjunction with certain other things, shows us how the
narrative is to be understood. Similarly in poems like *Tithonus* or *The
Lotos-Eaters* there is no story, the dramatic moment chosen is developed
by means of images and the moral element in it is brought out entirely
by evocation.

The dramatic moments in these poems present recurrent situations
in the life of rational choice which, by nature, belongs to reasoning
beings, and it is these recurrent situations which prompt the choice of
story. *The Lotos-Eaters* neither condemns nor approves the mariners,
it simply evokes the utter weariness which follows strain and effort, and
the sweetness of the promised rest:

> There is sweet music here that softer falls
> Than petals from blown roses on the grass,
> Of night-dews on still waters between walls
> Of shadowy granite, in a gleaming pass;
> Music that gentlier on the spirit lies,
> Than tir'd eyelids upon tir'd eyes;
> Music that brings sweet sleep down from the blissful skies.

The passage suggests and creates an impression of the sensuous quality
of rest, and it does so by means of images which are themselves
thoroughly wholesome. This music is not like the song of the sirens
which lulls the sense 'and in sweet madness robs it of itself'; it retains,
and so imparts to the sleep offered, an element of normality:

> Music that gentlier on the spirit lies,
> Than tir'd eyelids upon tir'd eyes.

It is easy to miss, not be conscious of, the fact that the sense of rest, of
sleep built up in this passage is entirely created in terms of music so that
there is an exchange of emotional and imaginative effect in the poem

which gives it imaginative density. But to the normal mind there is, in spite of the wholesomeness of the music, something alien about the island and its natives:

> whoso did receive of them,
> And taste, to him the gushing of the wave
> Far far away did seem to mourn and rave
> On alien shores; and if his fellow spake,
> His voice was thin, as voices from the grave;
> And deep-asleep he seem'd, yet all awake,
> And music in his ears his beating heart did make.

The thin voices which mourn and rave all suggest the alien world of death, especially to a reader of Homer who would catch here the echo of the thin ghost voices summoned back by Ulysses. Many of the associations Tennyson evokes suggest great want of strength and energy, and this sense of languor is heightened by the movement and sound of the verse:

> And in the stream the long-leaved flowers weep,
> And from the craggy ledge the poppy hangs in sleep.

By creating both awarenesses in the reader, that of strong and natural attraction, and that of dangerous temptation, the poem not only catches the quality of the moment at which the mariners arrive at the island, but also presents this moment as the type of something in the human situation itself. For it is not the island only which remains in the reader's mind, but the contrast of rest on the land, and toil on the sea, and here we suppose the poem's significance to lie.

We cannot, however, leave *The Lotos-Eaters* without remarking that the transference of our attention from a particular situation to the general condition of men is achieved by the use of what is very nearly a stock metaphor:

> Let us alone. What pleasure can we have
> To war with evil? Is there any peace
> In ever climbing up the climbing wave?

The toils of normal life are here associated with, and indeed deliberately identified with those of the mariners at sea. This is especially so in the last verse, the revised version of which strengthens this association. But the sailors of *The Odyssey* were not fighting with evil, nor settling civil order—unless Poseidon be taken as standing for these things—and in ascribing these activities to them Tennyson has made their labours

represent the troubles of the whole toiling race of men. He does, as I
have said, use common images in his poems; universal symbols which
we find in the common deposit of myth and legend, but common images
are not always of this august kind. Tennyson, in fact, was able to make
his mariners represent mankind, not because his readers were familiar
with the symbolic possibilities of Homer, but because of the common
idiom which speaks of 'the sea of life', of 'battling with the waves of
sorrow', or 'a sea of troubles' and so on. For this kind of cliché the
Victorians had a very considerable capacity: the taste for it is easily seen
not only in the subject and problem pictures of the period, *The
Scape-goat*, *The Soul's Awakening* and so on, which, if everyone had
their due, represent a kind of pictorial wit, but also in the parodies of
Dickens and Thackeray. The address of Mr Stiggins to the elder
Weller in the Fleet Prison fully exemplifies the manner. This metaphor
embedded in common speech is accompanied by, and may well arise
from a fondness for stock dramatic situations:

> 'His little daughter, whose sweet face
> He kiss'd, taking his last embrace,
> Becomes dishonour to her race—'

Those death-beds, those forsaken maidens and dramatic returns at
which we smile sometimes, make it seem that the Victorian mind was
furnished with the oddments of sentimental melodrama, but they are
really more significant than that. The passage from *The Two Voices* is
to us melodramatic, to the Victorians it was emblematic of moral
horror. Within the framework of the Victorian consciousness these
stock situations have some of the force and potentiality which the older
legends had for the more primitive mind. Tennyson uses both for
both are common symbols. The general situation of *The Lotos-Eaters*
is borrowed from Odyssean legend, but there are built into it elements
which the Victorian could cheerfully claim for his own:

> Dear is the memory of our wedded lives,
> And dear the last embraces of our wives
> And their warm tears: but all hath suffer'd change:
> For surely now our household hearths are cold:
> Our sons inherit us: our looks are strange:
> And we should come like ghosts to trouble joy.

The return of a dead man or a man believed dead, to trouble the heir,
bears all the marks of a contemporary set-piece. Tennyson himself
was fond of it, and uses the motif again in *In Memoriam*, and at full

length in *Enoch Arden*. This most famous use of it endeared him to his own, and makes him suspect to a later generation. But in *The Lotos-Eaters*, in spite of its un-Homeric character, it sounds no jarring note. The truth is that Tennyson was an adept in transforming and using these embedded metaphors, and current legend-made conventions to his own purpose.

It is in the handling of stock situations, whether classical or contemporary, that his genius moves from the private to the public theme. And this is the bridge from the Tennyson of *Haroun Alraschid* to the Tennyson of *Audley Court*, *Edwin Morris*, and the final triumph of *Maud*. *Maud* is indeed a triumph for the Apostles' doctrine, because it abandons the Wordsworthian, and treats its subject in a Tennysonian manner. But discussion of the development of Tennyson's manner of comment on the modern scene must for the moment be postponed.

Chapter IV

In Memoriam A. H. H.

THE natural and gradual development of Tennyson's personality and talent, which we have been discussing in the last two chapters, was interrupted. In September 1833 Arthur Hallam died in Vienna. His death was the most significant single event in Tennyson's life and more than anything else it determined the course of his mind. But, if it is considered as an isolated event, too much influence has been ascribed to it. One would suppose sometimes that Hallam died and life stopped —or stopped at any rate for Tennyson—until the publication of the 1842 *Poems*. If this really were so the loss of Hallam would be of little significance in Tennyson's development. The experience of loss is not, in a sane mind, insulated from other experiences; it does not rob the mourner of ordinary affections, nor save him from routine irritations. It is, in fact, because the eternal absence of the friend subtly modifies the quality of existence that bereavement becomes poetically significant:

> He is not here; but far away
>   The noise of life begins again,
>   And ghastly thro' the drizzling rain
> On the bald street breaks the blank day.

Hallam's friendship with Tennyson, though intense, was not exclusive. He was engaged to Tennyson's sister, Emily, and his intimacy with the family provided a link between the Cambridge and the Somersby circles. When he died it was Tennyson's elder brother Frederick, not Tennyson himself, who said 'We have lost our sheet anchor'. Hallam's open and confident temperament had provided an antidote for the Tennysonian malaise, and Tennyson was bound to feel his loss not merely in solitary grief but in the business of day to day relationships.

The legend which represents Tennyson as deliberately absorbed in gloom for years after Hallam's death ignores the practicalities of his situation, some of which were created, and all of which were exacerbated by his bereavement. Emily, for instance, refused to take her loss rationally: she indulged in a prolonged bout of Gothic suffering which seems, for a time, to have damaged her health. Other anxieties followed. Tennyson's younger brothers succumbed to the family malady; Edward suffered a complete mental breakdown, Septimus hovered on the brink of nervous collapse. All the while the Somersby household was overshadowed by the disapproving control exercised from Bayons Manor. Matters did not much improve when old Mr Tennyson died, for, in death as in life, the old man adhered, not altogether unjustifiably, to his preference for the younger branch of his house. The tension between Somersby and Bayons was prolonged until Tennyson's family left Somersby in 1837. As the acting head of the household Tennyson could hardly afford the luxury of an all-exclusive grief. Some one had to arrange for the welfare of Edward and Septimus, someone had to soothe Emily, and see to the details of the family's moving house. The legend of an impenetrable and continuing gloom minimises, too, the obvious lightening of Tennyson's mind after the family's departure from Somersby. This is more than a mere lightening of gloom; it is a positive joy:

> Now rings the woodland loud and long,
>   The distance takes a lovelier hue,
>   And drown'd in yonder living blue
> The lark becomes a sightless song.

There was good reason for this joy. The family had moved away from dependence on Bayons; Tennyson was in love with and engaged to be married to Emily Sellwood; his brother Charles was, for the moment, happily married to Miss Sellwood's younger sister, Louisa. There is very little excuse for the picture of Tennyson stupefying himself with melancholy like a dope addict who cannot be weaned from opium.

This is not in the least to suggest that his grief was not overwhelming. Hallam Tennyson says that his father told him his sorrow 'for a while blotted out all joy from his life, and made him long for death in spite of his feeling that he was in some measure a help to his sister'.[1] But contemporary evidence gives no picture of a mind unresistant to this sense of desolation. 'Alfred', wrote one of his friends, within a month or two of the catastrophe, 'tho' much broken in spirits is yet able to avert his thoughts from gloomy brooding, and keep his mind in activity.'[2] Alfred had so kept his mind in activity that in the last months of 1833 and the early part of 1834 he had composed *The Two Voices*, a version of *Tithonus*, eight sections of *In Memoriam* and a first draft of *Morte d'Arthur*.[3] That these poems were composed at all at such a time is indicative of an innate strength of mind, and their content is surprising for a man reputedly limp with mourning. For one of the principal marks of the poetry of this period is the determination not to be overcome by sorrow. In Section lxxxv of *In Memoriam*, which was composed, in part, between the September and the Christmas of 1833, Tennyson says that the very quality of his grief and of his love for Arthur forces him to recognise the claims of other relationships:

> I woo your love: I count it crime
> To mourn for any overmuch;
> I, the divided half of such
> A friendship as had master'd Time.

The balanced attitude of this poem surprised Bradley so much that he suspected a revision. The poem was revised but the original version is, if anything, stronger than its successor in its determination to master grief.

> What ever ways my days decline
> I felt and feel, tho' left alone,
> His being working in mine own,
> The footsteps of his life in mine;
>
> And so my passion hath not swerved
> To works of weakness, but I find
> An image comforting the mind,
> And in my grief a strength reserved.
>
> My pulses therefore beat again
> For other friends that once I met;
> Nor can it suit me to forget
> The mighty hopes that make us men.[4]

The same sense of the world waiting upon effort, 'the mighty hopes that make us men', is expressed with more imaginative power in *Ulysses*. '*Ulysses*', Tennyson says, 'was written soon after Arthur Hallam's death, and gave my feelings about the need of going forward and braving the struggle of life perhaps more simply than anything in *In Memoriam*.' The odd thing is that *Ulysses* does not express a conception of effort for effort's sake. There is a note in it of promise and desire:

> Yet all experience is an arch wherethro'
> Gleams that untravell'd world, whose margin fades
> For ever and for ever when I move.
> How dull it is to pause, to make an end,
> To rust unburnish'd, not to shine in use!
> As tho' to breathe were life. Life pil'd on life
> Were all too little, and of one to me
> Little remains: but every hour is saved
> From that eternal silence, something more,
> A bringer of new things; and vile it were
> For some three suns to store and hoard myself,
> And this gray spirit yearning in desire
> To follow knowledge like a sinking star,
> Beyond the utmost bound of human thought.

It would be one-sided not to add that, for all this desire, *Ulysses* is a poem about the last adventure of an old man, and an old man to whom all the really important things have already happened. His age is stressed, even in the passage quoted, and with his age an element of unsatisfied longing for something lost, as well as something still to be found. Hallam's death seems to strike at the youth in Tennyson, to make him seek for a symbol amongst old men. *Tithonus*, after all, was intended as a pendent to *Ulysses*, and in its first version[5] expresses nothing so much as an old man's desire to have done with living, simply to become nothing. The determination to carry on, the determination to behave rationally and not like a sick girl, does not cancel out the enormity of Tennyson's loss, the great blank of grief and bewilderment:

> 'But now the whole ROUND TABLE is dissolved
> Which was an image of the mighty world;
> And I, the last, go forth companionless,
> And the days darken round me, and the years,
> Among new men, strange faces, other minds.'

It would be cruel and callous, as well as a falsification of the facts, to suggest that the effort to 'divert the mind' was made without a great deal of anguish, or not against the pressure of an overwhelming desire to yield to misery and to die. But it *was* made; and the making of it brought Tennyson out of his ivory tower.

It is this struggle between mood and will which determines the greatness of *The Two Voices*. Sir Harold Nicolson says:

> In *The Two Voices* we have a definite and disturbing picture of Tennyson's panic-stricken bewilderment at the blow that had fallen; a picture of him gazing in an agony of despair at the ashes of a faith and fire that had once been his; a picture of a lonely frightened spirit crouched broodingly over thoughts of death.[6]

This represents an important element in Tennyson's mood, but it does less than justice to the poem. *The Two Voices* does present the picture of a man in the throes of a misery so great that neither rational argument, nor moral demands can touch it. But Sir Harold is so impressed by the emotional weight of this desolation that, in his analysis of Tennyson, he not only gives *The Two Voices* greater importance than any of the contemporary poems which express a different attitude, but he also minimises, in the poem itself, the imaginative effect of Tennyson's resistance to the 'still small voice'. The poem, he says, 'is composed in the curious minor key, that flickering half-light between the sane and the insane, which, as in *Maud*, constitutes Tennyson's most personal and poignant note.'[7] A comparison of *The Two Voices* and *Maud* will reveal the flaw in this view. The note of incipient madness in *Maud* is struck by the young man's attention to the irrelevant, and by his strained emptiness, and absence of mind:

> Strange, that the mind, when fraught
> With a passion so intense
> One would think that it well
> Might drown all life in the eye,—
> That it should, by being so overwrought,
> Suddenly strike on a sharper sense
> For a shell, or a flower, little things
> Which else would have been past by!

His mental life is dominated by inchoate images, the 'hard mechanic ghost' which follows him everywhere, the 'shadow still the same'. He is distracted by illusory visions and terrors. Tennyson's insight here is remarkably sensitive. Insanity has no standard of reference, it cannot argue. A similar incoherence is evident in *Supposed Confessions*:

> my own weakness fools
> My judgment, and my spirit whirls,
> Moved from beneath with doubt and fear.

The Two Voices is not in the least like this: its whole point is that it is a debate, that the voice is considered as a temptation, and answered obstinately from some inner and unfelt security which doubt and fear cannot move. The voice casts doubt on every possible comfort, but, significantly, what it does not alter is Tennyson's will to take comfort, to counter the suggestions of misery and see them for what they are:

> 'These words,' I said, 'are like the rest;
> No certain clearness, but at best
> A vague suspicion of the breast:'

Sir Harold would admit this determination of Tennyson's, but his contentions undermine its value. 'Tennyson', he says, 'is more convincing when he constructs the fabric of doubt, than when he endeavours to demolish this fabric with the tools of Faith.'[8] What else, one wonders, is to be expected? On an emotional level, the voice is quite right, not to be is to cease from misery, and is therefore infinitely desirable. If the voice were not convincing there would be no need for faith. But what is the fabric of doubt?

> Be near me when my light is low,
>> When the blood creeps, and the nerves prick
>> And tingle; and the heart is sick,
> And all the wheels of Being slow.
>
> Be near me when the sensuous frame
>> Is rack'd with pangs that conquer trust;
>> And Time, a maniac scattering dust,
> And Life, a Fury slinging flame.
>
> Be near me when my faith is dry,
>> And men the flies of latter spring,
>> That lay their eggs, and sting and sing
> And weave their petty cells and die.

The mental state expressed here was not intellectual doubt, but a condition three parts grief and overstrain, and one part native black-bloodness. It is not susceptible to cure by rational argument. The only thing that could relieve it would be a re-imagination of the human situation. So that when Tennyson argues in *The Two Voices*, when he gives reasons for living, of course they are none of them convincing because none of them touches the root of sorrow:

> The still voice laugh'd. 'I talk,' said he
> 'Not with thy dreams. Suffice it thee
> *Thy pain is a reality.*'

Emotionally, doubt has the upper hand, because it is itself an emotion. This certainly is the effect of individual exchanges in the poem, but the total effect is something else again. The tools of faith are neither convincing argument, nor yet emotional certainty. It is odd that Sir Harold, while asserting that Tennyson was a mystic wanting the courage of his mystical intuitions, should fail to recognise that courage when he sees it.

For Tennyson, like the mystic, asserts against the emotion of desolation the naked will to believe. It is a will to believe which is something more than mere obstinacy, and it sets before the suffering soul the reality of a truth which it knows, but in its grief is unable to feel:

> 'But thou,' said I, 'hast miss'd thy mark,
> Who sought'st to wreck my mortal ark,
> By making all the horizon dark.
>
> Why not set forth, if I should do
> This rashness, that which might ensue
> With this old soul in organs new?
>
> Whatever crazy sorrow saith,
> No life that breathes with human breath
> Has ever truly long'd for death.
>
> 'Tis life, whereof our nerves are scant,
> *Oh life, not death, for which we pant;*
> *More life, and fuller, that I want.'*

There is a distinction needed here between faith and dogma. The dogma, that is, the argument, of Tennyson's poem does not convince, is not well enough defined to carry any kind of conviction, but the faith—the insistence that underneath the illusion of sorrow there is somewhere a reality certainly carries conviction:

> 'Heaven opens inward, chasms yawn,
> Vast images in glimmering dawn,
> Half-shown, are broken and withdrawn
>
> Ah! sure within him and without,
> Could his dark wisdom find it out
> There must be answer to his doubt.'

Conviction in this case does not mean conversion to Tennyson's view on Tennyson's evidence, but the belief that Tennyson himself had grasped some certainty. The aesthetic effect of this does not appear in single images or the evocation of states of mind, but in the masculinity of the whole poem. It is not 'all over the place' like *Supposed Confessions*; it is supported by the argument and by an interior tension between the emotions of doubt and the believing will. For the will of the poet to live pulls against the emotionalism of a desire to give way and to die, and the exercise of moral discipline becomes a means of aesthetic control.

The development of Tennyson's mental life, and therefore of his poetry, was, during the seventeen-year period we are discussing, but especially in the ten years between 1832 and 1842, under the control of these two forces: it was a continuing battle between mood and will. In 1839 he wrote to Emily Sellwood:

> We must bear or we must die. It is easier perhaps to die, but infinitely less noble. The immortality of man rejects the thought, the immortality of man to which the aeons and the cycles are as hours and days.[9]

This passage reflects his preoccupations during this period; death, endurance, time and the nobility of man, and they are preoccupations to which the death of Hallam had driven him. *In Memoriam A. H. H.*, in which these themes are expanded, gathers and orders the moral experience of these years, and neither Tennyson's later life, nor his later work, can be understood without this record. This poem is a central and explanatory document in Tennyson's development, and though unpublished till 1850, must be seen as the background to the revisions and to the new work of the 1842 volume, and to *The Princess*, and even to the *Maud* volume of 1854.

II

To say that the poem is an important document in the history of Tennyson's mind is not to regard it as Mr Eliot regards it:

> It is a long poem made by putting together lyrics which have only the unity and continuity of a diary, the concentrated diary of a man confessing himself. It is a diary of which we have to read every word.[10]

This more or less states the present orthodoxy about the poem: the pleasure of reading *In Memoriam* is the pleasure proper to lyrical

7

poetry, and to autobiography; the enjoyment, that is, of the perfect evocation of mood, and of seeing in that evocation a man's mind unfold itself. Tennyson himself did not see the poem in this light:

> It must be remembered that this is a poem, not an actual biography. It is founded on our friendship, on the engagement of Arthur Hallam to my sister, on his sudden death at Vienna, just before the time fixed for their marriage, and on his burial in Clevedon Church. The poem concludes with the marriage of my youngest sister Cecilia. It was meant to be a kind of *Divina Commedia* ending with happiness.[11]

This was written in later years, when, in his role as the Ancient Sage, Tennyson subscribed to the legend of the sacredness of *In Memoriam*, so that when he says, in the same account of the poem, ' "I" is not always the author speaking of himself, but the voice of the human race speaking thro' him',[12] we perceive that the Laureate is wearing his oracular robes, and we wonder how far the statement tallies with his original inspiration. But his statements about the poem are so emphatic that it is fair to enquire how far we can accept Mr Eliot's description of it.

Certainly the word 'diary' is peculiarly felicitous, provided, that is, that we do not think of diaries as simply the records of personal introspection. This word suggests something of the quality of *In Memoriam*, the mixture of reminiscence, reflection and emotion that we should expect from a personal notebook, with the detail of daily life found in a journal. In *In Memoriam* our attention is not exclusively directed to a monotonously personal sorrow. We see Tennyson's friendship for Hallam as the centre and link of a web of relationships both at Somersby and at Cambridge, and we receive a picture not of the morbidly exclusive attachment of two young men for each other, but of Hallam as the central figure of an admiring group, and of Tennyson, lost in admiration and affection, on its fringes:

> The stern were mild when thou wert by,
> 　　The flippant put himself to school
> 　　And heard thee, and the brazen fool
> Was soften'd, and he knew not why;
>
> While I, thy nearest, sat apart,
> 　　And felt thy triumph was as mine;
> 　　And loved them more, that they were thine,
> The graceful tact, the Christian Art,

The special character of Tennyson's relations with Hallam are not disguised in this passage: it is, 'I, thy nearest', who 'sits apart', but the relationship is shown in the context of the social life which the two friends shared when:

> all in circle drawn
> About him, heart and ear were fed
> To hear him, as he lay and read
> The Tuscan poets on the lawn:
>
> Or in the all-golden afternoon
> A guest, or happy sister, sung,
> Or here she brought the harp and flung
> A ballad to the brightening moon:
>
> Nor less it pleased in livelier moods,
> Beyond the bounding hill to stray,
> And break the livelong summer day
> With banquet in the distant woods;
>
> Whereat we glanced from theme to theme,
> Discuss'd the books to love or hate,
> Or touch'd the changes of the state,
> Or threaded some Socratic dream.

It is this sense of a common life going on behind the friendship and behind the bereavement which gives *In Memoriam* something of the variety of a diary. The very fact that Tennyson's love for his friend was bound up with his most intimate concerns, with his family, and the intense intellectual life of his Cambridge circle, with his poetry, and even to some extent with his religion, made bereavement so much more desolating, so much more threatening both to the inner and the outer world. There are moments in the poem when grief is merely the intolerable pain in the breast:

> has the shock, so harshly given,
> Confused me like the unhappy bark
>
> That strikes by night a craggy shelf,
> And staggers blindly ere she sink?
> And stunn'd me from my power to think
> And all my knowledge of myself.

But the numbness of loss awakens to a passionate longing for the presence of the dead:

> Descend, and touch, and enter; hear
>   The wish too strong for words to name;
>   That in this blindness of the frame
> My Ghost may feel that thine is near.

Longing, not unnaturally, leads to reminiscence, and so to the consideration of the relationship which now exists between the living and
the dead. The circumstance of grief and loss colours old relationships,
and old discussions, and leads Tennyson to speculate about the state of
the dead, the reality of the bond of love, and the apparent contradiction
between the idealism of human love and the realities of the natural
world. The mind of the poet moves from lament to memory, and, as
in the apostrophe to Charles Tennyson on his wedding, to present joys.
The poem takes account of present incidents and present problems,
Tennyson notes events and argues problems in it just as one would
expect him to in the day to day record of a diary.

Yet it is precisely this characteristic of the poem's composition
which, in the long run, makes Mr Eliot's description of it inadmissible.
The sections of the poem, Tennyson says,

> were written at many different places, and as the phases of our
> intercourse came to my memory and suggested them.[13]

His note indicates that he had the habits of a diarist, but it is not a
description of *In Memoriam* as it exists. A diary records events and
reflections as they occur, and in the order in which they occur: it has
the continuity and the coherence of chronological order. There *is* a
chronological order in *In Memoriam* but it certainly does not represent
the order in which the poems were composed, and is conventional
rather than real. Indeed, with the exception of those poems which
deal with major events like the family's departure from Somersby, and
the marriage of Charles Tennyson, the sections which Bradley called
'time notes' do not refer to actual and datable happenings at all, but to
cycles of time, Christmas, spring, the return of the Anniversary of
bereavement. The conventional character of these poems is indicated
by the manner in which each one of them repeats and varies the theme
of its predecessor in the time scheme. These time poems are so presented
that they suggest that the events described happened in the three years
after Hallam died, yet the lyrics were not composed, as the entries in a
diary would be, contemporaneously with the events to which they are
linked. For example, Section lxxxv of the poem (This truth came borne
with bier and pall) was, in its earliest version, probably finished by the

end of 1833.[14] In the chronology of *In Memoriam* it is placed in the spring of 1835, and is immediately followed by a lyric which was actually written at Barmouth in 1839 (Sweet after showers ambrosial air), a poem which incidentally bears every mark of being the expression of a present emotion.[15] Besides this re-arrangement there is the fact that whole sections have been placed in the completed poem, and in some cases were specially written, to create the illusion of chronology.[16] Tennyson certainly wishes to give the impression of time passing, but he does it in a stylised manner very different from that of a diary.

This is exactly what we should expect. Although Tennyson speaks of 'short swallow flights of song', a phrase which suggests spontaneity in the expression of an immediate grief, he was never in his life satisfied with any such thing. His manuscripts show that his method was entirely different from that of the spontaneous poet. The Trinity manuscripts[17] alone give some five versions of *The Gardener's Daughter*, and three of *The Two Voices*, and from these notebooks we discover that it was Tennyson's method to work from fragments of verse which he returned to and elaborated later. He wrote down odd lines and half lines of poems which then, or many years after, might become the germ of a finished work. Then he made a copy of these verses and from it elaborated two or three drafts of the poem from which his final work would be created. And, after all this, the poem was privately printed in a trial edition, circulated for the criticism of friends, and only when this was done did it reach the consummation of publication. There is every sign that *In Memoriam* went through every stage of this process and it is possible to observe this creative work as it was happening. Hallam, Lord Tennyson says:

> On the evening of one of these sad winter days [i.e. immed-
> iately after Arthur Hallam's death] my father had already
> noted down in this scrap-book some fragmentary lines, which
> proved to be the germ of *In Memoriam*:

> > Where is the voice I loved? ah where
> > Is that dear hand that I would press?
> > Lo! the broad heavens cold and bare,
> > The stars that know not my distress!

> > The vapour labours up the sky,
> > Uncertain forms are darkly moved!
> > Larger than human passes by
> > The shadow of the man I loved,
> > And clasps his hands, as one that prays [18]

The ideas and images of this early expression of grief can be traced in the finished sequences of *In Memoriam*. The 'Vapour labouring up the sky' becomes

> The wild unrest that lives in woe
> Would dote and pore on yonder cloud
>
> That rises upward always higher,
>   And onwards drags a labouring breast,
>   And topples round the dreary west,
> A looming bastion fringed with fire.

The 'dear hand that I would press' is a constant motif in the poem:

> Doors, where my heart was used to beat
> So quickly, waiting for a hand,
>
> A hand that can be clasped no more—

or:

> And hands so often clasp'd in mine,
> Should toss with tangle and with shells.

The 'stars that know not my distress' become an image of that struggle of grief against an impersonal universe which dominates the progress of the poem:

> 'The stars,' she whispers, 'blindly run;
>   A web is wov'n across the sky;
>   From out waste places comes a cry,
> And murmurs from the dying sun.'

But if the passage quoted by Hallam Tennyson is the germ of *In Memoriam* it was not its beginning. Between September and December of 1833 Tennyson had composed a number of lyrics (Section ix of the poem 'Fair ship that from the Italian shore' is said to have been the first written) which formed the nucleus of the work. Rough drafts of some of these exist in the Trinity notebooks, and there are fair copies of some of them in the Heath Commonplace Book in the Fitzwilliam library.[19] In the Heath notebook the poems are numbered and arranged in such a way that they form a coherent group of verses on a theme. We know that Tennyson went on writing lyrics on the theme and in the metre of this first group of poems all the way through the thirties and forties. His friends describe him as adding to the 'Elegies' as they were then called, and writing out the new poems in the famous 'Butcher's Book', a long paged ledger notebook of the type then used for butcher's bills, and reading them aloud to the favoured few.[20] There is unfortunately no manuscript, at present available to us, of the earlier drafts of these poems,[21] but at least three versions of the completed poem, in the versions in which it existed before the edition of 1850, are still extant:(1) A manuscript which the present Lord Tennyson has lent to the Usher Gallery in Lincoln, (2) the Trinity manuscript, said to be the 'butcher's book', in the possession of Trinity College, Cambridge, (3) the proof copy of the 1850 edition which lacks, even at this stage, ten of the sections included in the final version. Both the Trinity and the Lincoln manuscripts show clearly that 'work' on the 'Elegies' meant correcting and polishing individual sections, and arranging them in a coherent order.[22] Mr Aubrey de Vere says that Tennyson had the poems set out on a ledger page so as to see more of them at once,[23] and some of the spacing and copying of the poems in both manuscripts show signs of this arrangement. The fact that most of the sections added to the poem in its final stages, and especially at the proof stage,[24] are repetition poems, recalling earlier lyrics in a way which brings out the coherence of Tennyson's theme does show Tennyson as concerned with the order of his work, and with the way in which that order brings out its meaning.

The question forced on us is: What then was Tennyson's view of the poem's order? He says that he did not write the various 'Elegies' with 'any view of weaving them into a whole, or for publication, until I found that I had written so many,'[25] although the careful numbering of the sections in the Heath notebook, and even in the Trinity notebooks, does suggest that, as early as 1833, he had already some idea that the poems could be fitted together. Some of the sections, like the collection of poems on the return of Hallam's body by sea have, of course, a natural relationship with each other, but it was not always easy to find a principle within the sections themselves which would bind them together and pull them into order, and still less to relate all the groups of lyrics together in one poem. But something of the way in which Tennyson moulded poems written on several subjects, in several moods and at several times, into a unit of meaning, can be discerned by tracing the genesis of the group of lyrics which runs from Section xxviii to Section xxxvii. This group included the first 'Christmas' poems, the 'Lazarus' poems, and the first of those in which Tennyson meditates on geological research. These poems are closely related to one another, and the whole group forms a sustained meditation on the theme of the absent dead, immortality, and love. First of all, Tennyson

presents his grief, his personal grief which is intensified for him by the
arrival of Christmas, but he presents it in the setting of a family
Christmas at Somersby:

> At our old pastimes in the hall
>   We gambol'd, making vain pretence
>   Of gladness, with an awful sense
> Of one mute Shadow watching all.
>
> We paused: the winds were in the beech:
>   We heard them sweep the winter land;
>   And in a circle hand-in-hand
> Sat silent, looking each at each.

But Christmas has two aspects; it is a family festival, made poignant
by the dead man's absence, and it is the celebration of the birth of
Christ. Although Tennyson is primarily concerned with the poignancy
of his grief in the midst of rejoicing, the fact that the rejoicing is for the
birth of Christ gives the whole of this meditation a framework of
reference with the Christian Revelation. It begins:

> The time draws near the birth of Christ;

and ends with a statement of the Incarnation:

> And so the Word had breath, and wrought
> With human hands the creed of creeds.

Three of the poems in the group, 'The time draws near the birth of
Christ' (xxviii), 'With trembling fingers did we weave' (xxx) and
'When Lazarus left his charnel-cave' (xxxiii), were among the first
poems to be written,[26] and were clearly meant to express not theological
speculation, but immediate grief. Even the Lazarus poem is, fundamentally, a poem on the same theme as the beautiful lyric 'O that
'twere possible', which was written at the time of Hallam's death, but
later became the germ of *Maud*:

> Ah Christ, that it were possible
> For one short hour to see
> The souls we loved, that they might tell us
> What and where they be.
>
> When Lazarus left his charnel-cave,
>   And home to Mary's house return'd,
>   Was this demanded—if he yearn'd
> To hear her weeping by his grave?

> 'Where wert thou, brother, those four days?'
> There lives no record of reply,
> Which telling what it is to die
> Had surely added praise to praise.

Tennyson, in fact, is treating the Lazarus story much as Browning treats it in *Karshish*, as a story of a man who could tell us about the after-life.

But if Tennyson's grief made him long to know about the after-life, the frame of revelation in which he thought about his grief brought him to consider the after-life in other ways. Hallam Tennyson says that his father thought the 'cardinal point of Christianity' was life after death, and when the three poems written on grief appear again in the Trinity manuscript as a group with the rest of Sections xxviii to xxxvii, the latent content both of the story of the birth of Christ and of the Lazarus story is brought out by the additions and developments of the first poems. Tennyson has added to the first two Christmas poems Section xxix 'With such compelling cause to grieve' which makes the transition from the personal grief of Section xxviii to the family trouble of Section xxx. *Now* Section xxx ends with the invocation to Christmas day:

> Rise, happy morn, rise, holy morn,
> Draw forth the cheerful day from night:
> O Father, touch the east, and light
> The light that shone when Hope was born.

We have already passed from grief, which is much stronger and more hopeless in the earliest manuscript version of the poem, to the hope contained in Revelation, for although 'the light that shone when Hope was born' is a kenning for the sun, it also refers to the new dawn of the after-life. From this we pass naturally to the Lazarus poems. The celebration of the birth of Christ links the family mourning for Arthur with the revelation of life after death, and the raising of Lazarus is a guarantee of that revelation.

It is perfectly clear that the Lazarus poem was not intended to carry this significance when it was first written. There are in the Trinity notebook two versions of 'When Lazarus left his charnel cave', but only one appears in the Heath notebook and that is a fair copy of the present Section xxxi. This clearly expresses what Tennyson wished to say at that time, that he longed to know what was after the grave. But in the final version of *In Memoriam* Tennyson includes the new poem Section xxxii 'Her eyes are homes of silent prayer', which he had, in fact, constructed from what was left of the two original versions of xxxi. He has done this, I think, for a purpose. Section xxxii describes St Mary Magdalen, and describes her as a type of unquestioning faith. Now this poem serves as a transition from the Lazarus poem to the poems of speculation about the validity of faith and love. For although the raising of Lazarus is a witness to survival, the revelation contained in it stopped short at a vital point:

> Behold a man raised up by Christ!
> The rest remaineth unreveal'd;
> He told it not; or something seal'd
> The lips of that Evangelist.

Because of this the Lazarus episode can stand for the ambivalence of revelation, and the story can lead to urgent questions about death. From this twisting together of the themes of revelation and death the speculative poems seem to arise naturally for their speculation is precisely about the need for and the value of revelation as a guarantee of known truth.

These poems, particularly Sections xxxiv and xxxv, show that they were composed at a different date and in a different mood from those of the first poems in the group. There is no sign of them at all in the notebooks of 1834 and 1835 at Trinity, and they are not in the Heath notebook. These sections of the poem were, clearly and admittedly, influenced by Sir Charles Lyell's *Principles of Geology*, a book which was published in 1833. Tennyson may have read it on its first appearance but he studied it, Hallam Tennyson says, 'for some months' in 1837.[27] Lines like these,

> The moanings of the homeless sea,
> The sound of streams that swift or slow
> Draw down Æonian hills, and sow
> The dust of continents to be,

bear the marks, not of a skim through of a fashionable book but of an imagination coloured by Lyell's descriptions and arguments: it would be sensible to suppose that these poems were composed in 1837 or later. Either, then, they were composed for, or deliberately linked with the Lazarus group of poems with which they stand in the Trinity manuscript. The connection is made through the figure of St Mary Magdalen who becomes the type of the devout Victorian lady, Tennyson's sisters, or his mother, whose faith was unquestioning: the antitype is the restless sceptic with his mind obsessed by geological doubt:

> O thou that after toil and storm
> > Mayst seem to have reach'd a purer air,
> > Whose faith has centre everywhere,
> Nor cares to fix itself to form,
>
> Leave thou thy sister when she prays,
> > Her early Heaven, her happy views;
> > Nor thou with shadow'd hint confuse
> A life that leads melodious days.

The Lady's, the Magdalen's, faith that the beloved survives is rooted in the revelation which her sceptical brother cannot accept. But revelation is not the only witness to life after death:

> My own dim life should teach me this,
> > That life shall live forever more.

The contrast between revealed truth and inner testimony allows Tennyson to introduce his poems of geological doubt, and with them a new theme and a new mood. The theme is the contrast of 'faith without form', that is without statements or dogmas, and faith linked with the 'flesh and blood' of Christ. The mood is the emotional depression which poisons an intellectual certainty. The horrors of the geological evidence threaten not the faith of the simple believer, but the promise of a faith without form. For the first time we hear the 'moanings of the homeless sea'. Geology seems to destroy the guarantee of 'my own dim life', and yet if there is no life beyond death, no purposed end to this animal existence, even the love between friends is unreal:

> And Love would answer with a sigh,
> > 'The sound of that forgetful shore
> > Will change my sweetness more and more,
> Half-dead to know that I shall die.'

Unless the soul is immortal even Tennyson's memories of Hallam are destroyed. He returns then to a need for revelation, to a need for a guarantee of survival outside subjective feeling, and beyond shaking by the evidence of fossil formations:

> And so the Word had breath, and wrought
> > With human hands the creed of creeds
> > In loveliness of perfect deeds,
> More strong than all poetic thought.

This section (xxxvi) ends this group of poems and gathers up the themes set out in the Christmas and Lazarus poems. Truth is admitted to be 'deep seated in our mystic frame', but this inner testimony is less important, and more vulnerable than 'Truth embodied in a tale':

> Which he may read that binds the sheaf,
>> Or builds the house, or digs the grave,
>> And those wild eyes that watch the wave
> In roarings round the coral reef.

But although this poem settles the claims of the two kinds of revelation, it is unlike the preceding poems in tone, and instead resembles the tone of the Prologue to *In Memoriam* which was written in 1849. Its direct reference to the validity of biblical revelation seems to belong to a much later date than the discussions of faith and form in Sections xxxiii and xxxiv. It cannot, however, be very much later since it appears in both the manuscripts and must therefore be dated sometime in the late thirties.[28] It looks as if Tennyson's hesitant return to Christian orthodoxy began rather earlier than we have generally supposed. We have, of course, to remember that Tennyson's adherence to Christianity is described in his own phrase 'Christianity is rugging at my heart': he was never exactly what one would describe as a pattern for the orthodox layman.

The Christmas-Lazarus group of lyrics shows that, in 'weaving' the Elegies together, Tennyson used verses composed at a later period of his bereavement, when reflection and endurance had matured his understanding, as a commentary on, and an interpretation of the poems composed in his first grief. The raising of Lazarus was at first a symbol of his mute desire to know the state of the dead: later it is set in a context of speculation about the guarantees of faith, and is finally integrated into a reassertion of his adherence to Christian truth. He intended, clearly, to give the Elegies not only coherence and unity, but an extra dimension. Again and again he returns to old themes and restates them in such a way that the new poems cast a backward light on the original statement of grief or despair. This is very obvious in the Christmas and Anniversary poems, but not all the repetitions are as inevitable as these. Section cxix, for instance, repeats and reverses, the mood of Section vii:

> Dark house, by which once more I stand
>> Here in the long unlovely street,
>> Doors, where my heart was used to beat
> So quickly, waiting for a hand,
>
> A hand that can be clasp'd no more—
>> Behold me, for I cannot sleep,
>> And like a guilty thing I creep
> At earliest morning to the door.
>
> He is not here; but far away
>> The noise of life begins again,
>> And ghastly thro' the drizzling rain
> On the bald streets breaks the blank day.

> Doors, where my heart was used to beat
>> So quickly, not as one that weeps
>> I come once more; the city sleeps;
> I smell the meadow in the street;
>
> I hear a chirp of birds; I see
>> Betwixt the black fronts long-withdrawn
>> A light-blue lane of early dawn,
> And think of early days and thee,
>
> And bless thee, for thy lips are bland,
>> And bright the friendship of thine eye;
>> And in my thoughts with scarce a sigh
> I take the pressure of thine hand.

These two poems appear neither in the Trinity, nor in the Lincoln manuscript. The Lincoln manuscript contains a series of poems, cxv, cxvii, cxviii, which are concerned with the 'work of time', and which do not appear in the Trinity manuscript. It has, however, no version of Section cxvi, 'Is it then regret for buried time', which, in our editions, continues this theme. Instead, Tennyson has inserted, between Section cxvii and Section cxviii, this lyric:

> Let death and memory keep the face
>   Of thee and twenty summers, fair
>   I see it and no grief is there
> Nor time can wrong the youthful grace
>
> I see it and I scarce repine
>   I hear the voice that held me fast
>   Thy voice is pleasant in the past
> It speaks to me of me and mine.
>
> *The face is bright, the lips are bland*
>   *He smiled upon me eye to eye*
>   *And in my thoughts with scarce a sigh*
> *I take the pressure of his hand.*

The first two verses of this poem are the germ of Section cxvi which runs:

> Not all regret: the face will shine
>   Upon me, while I muse alone;
>   And that dear voice, I once have known,
> Still speak to me of me and mine.

The last is obviously the last verse of the lyric quoted above, and I think it probable that the whole lyric was built upon that single verse. Indeed, it is not unlikely that cxix was composed before, not after its twin poem, Section vii. R. H. Shepherd, in his account of the trial edition of *In Memoriam*, says that only two of the first twenty-four sections of the poem were omitted from that edition. Between them the Lincoln and the Trinity manuscripts contain twenty-two of these poems. The missing Sections are vii and viii. There is then a strong presumption that these poems were added to *In Memoriam* at the very latest stage of its development. And, if this is so, the poignant 'Doors where my heart was used to beat' (vii) was probably written not in the first agony of bereavement but in the tranquillity of recollection. I

would, indeed, conjecture that in rehandling the rejected poem which
I have just quoted, Tennyson discovered the basis both of Section cxix
and of Section vii in the phrase about the pressure of Hallam's hand, 'A
hand that can be grasp'd no more'. I suggest that vii and cxix were
deliberately created as companion-pieces which would emphasise,
within the movement of the whole poem, a development and contrast
in the experience of bereavement. In any case the rehandling of the
lyrics confirms the impression that their 'weaving together' was, in
the proper sense, artificial. Tennyson did not conceive of his poem as
the disjointed outpourings of a diary, but as a statement of a whole
experience, and he uses the methods of art to achieve fullness and unity
in his presentation of this theme.

He states the theme in the opening section of the poem:

> I held it truth, with him who sings
>   To one clear harp in divers tones,
>   That men may rise on stepping-stones
> Of their dead selves to higher things.

> But who shall so forecast the years
>   And find in loss a gain to match?
>   Or reach a hand thro' time to catch
> The far-off interest of tears?

All through *In Memoriam* Tennyson reaches out his hand for the 'far
off interest of tears': what he tries to find and express in the pattern of
his poem is the pattern of his experience of loss. This gives the work
a double movement; it is biographical in the sense that it records
events, and it is philosophical in the sense that it tries to discover and
record the perspective of those events. Unfortunately the traditional
accounts of the poem's division, Bradley's for instance, are concerned
almost exclusively with its biographical movement, and concerned
with it, what is more, as if it followed the course of true biography. This
creates difficulties. The departure from Somersby is recorded in the
poem as occurring before the third Christmas of Tennyson's bereavement. Hallam died in September 1833, and the Tennysons moved from
Somersby, and spent their first Christmas at High Beech, the Christmas
described in the third Christmas poem, in 1837. If the poem's chronology is taken literally we are forced to the conclusion that there were
two years in Tennyson's life without a Christmas. But it is not to be
taken literally. Bradley follows in his division of the poem the authorised
account of the arrangement of the Elegies in the Eversley edition of

Tennyson's poems, but there is another less authoritative, but certainly authentic, version of Tennyson's arrangements recorded by Tennyson's architect, James Knowles, who had it, he says, from Tennyson himself.[29] Knowles's account of the poem explains more than the authorised version, and is very illuminating, for in it the climactic moments of the poem fall, not as in Bradley's account, on the Christmas but on the Anniversary poems (lxxii and xcix). In this arrangement the chronology of the poem is seen to fall into a pattern of three years, two years of grief and an uncompleted third, and the movement of experience and reflection is knit into this pattern. For these three years are not literal biographical years but phases in the experience of bereavement. There is a year of almost unrelieved gloom and desolation, there is a year in which the poet seems to be struggling out of darkness and in which, although he has not entirely re-established himself, he is subject to moments of extreme joy, and there is, finally, a year in which, once for all, he lays hold of the promise which experience has opened to him. This threefold division of the poem does not of course destroy the possibility of subordinate movements within its main phases; indeed Knowles's account allows for nine separate parts of the poems, although his divisions, unlike those used by Bradley, do not necessarily coincide with the so-called 'time notes'. On the other hand, the fact that the poem is developed in three phases gives a significance to the time poems which they would not otherwise have. The motif, for instance, of the church bells which first appears in the first Christmas poem, is caught up again in the third Christmas poem where it emphasises the fact that Tennyson has entered on a new existence:

> A single peal of bells below,
>> That wakens at this hour of rest
>> A single murmur in the breast,
> That these are not the bells I know.

> Like strangers' voices here they sound,
>> In lands where not a memory strays,
>> Nor landmark breathes of other days,
> But all is new unhallow'd ground.

The bells appear again in the New Year poem which follows immediately after the third group of Christmas poems:

> Ring out, wild bells, to the wild sky,
>> The flying cloud, the frosty light:
>> The year is dying in the night;
> Ring out, wild bells, and let him die.

This newness takes significance from the fact that, with the second of the Anniversary poems (xcix), we entered into the last phase of grief, the phase when the poet finally leaves behind him the gloom of bereavement. The second Anniversary poem is followed immediately by the poems on the departure from Somersby. On the night before he left his childhood home Tennyson dreamt of Arthur, a prophetic dream in which the Muses sing:

> And one would chant the history
> Of that great race, which is to be,

This theme of newness, of freshness and the great things that are to come is the theme of the bells:

> Ring out old shapes of foul disease;
> > Ring out the narrowing lust of gold;
> > Ring out the thousand wars of old,
> Ring in the thousand years of peace.
>
> Ring in the valiant man and free,
> > The larger heart, the kindlier hand;
> > Ring out the darkness of the land,
> Ring in the Christ that is to be.

All this sense of a change in life and hope is underlined when in Section cvii, which follows the apostrophe to the bells of the New Year, we find that we are celebrating not the anniversary of Arthur's death but that of his birth. New life, new power, Tennyson's return to the world of hope is after this the dominating theme of the rest of the poem.

All this gives point to Tennyson's description of *In Memoriam* as 'a kind of *Divina Commedia*, ending with happiness', for in a far-off tentative manner, the poem finds a pattern in grief not unlike the threefold order of the *Divine Comedy*. The chronology of *In Memoriam* is seen to exist not for its own sake but to serve the poem's larger purpose, and the biography is formalised to show the total shape of the experience: the poem is precisely *not* a diary. This formalisation is emphasised by the repetitions which we have already discussed, and we can perceive through the whole work Tennyson consciously striving for the unity of his poem, striving, that is, to see and present his loss in perspective, and as a whole experience rather than as moments of woe and joy. This is an activity Sir Harold Nicolson calls mechanical, and which he compares unfavourably with the lyric inspiration which made the expression of Tennyson's first grief so poignant. This comparison is scarcely just: a sequence of lyrics, even a sonnet sequence, is something other than the sum of its parts, and it was natural that Tennyson should wish to present his poem as the expression of a coherent experience rather than as an anthology of feelings. His formal arrangements are made to unify, to bring out the significance he discovered in the long weariness of bereavement. As a whole the poem has a meaning which the single lyrics have not, and the poet is after all justified in exercising his craft to bring out the meaning.

III

So the formality of *In Memoriam* underlines its meaning. Are we then to turn our attention from the superb expression of broken moods and desolating griefs to 'the message' of the poem? Must we again delve into Tennyson's half-comprehending and totally unconvincing reconciliation of the religious and the scientific conceptions of the universe? Do we begin once more to write theses on Tennyson as a thinker? The answer to this last question is of course, No. The poem's meaning is the poem itself; there is no detachable Tennysonian message for a lost generation, only the understanding of a common experience displayed in and through experience. But it is necessary to pause and consider the matter of science and religion so as to be clear not about Tennyson's moral, but about his subject. The actual form of *In Memoriam*, its division into sections dealing with the various facets of Tennyson's experience and reflection, leads to a good deal of misunderstanding. Readers and critics persistently take the part for the whole and assume that what is true of one section is true of the entire poem. So, while Maurice was praising *In Memoriam* for its assurance of a future state, and for its reconciliation of 'the highest religion and philosophy with the progressive science of the day', the Church papers were lamenting that the author did not make use of the consolations of religion, and while modern writers, like Mr Eliot and Professor Willey, find the poem more conspicuous for its agnosticism than for its faith, so devout a woman as Emily Sellwood, Tennyson's fiancée, consented to renew her engagement to Tennyson after reading the Elegies, although, before this, she and her family had hesitated about the marriage on religious grounds. All these divergent views of the poem can be justified by sections of the poem. But even those sections of *In Memoriam* which are directly concerned with religion or speculation take a

8

different colour when they are seen not as discussions of the relations
of science and religion, but as the expression of certain phases in the
management of loss and grief.

Tennyson is not in any way an archetypal case of Victorian scepticism.
He is hardly a sceptic at all since for him doubt was precisely doubt, a
moody inapprehension of the difference between true and false, a
colour of the personality, not a clear recognition that this or that
belief could not be upheld by the evidence. Science in all probability
had very little to do with his abandonment of traditional Christianity:
certainly he did not give up his faith because Sir Charles Lyell could be
got to admit, after dinner, that the world was probably 50,000 years
old. *Post hoc, ergo propter hoc* is always a fallacious argument, but in this
case even the *post hoc* does not hold. *The Principles of Geology* was
published from 1830 to 1833 and it is clear that unbelief troubled
Tennyson and his set well before that. Both Hallam and Sterling had
'doubts', and Tennyson's own *Supposed Confessions of a Second-rate
Sensitive Mind* was composed in 1829. *Supposed Confessions* does not
present a state of unbelief caused by contradictions between the religious
and scientific accounts of the universe; its want of faith arises from an
inability to commit the free reason to dogma:

> 'Shall we not look into the laws
> Of life and death, and things that seem,
> And things that be, and analyse
> Our double nature, and compare
> All creeds till we have found the one,
> If one there be?'

In fact the root of this is not nineteenth-century science, but eighteenth-
century rationalism. This absence of scientific reasoning against
religion is the more interesting because among the Cambridge group of
friends Tennyson himself had the strongest interest in natural science
in a period in which scientific investigation was beginning to stretch
out into new fields. We know that Tennyson had read Herschel before
he went up to Cambridge, and that Buffon's work was in his father's
library, we may suspect that he was acquainted with Von Baer's work
on embryology.[30] His tutor, William Whewell, himself a Professor of
Mineralogy, and a friend of Lyell's, discussed the nebular hypothesis in
his Bridgwater Treatise of 1833, eleven years before the immense stir
caused by *Vestiges of Creation*. Chambers, the author of that work, did
not invent modern astronomy, any more than Lyell invented geology

or Darwin the biological sciences, and traces of the new science appear in Tennyson's work well before the commencement of its great battles with religion. 'Great Nature' he says,

> 'Through five cycles ran
> And in the sixth she moulded man.'

and he is remembering the *Époques de la Nature* not the *Principles of Geology*, just as in his plea to man to work out the Ape and the Tiger, and in his sense of man's evolution from the beast, he is not anticipating Darwin but recollecting Lamarck. For the truth is that in the Victorian period the great discoveries were, as it were, in solution in the minds of scientists before they were finally formulated, and Tennyson seems to have picked up a good many of the more advanced notions of his period. But he was certainly no more than an amateur in science, and not enough of a philosopher or a scientist to relate these discoveries together in any system which should be inimical to Christianity.

There was no reason why he should do so. We are accustomed to consider Victorian science and scientists as necessarily the enemies of religion, but this enmity is a late Victorian phenomenon. Although some scientists, like Priestley, and like the French scientists in the late eighteenth century, had regarded science as belonging to the realm of reason, and had rejected religion, their rejection of faith was made on philosophical rather than on scientific grounds. The scientists of the early nineteenth century did not feel it a duty to proclaim, nor had they been goaded into declaring, a specifically *scientific* antagonism to revealed religion. Whewell, whose importance here lies in his relation to Tennyson, was clearly contented by the reasoning which inspired Paley's *Natural Theology*. Darwin tells us that he himself was satisfied by Paley at this period, and describes the Cambridge group of scientists of which Whewell was a member as largely orthodox in their beliefs.[31] Lyell is more bad-tempered about religion: he is clearly exasperated by the diversion of geological investigation to the pursuit of the evidences of Noah's flood, but his objections here are practical not philosophic, and are extended not only to those Christians who wished to prove, geologically, that Noah's flood did happen, but also to those rationalists who wanted geology to prove that it did not. Lyell's own philosophy is, like Whewell's, basically Paleian. Science, in laying bare the mysteries of nature, reaches out to and reveals the underlying law which governs all things, and law reveals the Law-giver and the Designer. At this period, though later he supported Darwin, Lyell rejects the evolutionary theories which were in the air, and it was the success of the theory of the evolution of the species which created the divorce between scientific and teleological reasoning. The theory to which Lyell adhered was that the species of things are fixed: they operate within their limited area, and according to the laws of their being and environment. His great theme is the universality of law; and law, for that period, was a concept common to natural science and to natural theology. The laws of nature are the laws by which God created and rules the world. How far this view of things was accepted in Tennyson's circle may be seen from Arthur Hallam's remarks on prayer:

> With respect to prayer, you ask me how I am to distinguish the operations of God in me from the motions in my own heart? Why should you distinguish them or how do you know there is any distinction? Is God less God because He acts by general laws when He deals with the common elements of nature . . . ? [32]

Something very like this is the thesis of the quasi-scientific *Vestiges of Creation* so familiar in notes to *In Memoriam*, in which the ingenious Robert Chambers moves a step beyond Paley and attempts to show that the whole variety of natural phenomena was created by God at one remove. The Almighty Mechanic did not himself put together the contrivances of the creation, but simply set into motion a series of laws which, operating in varying circumstances, would infallibly call into being organic gadgets suitable to those circumstances. Chambers is half-way to a theory of natural selection, but he is not, it is obvious, thinking in terms acceptable to the hey-day of scientific agnosticism. He is simply carrying the tradition of an older school, a tradition which Tennyson and his friends seem to have accepted, one step further forward. This school does not set the scientific account of the universe against the religious—it expects one to contribute to the other.

The Paleian apologetic enshrines a perfectly respectable form of Christianity and easily justifies the faith of him

> that after toil and storm
> Mayest seem to have reach'd a purer air,
> Whose faith has centre everywhere,
> Nor cares to fix itself to form.

It would, however, have peculiar difficulties for Tennyson. It offers no guarantees to a mind whose doubt is primarily non-rational, and against his mother's gentle piety, or the fiery Calvinism of his Aunt

Bourne, it looks like infidelity. Tennyson was not the man to build his soul on the 'evidences of religion'. 'Nothing', he said, in later life, 'worthy proving can be proven,' and that 'nothing' includes even the existence of the self. This leaves him without reason's first premise; his temperament demands the absolute 'it is so' of authority to warrant his own experience. This, in a sense, Hallam may be said to have supplied. Hallam is the hero of Section xcvi:

> Perplext in faith, but pure in deeds,
>   At last he·beat his music out.
>   There lives more faith in honest doubt,
> Believe me, than in half the creeds.
>
> He fought his doubts and gather'd strength,
>   He would not make his judgement blind,
>   He faced the spectres of the mind
> And laid them: thus he came at length
>
> To find a stronger faith his own;
>   And Power was with him in the night,
>   Which makes the darkness and the light,
> And dwells not in the light alone.

It was Hallam's certainty in his non-dogmatic religion that Tennyson took over and that cured him of the theological megrims expressed in *Supposed Confessions*. Hallam was his guarantor.

The shock of Hallam's death, then, at once shattered all this. We are not faced with a man who is now losing the faith of his childhood. It is not Tennyson's belief in *creeds* which now cracks, but his secure awareness of a purposeful universe. Death poses the question, 'Is this the end, is this the end?' makes 'dust and ashes all that is', and what it particularly makes dust and ashes of is friendship:

> If Death were seen
> At first as Death, Love had not been,
> Or been in narrowest working shut,
>
> Mere fellowship of sluggish moods,
>   Or in his coarsest Satyr-shape
>   Had bruised the herb and crush'd the grape,
> And bask'd and batten'd in the woods.

The world itself, all that matters in it, has taken the colour of doubt from death, so that what Tennyson is saying is not 'What nonsense all this makes of the theology of simple faith', but 'how necessary it makes it!' In the long run Tennyson's longing for Arthur, his recall of his spirit, is simply a demand for some authoritative assertion, some oracle who will promise that real things are real.

It is at this point that the activities of science, which were in Tennyson's mind, as in those of his friends, the wonders of the 'mother-age', begin to take on a sinister complexion. The conclusions of the astronomers, the zoologists and the geologists intensify the desolations of bereavement:

> 'The stars,' she whispers, 'blindly run;
> A web is wov'n across the sky;
> From out waste places comes a cry,
> And murmurs from the dying sun:'

The villain of *In Memoriam* is certainly geology, but not because geology was antagonistic to religion. Sir Charles Lyell was not writing polemic. His wish in the *Principles of Geology* was precisely to establish principles: once for all to settle the controversies which inhibited the accurate study of rock formations. He had first of all to deal with the current theory that every change in rock str atification and every loss of species which the fossil remains revealed were the results of extensive and long-finished catastrophes, and then, by the study of fossil remains in rock strata, to supply a method of determining the chronological relationships of geographically separated rock formations. He was concerned with two kinds of evidence, that of organic remains, which brings him into the world of zoology and to the discussion of species and their history, and that of the rocks themselves and their structure. With enormous patience and admirable erudition Lyell brings evidence from mineralogy, from archaeology, from history, from marine biology, and from other sources, to indicate that the natural laws which brought about the ancient change in the surface of the earth are the laws which still operate. The face of things is still changing, and the principal agents of its change are water and fire—earthquake and volcanic eruption, and the less spectacular forces of tidal wash, and running waters. As for the destruction of species—Lyell sets his face against any theory of mutation, and discusses instead the environmental disturbances which bring about the increase or disappearance of any given species. These forces continue, and of them the most important is the battening of one species on another. The catastrophes which made the world what it is are not happily past at all. Lyell is not discussing these matters as a metaphysician; his desire is to get on to his real problem, the chronology of rocks, but he has to discuss the whole question of change through two of his three volumes in order to establish the cardinal point of his hypothesis, the principle of the uniform operation of the laws of nature now and from the beginning of time, and with it the principle of the non-exceptional nature of geological change.

But his arguments carry metaphysical consequences. What he told the unsuspecting Victorian public was that change is the order of the universe. The ancient and eternal hills once were not, and in time will not be. Such a doctrine has a more insidious effect, especially on the imagination, than the overturning of Archbishop Ussher's erroneous chronology of the Creation. It was possible, then, to equate the ages of the earth's formation with the six days of the Creation and there is a grandeur in this conception which adds to the dignity of man as the Lord of the Universe:

> When first the world began
> Young Nature thro' five cycles ran,
> And in the sixth she moulded man.
>
> She gave him mind, the lordliest
> Proportion, and, above the rest,
> Dominion in the head and breast.

But the *Principles of Geology* asserts that this process of creation is not over, and it robs the imagination of the contemplation of a finished order. Lyell's analysis continually returns to the flux of things:

> Imperfect as is our information of the changes they [that is, deltas] have undergone within the last three thousand years, it is sufficient to show how constant an interchange of sea and land is taking place on the surface of our globe. In the Mediterranean alone, many flourishing inland towns and a still greater number of ports, now stand where the sea rolled its waves since the era when civilised nations first grew up in Europe.[33]

And he quotes with approval the Scottish geologist, Hutton:

> In the economy of the world I can find no traces of a beginning, no prospect of an end.[34]

This kind of statement, repeated over and over again, and accompanied by an immense amount of data about the geological changes involved, is not compatible with the imagination of stability. It confirms what

Tennyson had always sensed, and justifies the queer apprehension of
change and flux which appears in his juvenile poems:

> The world was never made;
> It will change, but it will not fade.
> So let the wind range;
> For even and morn
>   Ever will be
>   Thro' eternity.
> Nothing was born;
> Nothing will die;
> All things will change.

This is an apprehension which was clearly part of his personality. He
was by temperament enormously uncertain of the solid actuality of
things: nine-tenths of his doubt is the acute awareness of transience.
Between his moods and their geological justification Tennyson is
caught in a classic dilemma: if all things change and move then there
is nothing of which one can say 'It is'. The actual transience of the
physical world, revealed by geology, is, however, less important than
the shadow which it casts on human values:

> Might I not say? 'Yet even here,
>   But for one hour, O Love, I strive
>   To keep so sweet a thing alive:'
> But I should turn mine ears and hear
> The moanings of the homeless sea,
>   The sound of streams that swift or slow
>   Draw down Æonian hills, and sow
> The dust of continents to be;
> And Love would answer with a sigh,
>   'The sound of that forgetful shore
>   Will change my sweetness more and more,
> Half dead to know that I shall die.'

This is the poetic expression of Lyell's prosaic account of the silting up
of deltas: geology throws even darker shadows. Investigations into
fossil remains reveal the extinction of species, a process which, true to
his principle, Lyell sees as happening according to law:

> Every species which has spread itself from a small point over
> a wide area must . . . have marked its progress by the diminu-
> tion or entire extirpation of some other, and must maintain
> its ground by a successful struggle against the encroachment
> of other plants and animals.[35]

He remarks, with a certain complacency, that, given the normal operation of cause and effect, 'the successive destruction of the species must now be part of the regular and constant order of nature'.[36] Even this is less sinister than his earlier remarks on earthquakes:

> This cause [that is, the agency of subterranean movements] so often the source of death and terror to the inhabitants of the globe, which visits in succession, every zone and fills the earth with monuments of ruin and disorder, is, nevertheless, a conservative principle in the highest degree and above all others necessary to the stability of the system.[37]

In both these discussions, Lyell is concerned with the economy of nature—his eye is on the whole system. But a chill falls on the less objective mind when it contemplates the death and terror of human beings as a concomitant of this essential of 'the stability of the system'. How it struck Tennyson's mind we all know:

> 'So careful of the type'? but no.
> > From scarped cliff and quarried stone
> > She cries, 'A thousand types are gone:
> I care for nothing, all shall go.
>
> Thou makest thine appeal to me:
> > I bring to life, I bring to death:
> > The spirit does but mean the breath:
> I know no more.' And he, shall he,
>
> Man, her last work, who seem'd so fair,
> > Such splendid purpose in his eyes,
> > Who roll'd the psalm to wintry skies,
> Who built him fanes of fruitless prayer,
>
> Who trusted God was love indeed
> > And love Creation's final law—
> > Tho' Nature, red in tooth and claw
> With ravine, shriek'd against his creed—
>
> Who loved, who suffer'd countless ills,
> > Who battled for the True, the Just,
> > Be blown about the desert dust,
> Or seal'd within the iron hills?

The facts of nature appear to deny the dream,

> That not a worm is cloven in vain;
> That not a moth with vain desire
> Is shrivell'd in a fruitless fire,
> Or but subserves another's gain.

This is not intellectual conviction but terrified imagination. Bereavement had thrust on Tennyson the question 'Is this the end, is this the end?', and he finds the picture of a world empty and purposeless without Hallam (My prospect and horizon gone) confirmed by the nightmare of nature. It need not be said that his final convictions do not lie here. He *fears* the world may be really like this, but he does not *know* it.

What finally cured him of this disease of the imagination was a growing awareness of the value of human love. The almost pathetic assertion of his later days is the corner-stone of his world:

> 'Peace, let it be for I loved him and love him forever, the dead are not dead but alive.'

The prop of his conviction, then, is neither science nor religion nor yet their reconciliation. There were elements in both the scientific and the religious view of things which were built into his emotional universe, but to discern them we need to return to the structure of *In Memoriam*.

IV

In Memoriam began as isolated lyrics, a good many of which express a moment's awareness of a moment's state of mind, and there are therefore many strains in it which are recurrent, but autonomous. Grief, immortality, Hallam's fame, questions of faith—Tennyson's problem in 'weaving the lyrics together' was to find a place for all these, but a place in which, while each succeeding lyric should be subordinate to an overriding theme, each should retain and express a quality of mood, or a stage in reflection not found elsewhere. This was not so much a problem of construction as a problem of meaning: the overriding theme must be uncovered in the experience described. The first section of the poem sets the course:

> But who shall so forecast the years
> And find in loss a gain to match?
> Or reach a hand thro' time to catch
> The far-off interest of tears?

The skill with which this section both sets the tone of the poem and introduces the theme of overwhelming sorrow with which it begins is remarkable. Men may indeed rise on stepping-stones of their dead selves, but here we are at the beginning—the possible fruit of sorrow cannot comfort sorrow, and the note is a note of unbearable loss. On the other hand we have already been pointed to the significance of sorrow and love:

> Let Love clasp Grief lest both be drown'd,
>   Let darkness keep her raven gloss:
>   Ah, sweeter to be drunk with loss,
> To dance with death, to beat the ground,
>
> Than that the victor Hours should scorn
>   The long result of love, and boast,
>   'Behold the man that loved and lost,
> But all he was is overworn.'

If love has any value at all it implies grief in loss, and this justifies the extreme sorrow of the first part of the poem, but it is not until the end that the full power of love is discerned. For it is the victor Hours which are indeed to bring out the 'long result of love'. Experience interprets experience, and not until the last sections of the poem will we understand the full significance of the first:

> The love that rose on stronger wings,
>   Unpalsied when he met with Death,
>   Is comrade of the lesser faith
> That sees the course of human things.
>
> No doubt vast eddies in the flood
>   Of onward time shall yet be made,
>   And throned races may degrade;
> Yet O ye mysteries of good,
>
> Wild hours that fly with Hope and Fear,
>   If all your office had to do
>   With old results that look like new;
> If this were all your mission here,

                    *   *   *

> Why then my scorn might well descend
>   On you and yours. I see in part
>   That all, as in some piece of art,
> Is toil coöperant to an end.

This belief that time reveals the pattern of sorrow gives the poem its unity of tone, and it justifies, not only the biographical arrangements which we have already discussed, but also the recurrent echo-poems which take up and modify earlier expressions of mood. Biography and verbal echo are no more than a means of expressing the single persistent theme with which the poem opened: that love gives value to sorrow. This conviction appears throughout the poem and is summed up in words so familiar that their force is blunted:

> This truth came borne with bier and pall,
>   I felt it, when I sorrowed most,
>   'Tis better to have loved and lost,
> Than never to have loved at all—

Time and love are the dominant motifs of *In Memoriam*, and most of the other issues Tennyson discusses are included in them. The question about immortality is no more, and no less, for Tennyson than the insistent problem of whether love is permanent. Does Death cancel the bond or no? If the soul does not survive, if there is nothing but animal life, love itself has no validity. On the other hand, if the soul survives, what interest does it, in its newer world, take in the concerns of the living? But Love itself answers both the problems:

> And strangely on the silence broke
>   The silent-speaking words, and strange
>   Was love's dumb cry defying change
> To test his worth; and strangely spoke
>
> The faith, the vigour, bold to dwell
>   On doubts that drive the coward back,
>   And keen thro' wordy snares to track
> Suggestion to her inmost cell.
>
> So word by word, and line by line,
>   The dead man touch'd me from the past,
>   And all at once it seem'd at last
> The living soul was flash'd on mine,
>
> And mine in his was wound, and whirl'd
>   About empyreal heights of thought,
>   And came on that which is, and caught
> The deep pulsations of the world.

The answer to Tennyson's anxious demand for reunion, for experience of the survival of the beloved dead carries him to the centre of being. Though 'stricken through with doubt' the memory of this experience colours daily life as the bereavement had coloured it. Both have their roots in the relationship of personal love between Tennyson and Hallam.

If this experience carries Tennyson to the centre of being it also carries him outwards from himself. Reflecting on Arthur's virtues, and strengthened by contact with him, he comes to a resolution:

> I will not shut me from my kind,
>   And, lest I stiffen into stone,
>   I will not eat my heart alone,
> Nor feed with sighs a passing wind:
>
> What profit lies in barren faith,
>   And vacant yearning, tho' with might
>   To scale the heaven's highest height,
> Or dive below the wells of Death?
>
> What find I in the highest place,
>   But mine own phantom chanting hymns?
>   And on the depths of death there swims
> The reflex of a human face.
>
> I'll rather take what fruit may be
>   Of sorrow under human skies:
>   'Tis held that sorrow makes us wise,
> Whatever wisdom sleep with thee.

Love and sorrow teach him the lessons of the moral life, and they give a more strenuous appeal to the attractions of the dream of progress. The development to which they invite us is not the easy contemplation of the 'fairy tales of science and the long result of time', but a progress in which human beings take an active and a suffering part. Time and love and grief have all a place in the soul's development:

> Arise and fly
> The reeling Faun, the sensual feast;
>   Move upward, working out the beast,
> And let the ape and tiger die.

The modern mind can scarce endure this; moral endeavour is not its ideal, and it recognises that the energies of the ape and tiger are not

without their place in the higher life of man. Still, the point is clear:
moral endeavour, whatever else it entails, is not a matter of self-
cultivation. It requires the emergence from a private world. Love for
Arthur leads Tennyson outwards to other friends that still remain.

This theme of Love explains why it is that Tennyson, in discussing
the structure of his poem, chose to associate it with Dante. Dante was
a link with Hallam, who, for his age, was a gifted connoisseur of
Italian poetry, and a student of Dante in a period when the poet,
though beginning to be fashionable, was still a little out of the way.[38]
Hallam's studies made Tennyson familiar with the convention in
which he expresses his understanding of friendship. For though *In
Memoriam* bears no direct relationship to *The Divine Comedy*, it was in
Dante's poem that Tennyson discovered a pattern appropriate to his
experience. In some sense Arthur is his Beatrice, love of him leads
Tennyson through the hell of the first year of his loss, and as Beatrice
appears to Dante at the end of the *Purgatorio*, so Arthur is restored to
Tennyson in the experience described by Tennyson as occurring in the
poem's second phase. Besides, for Dante, the way from loss to the
experience of the highest things was by way of love: the *Paradiso*
presupposes the *Vita Nuova*. Hallam had translated the *Vita Nuova*, and
written a commentary on it, and sometimes it seems as if Tennyson
had picked up from him not so much its doctrine as its idiom. Love
becomes, as in that poem, a third person between him and his
friend:

> Love is and was my Lord and King,
> And in his presence I attend
> To hear the tidings of my friend,
> Which every hour his couriers bring.

The awareness of Dante which Tennyson gained from Hallam's
studies gave him the entrée into what lies behind Dante, the whole
corpus of a doctrine about love which the European tradition had taken
over from Plato. For the most part the love of which Tennyson speaks
in the poem is too exclusively personal to be personified: it is the bond
between him and Hallam. But as the poem progresses, it takes on a
quasi-autonomous existence—and becomes a platonic entity whose
existence guarantees all its lesser manifestations of the phenomenal
world. Dante's personification of Love as Power exactly suits
Tennyson's feeling that the power of his friendship with the dead
delivered him from the shadows of his own mind.

It is this emphasis on Love which, for many, gave the poem its Christian flavour. Love, which means Tennyson's love for Hallam, is identified by means of that semantic sleight-of-hand which confuses philosophers, with the 'love' of Christianity which is an attribute and a name of God. This is partly Tennyson's fault. The Prologue to the poem begins confusingly, 'Strong Son of God, immortal Love'. But the Prologue is an after-thought written when *In Memoriam* was finished, and, as Henry Sidgwick shrewdly remarked, is too Christian and too certain for the body of the work.[39] Tennyson is an eclectic; if the love that delivered him from desolation could be identified with the Son of God—well and good, but there is no suggestion in *In Memoriam* itself that it is anything other than friendship. Faith is not conquering science. Faith has nothing to do with it, or not in any religious sense. But the facts of science, the geological revelation of transience, are as nothing beside love's guarantee of permanence:

> There rolls the deep where grew the tree.
> O earth, what changes hast thou seen!
> There where the long street roars, hath been
> The stillness of the central sea.

*   *   *

> But in my spirit will I dwell,
> And dream my dream, and hold it true;
> For tho' my lips may breathe adieu,
> I cannot think the thing farewell.

This is still Sir Charles Lyell's doctrine, almost verbatim, but Tennyson's imagination of the facts has changed. Lyell himself had established as the corollary of his principle of change, the principle of the permanence of law. The quotation from Playfair on the title page of the *Principles of Geology* reads:

> Amid all the revolutions of the globe the economy of Nature has been uniform, and her laws are the only things that have resisted the general movements. The rivers and the rocks, the seas and the continents have been changed in all their parts, but the laws which direct those changes and the rules to which they are subject have remained invariably the same.

This Tennyson seems to accept and to find comforting:

> The fame is quench'd that I foresaw,
> The head hath miss'd an earthly wreath:
> I curse not nature, no, nor death;
> For nothing is that errs from law.

Law, after all, implied purpose and significance to a pre-Darwinian age.
Science provided Tennyson not only with a conception of order, but
with the principle of progress. All this work of creation and destruction
is not a succession of meaningless changes, it moves towards the
crowning miracle of man. Lyell himself rejected any notion of evolutionary process, but he gives, in order to refute it, a careful account of
the evolutionary theories of Lamarck. Chambers, in *Vestiges of Creation*,
is less cautious about Lamarck and himself sees the end of the physical
processes he describes, and the culmination of the work of natural law
in some future 'crowning race'. Tennyson probably picked up the
dream of 'some far-off divine event' from these writers, but if he did
he had, I suspect, no sense of acquiring a new idea or a new purpose.
The desire for, and the straining towards the vision of the perfect race
of man living an idyllic life in bliss and concord was part of the
romantic inheritance. It is only at this time that it begins to be linked
to the laws of the physical and the biological sciences. Tennyson also
links it to the purpose of God:

> That God, which ever lives and loves,
>   One God, one law, one element,
>   And one far-off divine event,
> To which the whole creation moves.

This looks like the reconciliation of science and religion. In fact
science and religion are very minor elements in the synthesis of thought
and feeling which these verses represent. Love, endurance, memory,
suffering and rapture have more to do with the matter, and religion,
where it enters into the poem, is conceived of not in terms of doctrines
which have to be aligned with the new dogmas of science, but in
terms of persons and relationships which are as much a part of experience as the facts of science.

V

In Memoriam is the archetypal poem of the mid-Victorian age. This
is not, I think, because Tennyson is concerning himself with the
stresses and strains of the Victorian intelligentsia: the appeal of his
poem is very much wider—he had indeed the luck to write a great
poem which was also a popular poem. Yet this was not entirely luck.
In the last chapter we remarked that Tennyson's use of myth, and of
popular idiom universalised a personal experience, and the remarkable
thing about *In Memoriam* is not the evocation of a purely personal

sorrow so much as the extent to which private grief has been, slowly and surely, thrust into perspective, impersonalised until it comes to reveal the pattern of any bereavement. Tennyson continually measures his own grief against the known and common sorrows of his age, an age in which, it should always be remembered, a young death was the rule rather than the exception. There is a famous passage which Queen Victoria altered with her own hand, and which comforted her in the loss of Albert:

> Tears of the widower, when he sees
> A late-lost form that sleep reveals,
> And moves his doubtful arms, and feels
> Her place is empty, fall like these.

In the same metaphor Tennyson refers to his 'widowed race'. This term does not, I think, imply any particular quality in his relationship with Arthur (the aged Tennyson, grumbling about late Victorian sentimentality, declared that in Hallam's lifetime he never called him 'dearest'): its value is that it provides a measure for his grief. Then again the analogy of widowing provides a means of transfer, a means by which the emotion of the poem comes to stand for the tears of all the bereaved—as it did for Queen Victoria's. This universalising of emotion is taken further in the various analogies in which Tennyson attempted to explain his sense of desolation:

> A happy lover who has come
> To look on her that loves him well,
> Who 'lights and rings the gateway bell,
> And learns her gone and far from home;
>
> He saddens, all the magic light
> Dies off at once from bower and hall,
> And all the place is dark, and all
> The chambers emptied of delight:

*   *   *

> Could we forget the widow'd hour
> And look on Spirits breath'd away,
> As on a maiden in the day
> When first she wears her orange-flower!

*   *   *

9

> O mother, praying God will save
>   Thy sailor,—while thy head is bow'd,
>   His heavy-shotted hammock-shroud
> Drops in his vast and wandering grave.

These situations belonged to the life of the Victorians but they also belonged to their mythology. Their novels, their plays, their subject pictures always return to this kind of thing; though they do not move us these situations spoke to our ancestors of common and simple profundities. The interesting and unexpected fact about these commonplace analogies in his poem is that Tennyson uses them to *argue* his reader into a knowledge of his experience and his theme:

> I know that this was Life, —the track
>   Whereon with equal feet we fared;
>   And then, as now, the day prepared
> The daily burden for the back.
>
> But this it was that made me move
>   As light as carrier-birds in air;
>   I loved the weight I had to bear,
> Because it needed help of Love.

This use of the stock analogy as a means of setting out the nature of a situation or the quality of a person is one that we have observed in *Isabel*. We need not suppose that implies any falseness in Tennyson's account of things, any attenuation of experience. It is true, for example, that the mother praying for her son is a stock figure inviting a stock response, that is the reason why Tennyson introduces her into his poem, but the desolation which he is feeling is vivid in the language:

> His heavy-shotted hammock-shroud
> Drops in his vast and wandering grave.

The unemphatic accuracy of the description of sea burial, the hammock weighted with lead, comes with a shock after the conventional picture of the praying mother, and the shock is in part a response to the movement of the last two lines. Sea burial returns at that moment in the poem when Hallam's body was still on the high seas, to the immediate grief, and relates the unidentified, general 'sailor' to the particular loss. For we are not only concerned here with individuals grieving but with the enormous desolation—vast and wandering—of unexpected bereavement which is shared by the poet and his types. Similarly, Tennyson taking up the image of 'the path of life', a figure so embedded in the language that it is scarcely recognised as a metaphor, reimagines it:

I wander, often falling lame,
    And looking back to whence I came,
Or on to where the pathway leads;

    And crying, How changed from where it ran
      Thro' lands where not a leaf was dumb;
      But all the lavish hills would hum
    The murmur of a happy Pan.

This is still general enough, considered as description of a road, but the detail, for instance the 'lavish' hills, imparts within the general pattern a knowledge of the particular quality in the relationship which Tennyson is describing.

This method of particularising common symbol or common idiom is the method which we saw Tennyson developing in *The Lotos-Eaters* and in *Isabel*, and it is the means by which he conveyed the understanding of his experience to the Victorians. For *In Memoriam* is less a great emotional than a great reflective poem: it is not the mood of the mind but the significance of that mood which Tennyson wishes to convey, and it is not only in the detail of the poem, but in its movement and structure that he adapts a common symbol. The whole movement of the poem discovers to us the theme of change in permanence, and its recurrent imagery, like the imagery of a Shakespearean play, expresses and declares the theme. I mean of course the imagery which gives the poem its singular beauty, the imagery derived from natural change, from the return of the seasons, the coming of night and day, the transience of weather:

    Witch-elms that counterchange the floor
      Of this flat lawn with dusk and bright.

In the natural order, change is inevitable but things remain the same. Wild autumn expressed Tennyson's grief:

    Tonight the winds begin to rise
      And roar from yonder dropping day:
      The last red leaf is whirl'd away,
    The rooks are blown about the skies;

    The forest crack'd, the waters curl'd,
      The cattle huddled on the lea;
      And wildly dash'd on tower and tree
    The sunbeam strikes along the world.

But spring returns:

> Dip down upon the northern shore,
>   O sweet new-year delaying long;
>   Thou doest expectant nature wrong;
> Delaying long, delay no more.

★   ★   ★

> O thou, new-year, delaying long,
>   Delayest the sorrow in my blood,
>   That longs to burst a frozen bud
> And flood a fresher throat with song.

The sense of change is evident, too, in the repeated poems which 'change the sky': the seasons may be the same, but much is altered. Time is the theme of the poem, but it is also its machinery—its cycles represent the great discovery of the years of grief—that there is no real destruction, that under the forms of change there is reality and stability.

> No lapse of moons can conquer love.

Chapter V

Out of the Wood

ALTHOUGH Hallam's death did not reduce Tennyson to the moral imbecility described by the critics, and though he was able to use it, as *In Memoriam* shows, as the source of a creative apprehension of the moral world, the immediate experience of bereavement renewed the psychological problems of his early youth. In his desolation of mind he was again aware of the unreality both of the inner and of the outer world, and, for a while, the 'moanings of the homeless sea' possessed his imagination. But, as we have seen, he did not in this revived awareness of an uncertain world return to the bolt holes of his adolescence. Hallam's life no less than Hallam's death had left its mark on his personality. In five years of a sane friendship the world of fantasy had lost its compelling power. The fragile escape worlds of the Arabian Gardens and the Merman's caverns were closed to Tennyson in his new grief; he had to endure what he could not now avoid. The symbols of escape remain in his poetry, the enchanted places are still there but they are seen now as views in the distance, and are thought of as countries travelled to across dangerous seas. The 'Happy Isles' and the 'Island-Valley of Avilion' are types of a happy world beyond death; Hallam has travelled to them, but the living cannot reach them. Even sleep is no longer the route to escape. When Tennyson dreams in *In Memoriam* he dreams at first of his waking grief and of the happy past which, in dream, is stained with present trouble. When he does dream of peace, peace is distant: in the last, the happiest, of the dream poems in *In Memoriam* Arthur travels to him in a great ship across great seas. This dream ship is the transformation of the 'fair ship' which carried Hallam's body from Italy to England, and it is the same ship in which Ulysses sets sail from Ithaca and in which King Arthur, surrounded by weeping queens, is carried on his way to Avilion. Paradise is not altogether lost but it is distant, and at present unattainable. The imagination, deprived of the immediate escape to fantasy, is forced to attend to the nearer world of sight and sense, the world of ordinary relationships in which grief has to be endured. If Hallam's death darkened Tennyson's problem it also helped him to find, by painful experience, some kind of solution for it, and, in particular, it drove him to seek a balance between the demands of inner solitude and the claims of relationship and society.

As we saw in Chapter III Tennyson had already committed himself to finding a function in society. He had decided that the Palace of Art must be deserted for the Cottage in the Vale. Hallam's dying did not force him into any new choice of action, but it did, in a sense, make the lowly cottage real: the intellectual decision to leave the delights of self-cultivation became, after Tennyson's bereavement, a condition of his moral personality. How serious, and yet how shallow, that intellectual decision was in 1833, before Hallam's death, is shown by a group of poems which Tennyson composed in the summer between the disastrous failure of the 1832 volume, and the still greater disaster of the autumn.[1] This group includes, as well as *The Gardener's Daughter*, *St. Simeon Stylites* and the twin poems *St. Agnes* and *Sir Galahad*. The theme of *St. Simeon Stylites* is the corruption of self-cultivation. St Simeon, though an ascetic, is first cousin to the Soul in *The Palace of Art*, for like the Soul, he pursues salvation in isolation from his fellows. In the maceration of his body, Tennyson thinks, he destroys nature and insults God. The poem did not need an explicit moral; the mere presentation of St Simeon's practices would, to a Victorian mind, be a sufficient comment on the saint. Tennyson's own distaste for asceticism is not, either here, or later in the *Idylls of the King*, a simple revulsion from the horrors of mortifying the flesh. It is a strong and protestant distaste for 'cloistered virtue', for the self-cultivation of a particular kind of religious temperament. It would be shared by his contemporaries. But his attitude was ambivalent, and so was theirs. The long popularity of *St. Agnes* and *Sir Galahad* betrays in the Victorian mind a wistful longing for a more romantic morality than that bequeathed to them by their Puritan ancestors. The theme of *St. Agnes* and of *Sir Galahad* is like that of *St. Simeon Stylites*: they are also about solitude and salvation but treat these things rather differently. In his description

of the young saints, Tennyson conveys the artificiality and the hypnotic
fascination of a certain kind of religious imagination:

> Break up the heavens, O Lord! and far,
>   Thro' all yon starlight keen,
> Draw me, thy bride, a glittering star,
>   In raiment white and clean.

This whiteness and this glitter run all through the texture of St Agnes,
and appear again in *Sir Galahad*:

> Fair gleams the snowy altar-cloth,
>   The silver vessels sparkle clean,

This is easily recognisable as that bane of the later Victorian consciousness, the blend of aestheticism and romanticised religion, and it is significant that both these poems were favourites with the Pre-Raphaelite
painters. But Tennyson did not anticipate the Pre-Raphaelite use of
religion as the instrument of aesthetic thrill. He is conscious of the
sensuous quality of religion but he is equally conscious of its reality, and
can without insincerity enjoy his imagination of purity and saintliness in
St. Agnes' Eve just as in a finer poem, finer because less pretentious, *Sir
Launcelot and Queen Guinevere*, he enjoys his imagination of a mediaeval-
ised enamelled May. The real spiritual strife of sanctity is perhaps better
realised in the grotesque contortions of St Simeon than in the raptures
of St Agnes, but two things redeem *St. Agnes* as a poem, and give a
relevance both to its own subject matter, and to Tennyson's situation.
One is the image of purity:

> Make Thou my spirit pure and clear
>   As are the frosty skies.

the other the last four lines of the poem:

> The sabbaths of Eternity,
>   One sabbath deep and wide—
> A light upon the shining sea—
>   The Bridegroom with his bride!

These descriptions, although conventional, are more truly a product of
the mystical imagination than the play with altar linen and decorations:
frosty skies, and the light upon the seas convey suggestions of great
depths of barren light and darkness which are more in tune with the
subject than tapers and snowdrops. It is clear enough in *St. Agnes* that,
in spite of the artificiality with which he overlaid it, Tennyson could not

really eradicate from his imagination the quick sensitiveness to solitude, nor the sense of those values which, in *St. Simeon Stylites*, he attempts to deny.

This group of poems does seem to show that in the early part of 1833 Tennyson's choice of the Cottage in the Vale was a surface choice. It was deliberately made and conscientiously pursued, but in *St. Simeon Stylites* as in *The Palace of Art* Tennyson behaves like a man who, while displaying the evils of drink, has very little faith in the pleasures of temperance. The Pillar and the Palace were at least realities, the Cottage in the Vale scarcely exists. Tennyson attempted to make it real in *The Gardener's Daughter*, but this is a poem of so conscious a polish and so laboured a detail that in some ways it is more fantastic than *Recollections of the Arabian Nights*. In it Tennyson makes exactly the same mistake as the early Pre-Raphaelites made, the mistake of supposing that realistic art requires the collection of minute detail. The meticulous accumulation of small realities produces a kind of beauty but it is certainly not the beauty of the objective world:

> Ere an hour had pass'd,
> We reach'd a meadow slanting to the North;
> Down which a well-worn pathway courted us
> To one green wicket in a privet hedge;
> This, yielding, gave into a grassy walk
> Thro' crowded lilac-ambush trimly pruned;
> And one warm gust, full-fed with perfume, blew
> Beyond us, as we enter'd in the cool.
> The garden stretches southwards. In the midst
> A cedar spread his dark-green layers of shade.
> The garden-glasses glanced, and momently
> The twinkling laurel scatter'd silver lights.

The diction of this meticulous description is itself elaborate and artificial and transports the Gardener's Daughter into a world as unreal as that of the pastoral convention:

> she, a Rose
> In roses, mingled with her fragrant toil,

Some of this care in description and diction arises from Tennyson's attempt to meet the critics of the 1832 volume, but the more we look into it the more the Cottage in the Vale seems to have the characteristics of Marie Antoinette's dairy at the Petit Trianon. It is not that Tennyson was not trying to put his decision into operation, but that he had not, at this stage, any creative grasp of what it was he had chosen. His grief for

Hallam jerked him into a realisation of his choice, the realisation of what it meant to live in the real world in relationship to others of his own kind. Indeed that relationship came to be a necessity of his existence:

> I will not shut me from my kind,
>   And, lest I stiffen into stone,
>   I will not eat my heart alone,
> Nor feed with sighs a passing wind:

★   ★   ★

> What find I in the highest place,
>   But mine own phantom chanting hymns?
>   And on the depths of death there swims
> The reflex of a human face.

> I'll rather take what fruit may be
>   Of sorrow under human skies:
>   'Tis held that sorrow makes us wise,
> Whatever wisdom sleeps with thee.

It was the realisation of his need which made his choice real and vivid to him.

This new condition in Tennyson's awareness of the world is apparent all through the *Poems* of 1842. This volume had four distinct strata. The foundation of the collection is a selection of poems from the 1832 volume: these have been revised and remodelled. Then there is the group of poems which we have been discussing which were composed after the publication of the 1832 volume, but before Hallam's death. After these come poems like *Break, Break, Break* and *Ulysses* which are direct reflections on bereavement, and finally a heterogeneous collection of lyrics and idylls which Tennyson was working on in the late thirties. Miss Joyce Green, in an essay on the revisions of the 1832 volume,[2] shows how Tennyson's intention in collecting and arranging all this work for the 1842 volume was not so much to placate or satisfy the critics of his earlier work, as to present a collection of poems which should be homogeneous in tone and theme. The tone and theme of such a collection would, of course, be dictated by Tennyson's mood in the late thirties and not by that of his undergraduate years. This would require considerable revision of the undergraduate poems, and Miss Green, in a compelling analysis, shows how these revisions support Tennyson's new theme of a determination to face and not to escape the world. The new collection of poems was both to satisfy Tennyson's

aesthetic conscience and his moral determination not to withdraw from
the world into the weak indulgence of sorrow. The most telling
evidence which Miss Green offers for her thesis is the withdrawal of *The
Hesperides* not only from the 1842 volume but from all subsequent
editions of the *Poems* issued in Tennyson's lifetime. *The Hesperides* is a
poem of whose artistic merit there can be no doubt, and modern
criticism regards it as of the essence of Tennysonian verse. Miss Green
remarks that *Tithonus*, the companion poem to *Ulysses*, was also
excluded from this volume and not published until decades later. Both
The Hesperides and *Tithonus* are in different ways poems of escape;
they show the poet enamoured of escape, and *Tithonus*, in its earliest
versions,[3] presents a mood of weariness and willingness to give up the
struggle. They are not in the least in tune with the determination:

> To strive, to seek, to find, and not to yield.

The omission of these poems, Miss Green contends, makes it clear that
the new collection was meant to present the public with something
other than a poetic day-dreamer. Tennyson was deliberately assuming
a new persona: the poet of the 1842 volume is not altogether a preacher
of morality, but he is certainly not a neurotic escapist.

Unfortunately the demands of the controversy with which she is
concerned prevent Miss Green from giving to the new poems in the
1842 volume the same admirable attention which she gives to the
revision of the 1832 poems. They also prevent her from examining, in
any detail, the relations between the 1842 volume, *In Memoriam*, and
The Princess. The theme of *In Memoriam* was not, as we have seen, the
experience of a solitary mind. Grief reaches out for companionship
and it is in fact in relationship rather than in solitude that the centre of
being is reached:

> So word by word, and line by line,
>   The dead man touch'd me from the past,
>   And all at once it seem'd at last
> The living soul was flash'd on mine,
>
> And mine in his was wound and whirl'd
>   About empyreal heights of thought,
>   And came on that which is, and caught
> The deep pulsations of the world.

Hallam, the lost friend, became in a sense the pivot of Tennyson's
relationship with the world:

> Strange friend, past, present, and to be;
> Loved deeplier, darklier understood;
> Behold, I dream a dream of good,
> And mingle all the world with thee.

Tennyson came, at last, to remember Hallam in the urbane world of college friendships and social amusements, to which, for his friend's sake as well as for his own, he gave an increasing value. It is this sense of the value of the world in all its aspects, as contrasted with the solitary mind, which is the common element in all Tennyson's writings in the late thirties and forties. The rule he laid down for himself, 'I will not shut me from my kind', had for him poetic as well as psychological and moral significance.

But the poet of the 1842 volume is not a poet of what is conventionally called 'social realism'. He is not, that is, though he was writing in the 'hungry forties', primarily concerned with the social conditions of the working class. The real world had come into focus, but for him the 'real world' was the world in which he passed his life, the world of intelligent, cultured Victorians of the upper middle class, not the struggling energetic communities of an infant industrial society. Tennyson was as likely to be at home among manufacturers or Chartists as Pope would be in Newgate, or Dickens in the drawing-rooms of Sir Leicester Dedlock. It was his own, and not an alien environment, which pressed itself on him, and it is the minutiae of that comfortable existence which begin to command attention:

> There, on a slope of orchard, Francis laid
> A damask napkin wrought with horse and hound,
> Brought out a dusky loaf that smelt of home,
> And, half-cut-down, a pasty costly-made,
> Where quail and pigeon, lark and leveret lay,
> Like fossils of the rock, with golden yolks
> Imbedded and injellied;

The pie is treated with the elaborate attention given to the description of Arthur's sword hilt, or of Queen Guinevere's gown, but it is, so to speak, an *actual* pie, it has the dimensions of a particular time and place. It is Tennyson's attention to details of this kind which enables him once and again to objectify the real fears and fancies of his class and period, to show it as secure, and yet under threat. James, in *Walking to the Mail*, says that Sir Edward Head

> shudder'd, lest a cry
> Should break his sleep by night, and his nice eyes
> Should see the raw mechanic's *bloody thumbs*
> *Sweat on his blazon'd chairs,*

Sensitiveness to his own circle and their habits of life made him aware
not only of social change but also of the strains and stresses which were
already distorting the political and economic life of Victorian England.
It is in the conversation poems of the 1842 volume, the Southeian
interludes, in which Tennyson tries to reproduce the halcyon days of
Apostolic discussion, that these strains and stresses appear. *Audley Court,
Edwin Morris, Walking to the Mail* represent friendly discussion amongst
young men gathered together on some social occasion, or, like so
many of the Victorian intelligentsia, walking together in romantic
country, and these poems serve to introduce some anecdote, or lead,
with a curious naturalness, to the discussion of a particular social
problem:

> sir, you know
> That these two parties still divide the world—
> Of those that want, and those that have: and still
> The same old sore breaks out from age to age
> With much the same result. Now I myself,
> A Tory to the quick, was as a boy
> Destructive, when I had not what I would.

The speaker illustrates his point with the anecdote about the sow and the
schoolboys. A pleasant conversation piece in fact disguises and presents
the serious play of opinion upon the Chartist problem. The strains
which made up the mood of contemporary politics are presented to
us under the conditions and in the manner in which opinion was likely
to be expressed. It is obviously not concerned with the tense emotion
and anger of the social crusader, nor with the misery and compassion
evoked by actual experience of the conditions of the poor. This is the
drawing-room conversation of the serious and politically alert and as
such it is valuable enough to the social historian; it has, also, a poetic
reality which is absent from the more extravagant diatribes both of
Tennyson himself and of some of his later contemporaries. Tennyson
spreads himself, for instance, in the elaborate and idealistic poem *The
Golden Year* in which one of the group of friends is represented as a
poet singing the hopes of Victorian progress; his song is not so successful as the denial of idealism which it provokes:

'What stuff is this!
Old writers push'd the happy season back,—
The more fools they, —we forward: dreamers both:
You most, that in an age, when every hour
Must sweat her sixty minutes to the death,
Live on, God love us, as if the seedsman, rapt
Upon the teeming harvest, should not plunge
His hand into the bag: but well I know
That unto him who works, and feels he works,
This same grand year is ever at the doors.'

This cantankerous speaker one suspects to be Carlyle, for this is both
his manner and his sentiment, and the passage has an authenticity which
the rest of the poem has not. Even allowing for a generation so peculiarly
unreticent in the idiom of its conversation as the early Victorians (one
wonders how they could write such letters or say such things) it seems
unlikely that any group of people would discuss the prospects of their
society in the terms of *The Golden Year*:

When wealth no more shall rest in mounded heaps,
But smit with freër light shall slowly melt
In many streams to fatten lower lands,
And light shall spread, and man be liker man
Thro' all the seasons of the golden year.

*　　*　　*

Fly, happy, happy sails, and bear the Press;
Fly happy with the mission of the Cross;
Knit land to land, and blowing havenward
With silks, and fruits, and spices, clear of toll,
Enrich the markets of the golden year.

The advantages of a free press and free trade, the great liberal creed, are,
it is true, presented here as part of a song and not part of a conversation,
but it is a very mediocre song, and it is mediocre because Tennyson has
left the particular vision of the present moment for legendary havens
overflowing with (duty free) silks and spices. Legend creeps upon him
even in the conversation of friends.

This weakness in *The Golden Year* reveals Tennyson's difficulty in the
management of the 1842 volume. Social realism, say of the kind attempted in Mrs Gaskell's novels, or in the poetry of Crabbe or even of
Cowper, was not only outside the scope of Tennyson's experience,
but alien to his imagination. The 1842 volume includes, in a revised
form, most of the poems in the 1832 volume, and it seems that Tennyson

was neither willing nor able to deny himself that vision of reality
which made the earlier volume what it is. Neither his conscience, nor
the strains of his bereavement made any radical change in the structure
of his personality, or in the nature of his talent; they widen his vision,
but do not destroy its quality. Because of this both the 1842 volume
and *The Princess* present a paradox. In both Tennyson is speaking from
the security of his place in a familiar society which he describes in
authentic detail, and in both he presents elaborate worlds of fantasy and
legend. The *mores* of the fairy tale and the *moeurs* of the Victorian
élite jostle one another in surprising confusion, and yet the final effect
is not inharmonious. Single poems show this juxtaposition of the two
worlds even more clearly than the collection as a whole. *The Talking
Oak* has a conventional Victorian maiden as the heroine of a fantastic
burlesque:

> She left the novel half-uncut
> Upon the rosewood shelf;
> She left the new piano shut:
> She could not please herself.

Will Waterproof's Monologue uses and burlesques the material of the
legend of Jupiter and Ganymede, but in doing so it gives the chophouse,
The Cock, where Tennyson ate steak and drank porter with his friends,
an unreal, legendary quality. In this mêlée we can discern the emergence,
and indeed the solution, of a new poetic problem, the problem of
relating the two worlds which now possessed Tennyson's imagination,
the world of fantasy, the dream prison of *The Lady of Shalott*, and the
world of social life and human relationships. In his struggle with this
problem Tennyson reveals a new and attractive side of his personality.
For what appears in the 1842 volume is the Tennyson of a grotesque,
sometimes macabre humour, a Tennyson who dismissed the melancholy
of his youth as incipient gout, a Tennyson with a relish for the folk tale
and a genius for transforming anecdote, ancient or modern, and even
the despicable material of the sentimental novel into comment on
society.

His reconciliation of the two worlds of his imagination begins with
the choice and handling of his material. The sources of the 1842 poems
are many and various, and the manner in which they are treated is
sometimes very surprising. Susan Ferrier's *The Inheritance* (a novel which
is a cross between a 'silver fork' novel, a 'tale of terror', and an
evangelical tract) is very successfully translated into the ballad of

Lady Clare, while the story of the Goose that laid the Golden Eggs is transformed into an allegorical satire on radical agitation. *Lady Clare* in particular displays the poet's capacity to unify: to sift from Miss Ferrier's narrative and moral sophistications an essential ballad theme was something of an imaginative triumph. In his recreation of the story Tennyson takes the world of Miss Ferrier's novel, which was the world of his own time, and transfers it to the world of the ballad makers:

> 'If I'm a beggar born,' she said,
> 'I will speak out, for I dare not lie.
> Pull off, pull off, the brooch of gold,
> And fling the diamond necklace by.'

But in *The Goose* as again in *Amphion* and in *Locksley Hall*, Tennyson's method is rather to relate the fairy tale or legendary world to the immediate problems of society. There is a kind of interaction between present realities and the inventions of fiction which persists all through the 1842 volume whether the source material of a given poem lies in novelette, eastern tale, or classical legend.

Tennyson's method of relating the two worlds is best shown perhaps in the way in which, in his revision of *The Sleeping Beauty*, he sets the fairy tale into the milieu of present society. *The Sleeping Beauty* was a poem of the 1830 period, included in *Poems, Chiefly Lyrical*. In the 1842 volume it is given a double setting: the description of the Princess's charmed sleep, the subject of the original lyric, is given a context in an account of her father's court, and the whole tale is set into the Prologue and Epilogue of a modern love story in which, for his own purposes, a lover recounts the tale to his beloved. This revised version of the poem is called *The Day-Dream*. *The Sleeping Beauty* in its original form is a classical example of the dream/tower/enchanted maiden poem:

> She sleeps, nor dreams, but ever dwells
> A perfect form in perfect rest.

In *The Day-Dream* this central description of an enchanted maiden is subordinated to the main movement of a story which draws her out of charmed sleep into the outer world, and which sets the outer world into domestic and social motion:

> 'Pardy,' return'd the king, 'but still
> My joints are somewhat stiff or so.
> My lord, and shall we pass the bill
> I mention'd half an hour ago?'

> The Chancellor, sedate and vain,
>   In courteous words return'd reply:
> But dallied with his golden chain,
>   And, smiling, put the question by.

The chill, enchanted stillness of *The Sleeping Beauty* is not lost in *The Day-Dream* but is set against a strong awareness of animation. In the time of the Princess's charmed sleep the court remains immobile, spellbound, but it is spellbound in the attitudes and with the arrested promise of life. There is besides a longing for the Prince's coming, for the breaking of the spell, which is absent from *The Sleeping Beauty*:

> When will the hundred summers die,
>   And thought and time be born again,
> And newer knowledge, drawing nigh,
>   Bring truth that sways the souls of men?
> Here all things in their place remain,
>   As all were order'd, ages since.
> Come, Care and Pleasure, Hope and Pain,
>   And bring the fated fairy Prince.

This longing is very much in harmony with the 1842 volume in which Tennyson's desire to grasp at what time promises, his eagerness for new knowledge and new hopes is expressed in poems as dissimilar as *Locksley Hall* and *The Golden Year*. But the Fairy Prince is heralded by something at once more profound and more familiar than the trumpet notes of Victorian liberalism:

> Come, Care and Pleasure, Hope and Pain
>   And bring the fated fairy Prince.

When he comes to waken the Sleeping Beauty he is not accompanied by Progress in golden laurels: he brings with him the ordinary concerns of daily existence as they are exemplified by the activities which came to a sudden stop when the Princess pricked her finger:

> Roof-haunting martins warm their eggs:
>   In these, in those the life is stay'd.

Warmth and life is stayed by enchantment and the Prince restores them.

The themes of the legend are repeated and emphasised in the love story which is its setting. In telling the fairy tale the lover insistently recalls his Flora both to personal and to impersonal hopes. He harps on the expected advance of mankind:

> So sleeping, so aroused from sleep
> Thro' sunny decades new and strange,
> Or gay quinquenniads would we reap
> The flower and quintessence of change.

But he returns again to the theme of personal affection:

> My fancy, ranging thro' and thro',
> To search a meaning for the song,
> Perforce will still revert to you;
> Nor finds a closer truth than this
> All-graceful head, so richly curl'd,
> And evermore a costly kiss
> The prelude to some brighter world.

The enchanted maiden bound in sleep, no longer satisfies the mind. She must awake to animation and reality. Tennyson has remodelled his fairy tale so that it is no longer, as in *Poems, Chiefly Lyrical*, a symbolic tale of the soul in isolation, but rather a lesson on the return to human reality.

The Day-Dream is not the only poem in which a fairy tale or legend is given a prologue and an epilogue which link it to contemporary life. *Godiva* opens with a modern scene:

> I waited for the train at Coventry;
> I hung with grooms and porters on the bridge,
> To watch the three tall spires; and there I shaped
> The city's ancient legend into this:—

and it has a modern moral. *Morte d'Arthur* is given an elaborate framework in the Christmas festivities among a group of friends; *The Princess* has a similar setting in the mid-summer holidays. These poems are adaptations of the conversation poems which we have just discussed; the conversation between friends is used to introduce not a contemporary anecdote but a longer and more ancient story or even a fantasy. But the world of the Victorian country house is still visible and active behind the narrative. It seems as if by making this connection Tennyson tried to keep his everyday world and his poetic imagination in touch with one another. There are other poems, like *Amphion* and *Will Waterproof's Monologue*, in which the central story or theme is modern but the framework is legendary and fantastic. We might perhaps complain that this mode of writing still interposes a hard transparent wall of artificiality between the mind and its experience, that in these poems, as in *The Lady of Shalott*, we still see reality in a mirror. This

10

may be so; nevertheless the linking together of the fanciful and the real in the 1842 volume has a purpose related to present reality. It enables the fancied thing, the obsolete legend, to stand as a symbol for, a comment on the present world. The Epilogue to the *Morte d'Arthur* ends, for instance, with the peals of Christmas bells:

> when dreams
> Begin to feel the truth and stir of day,
> To me, methought, who waited with a crowd,
> There came a bark that, blowing forward, bore,
> King Arthur, like a modern gentleman
> Of stateliest port; and all the people cried,
> 'Arthur is come again: he cannot die.'
> Then those that stood upon the hills behind
> Repeated—'Come again, and thrice as fair;'
> And, further inland, voices echo'd—'Come
> With all good things, and war shall be no more.'
> At this a hundred bells began to peal,
> That with the sound I woke, and heard indeed
> The clear church-bells ring in the Christmas-morn.

In this passage the motifs of *In Memoriam* are repeated: the ship that brings the promise of a new state of things, the bells that ring in the 'Light that shone when Hope was born', and which later 'Ring in the thousand years of peace', these are linked here with the legendary Arthur, who, because of this relationship, becomes a symbol of the promise of progress, which, though constantly defeated, still returns, as well as a type of Hallam. *Godiva* points the connection of the legend with modern problems still more insistently:

> Not only we, the latest seed of Time,
> New men, that in the flying of a wheel
> Cry down the past, not only we, that prate
> Of rights and wrongs, have loved the people well,
> And loathed to see them overtax'd; but she
> Did more, and underwent, and overcame,

It is worth noticing that the artificiality of the diction in these poems is not altogether inappropriate to the world in which Tennyson lived. It is itself a link between the sober reality and the wild fantasy which existed side by side in Victorian England. A generation which takes mechanical aids for granted does not easily perceive that there really was an element of fairy tale in the Victorian world itself, a sense of the legends of human power realised which provoked not only the important but the mannered style. The Great Exhibition itself, a national legend both then and now, was reared after all not in ferro-concrete but in glass, it was a Gothic fantasy, a *Crystal Palace*. Railways, judging from Dickens's description of them, could appear as an enormous new world of strange and enchanting powers, and even when their mechanism was not understood they did produce metaphors:

Let the great world spin for ever down the ringing grooves of change.

Tennyson's description, in *The Princess*, of the Mechanics' Institute amusing itself with technical devices shows how fascinating the new state of affairs was:

> round the lake
> A little clock-work steamer paddling plied
> And shook the lilies: perch'd about the knolls
> A dozen angry models jetted steam:
> A petty railway ran: a fire-balloon
> Rose gem-like up before the dusky groves
> And dropped a fairy parachute and past:
> And there thro' twenty posts of telegraph
> They flash'd a saucy message to and fro
> Between the mimic stations; so that sport
> Went hand in hand with Science.

This is a kind of child's eye view of the Mechanical Age, naive, perhaps childishly indifferent to the uglier sides of engineering development, but displaying that extraordinary and near poetic pleasure which the human mind takes in the miniature, the elaborate and the mechanical. In a sense Tennyson had no need to create a link between the fairy tale and the contemporary world. He had the valuable gift of seeing his own world in the perspective of an imaginative vision.

It is perhaps because of this that Tennyson can make not only the fairy tale but the novelette into an instrument of comment. Any material which came to his hand was used in a similar way. The anecdote of the Ghost's 'flitting' with the family who tried to escape it is a folk tale of some antiquity, but in *Walking to the Mail* it is given a contemporary flavour and a relevance to the departure of the terrified aristocrat from his family. No more than the unfortunate farmer can he escape his ghosts by fleeing from them. The fear of the 'raw mechanic's bloody thumbs' has to be lived with and faced. The baronet's position is the position of society. It cannot 'flit' from the terrifying spirits called up by Chartism and hunger. What Tennyson does with the folk tale he does with the novelette. There are a good many novelettish tales in the 1842 volume—tales of lovers crossed by circumstances, *Edwin Morris, Lady Clare, The Lord of Burleigh* and *Locksley Hall*, and it is noticeable that many of them are concerned with the same situation, the parting of true lovers by their families and for social or financial reasons. This is a perennial theme in Tennyson's work and is treated at its fullest at a later period in *Maud* and *Aylmer's Field*. It is more than probable that Tennyson's obsession with it rose originally from a particular case of parental interference known to him, perhaps his brother Frederick's disappointment in love, perhaps the well-meaning delays imposed by Henry Hallam on the marriage of Arthur Hallam and Emily Tennyson, perhaps the breaking of his own engagement to Emily Sellwood. Whatever the reason, the problem of rank and love engaged his interest, and it was of course basic material for the novel writer, at least in that period. It is amazing how many oddments of story Tennyson found for the representation of disappointed or star crossed love. *The Lord of Burleigh* derives from Watford's *Tales of Great Families, Locksley Hall* from Sir William Jones's *Moallakat*; even *Œnone* is fundamentally the story of the deserted mistress. It may be that in such tales Tennyson was flattering the taste which produced the Ladies Annuals: certainly a later generation cannot take the subjects seriously and is amused, or irritated, rather than moved by the spectacle of Sarah Hoggins sinking under the burden of a position 'unto which she was not born'. But this is not Tennyson's only comment on a love situation. There is this passage in *Edwin Morris*:

> She went—and in one month
> They wedded her to sixty thousand pounds,
> To lands in Kent and messuages in York,
> And slight Sir Robert with his watery smile
> And educated whisker.

There is something grimmer and more significant here. This is a protest against a particular and vicious form of the cash nexus, and it seems to me that through some of these tales Tennyson is using Victorian taste to attack one of the vices of Victorian society, the pressure of rank and money on personal relationships. This theme is developed at greater length in the period of *Aylmer's Field*, but in the 1842 volume, and certainly in *The Princess*, the relationship of lovers, and afterwards of husband and wife, is seen to stand in the centre of society and is considered as the type of social relations. It is foolish to laugh at Tennyson's concern with domestic relationships—they were at the forefront of the Victorian ethical tableau, they are the basis of a literary convention, and Tennyson uses that convention, as most poets use the conventions of their period, as the medium of something else.

This habit of directing a story so that it becomes a comment is very much in keeping with Tennyson's oblique method of writing, and it leads, of course, to direct allegory. *The Goose, Amphion,* and more important than either, *The Vision of Sin* represent this mode of writing in the 1842 volume. In these poems, however, we are not dealing with true allegory, that is, with stories in which both actors and actions are designed to stand for some specific situation outside themselves, but with type stories, stories in which the action, though complete and satisfying in itself, points to, and reflects some other situation. It is no use trying to make an absolute identification, for instance, of the Stranger in *The Goose* with the radicals, but the story can still be taken as an allegory, and was meant to exemplify the consequences of political promises. The youth in the *Vision of Sin* is not a symbolic character: he is precisely 'a youth', and it is the tone of the poem rather than direct symbolism which conveys its meaning:

> And from the palace came a child of sin,
> And took him by the curls, and led him in,
> Where sat a company with heated eyes,
> Expecting when a fountain should arise:
> A sleepy light upon their brows and lips—
> As when the sun, a crescent of eclipse,
> Dreams over lake and lawn, and isles and capes—
> Suffused them, sitting, lying, languid shapes,
> By heaps of gourds, and skins of wine, and piles of grapes.

In this opening of the poem the enervated, febrile quality which later breaks into purposeless excitement is already present:

> Then they started from their places,
> Moved with violence, changed in hue,
> Caught each other with wild grimaces,
> Half-invisible to the view,
> Wheeling with precipitate paces
> To the melody, till they flew,
> Hair, and eyes, and limbs, and faces,
> Twisted hard in fierce embraces.

And this moves by a natural progression into that dessication of experience which sees human folly a shade too clearly:

> 'You are bones, and what of that?
>   Every face, however full,
>   Padded round with flesh and fat,
>   Is but modell'd on a skull.'

The quality of the poem arises from Tennyson's uncanny sensitiveness to shades of psychological experience, especially those experiences in which the sensuous apprehension of things turns sour and mouldy. It is this awareness of corruption which is the 'Vision of Sin'. The poem is another version of *The Palace of Art* and perhaps of *St. Simeon Stylites*, for the root of the evil is in self-indulgence. In *The Vision of Sin*, however, the manner of description is harder and less subjective; it is observed rather than felt, and, what is more, it is set against an awareness of another experience:

> And then I look'd up toward a mountain-tract,
>   That girt the region with high cliff and lawn:
>   I saw that every morning, far withdrawn
> Beyond the darkness and the cataract,
>   God made Himself an awful rose of dawn,
>   Unheeded:

This awareness of something untouched by the madness of the revellers saves the poem from mere dalliance with corruption; and then again Tennyson's grim humour, the macabre conversation of the 'man of ruined blood', not only adds to the reality of his ruin, but also distances it. We see this situation not as a fit of the miseries darkening the poet's world, but as a human possibility—a possibility which is a comment not only on human beings as they are in themselves but also on human society and ideals:

> 'He that roars for liberty
>   Faster binds a tyrant's power;
>   And the tyrant's cruel glee
>   Forces on the freer hour.'

But though the weight of the corrupted mood is reinforced by our knowledge that the real world is not all that far from the Vision of Sin, Tennyson's humour keeps that knowledge at a sane distance. A man can be warned but not obsessed by things which make him laugh, and there is something almost indecently ludicrous about the sinner:

> 'Death is king, and Vivat Rex!
>   Tread a measure on the stones,
>   Madam—if I know your sex,
>   From the fashion of your bones.

> No, I cannot praise the fire
> In your eye—nor yet your lip:
> All the more do I admire
> Joints of cunning workmanship.'

But still one is warned: the story is an exemplar, a type of self-indulgence and is meant to be applied to the normal world.

The world of these type stories and the world of reality which they are meant to illuminate are not, however, always in line with each other. Ulysses sails away to seek the Happy Isles, leaving Telemachus to the sphere of common duties, and Arthur leaving Bedivere desolate, travels to the Lake Island of Avilion:

> Where falls not hail, or rain, or any snow.

The Round Table, 'which was an image of the mighty world', is past, and the mind stretches forward to the earthly Paradise. 'Jam yesterday, jam tomorrow, but never jam today.' *Ulysses* and *Morte d'Arthur* are of course poems of the period immediately following Hallam's death, and it is clear that for some time, although Tennyson's mind stretched out to his fellows and to immediate reality, it was not altogether settled: his desires were ambivalent. The desire of Tithonus,* who like Ulysses is a persona of Tennyson, is altogether different—he does not want to 'follow knowledge like a sinking star', but to leave the 'ever silent spaces of the East' and return to the world of men:

> Why should a man desire in any way
> To vary from the kindly race of men,

The chief characteristic of that world is, more than anything, that it is subject to death:

> The woods decay, the woods decay and fall,
> The vapours weep their burden to the ground,
> Man comes and tills the field and lies beneath,
> And after many a summer dies the swan.

Though Tithonus rejects the splendid world of the dawn as unnatural to man, still the most desirable quality of the world natural to him is a negative one: in it he has the power to die. The hero of *Locksley Hall* is like Tithonus, his desires are ambiguous. He wants to escape into irresponsibility:

* *Tithonus* does not appear in the 1842 volume, but since it is a poem of the thirties, and belongs, both in subject matter and theme, to the period under discussion I include it here.

Ah, for some retreat
Deep in yonder shining Orient, where my life began to beat;

★   ★   ★

Or to burst all links of habit—there to wander far away,
On from island unto island at the gateways of the day.

Larger constellations burning, mellow moons and happy skies,
Breadths of tropic shade and palms in cluster, knots of Paradise.

He has, however, a sense of realism about the island paradise itself:

I, to herd with narrow foreheads, vacant of our glorious gains,
Like a beast with lower pleasures, like a beast with lower pains!

Mated with a squalid savage—what to me were sun or clime?
I the heir of all the ages, in the foremost files of time.

The last line here has alarming implications—the idealism which made
an unreal retreat of a South Sea Island looks like distorting the reality of
the present:

Thro' the shadow of the globe we sweep into the younger day:
Better fifty years of Europe than a cycle of Cathay.

Yet both the protagonist of the poem and his creator are well aware of
the contrast between the ideal and the real:

all things here are out of joint:
Science moves, but slowly slowly, creeping on from point to
point:

Slowly comes a hungry people, as a lion creeping nigher,
Glares at one that nods and winks behind a slowly dying fire.

Indeed it is the sense of present, intolerable trouble which creates the
desire for escape.

The stabilising of this curious see-saw action of Tennyson's mind
moving between two desires is most easily observed in *The Princess*
which in a more elaborate, and perhaps more significant form, presents
all the characteristics of the 1842 volume. It is not a great poem,
certainly not so good in its own kind as *Audley Court* or *Morte d'Arthur*
are in theirs, but is a remarkable one, and more interesting than critical
prejudice has normally allowed. Our immediate forebears found it dull
because it is pre-eminently Victorian; it reproduces with exactness the
overcrowded setting of the period:

And me that morning Walter show'd the house,
Greek, set with busts: from vases in the hall
Flowers of all heavens, and lovelier than their names,
Grew side by side; and on the pavement lay
Carved stones of the Abbey-ruin in the park,
Huge Ammonites, and the first bones of Time;
And on the tables every clime and age
Jumbled together; celts and calumets,
Claymore and snowshoe, toys in lava, fans
Of sandal, amber, ancient rosaries,
Laborious orient ivory sphere in sphere,
The cursed Malayan crease, and battle-clubs
From the isles of palm: and higher on the walls,
Betwixt the monstrous horns of elk and deer,
His own forefathers' arms and armour hung.

This, except that the house is Greek not Gothic, is the stuffy world of Balmoral and the Vicarage parlour with the collections of shells and fossils.[4] Perhaps for this reason the passage begins to have a period charm. But the charm is there because Tennyson has caught the exact note of his period and environment; the Arcadian story is set in a particular time and place. The holiday of the Mechanics' Institute, the parlour game played by a group of college friends with their ladies in the surroundings of a great house with all its atmosphere both of past glories and present prosperity—these are the things with which Tennyson was most at home. There is a group of intimate friends in the foreground, but progress and politics loom behind. Under the disguise of the tale, both burlesque and fairy tale, which the young men, elegantly disposed against the background of a Gothic ruin, tell 'from mouth to mouth', a great many newspaper and high table topics are aired—the new science, the corn question, the relations of landlord to tenant, and most of all the question of female education which Maurice's foundation of Queen's College, Harley Street, had brought into public notice.[5] In such circumstances these issues could be discussed with a certain objectivity. The relaxed mood of the party, the improbability of the story, and the element of burlesque—both men and women are guyed—give a distance to the subject. No one need feel personally involved. And, as in *The Golden Year*, more than one view of the main subject is presented: the extremist views of the Prince's father and of Princess Ida, and the middle, common-sense view of the Prince. A modern, reading with a wry mouth, may well feel that the Prince and Tennyson are

getting it both ways. The Prince can take a high-minded view of
marriage:

> Like perfect music unto noble words,

and indicate that the ideals of Ida and the proper education of the female
half of the race can be safely left to him—but beautiful as it all is, the
fact remains that women are to be educated for marriage while men are
educated for themselves:

> Yield thyself up: my hopes and thine are one:
> Accomplish thou my manhood and thyself;
> Lay thy sweet hands in mine and trust to me.

We need not waste time in abusing Tennyson for what, in his day, was
an advanced view. His theory about marriage has very little importance
in the history of female emancipation, and a great deal in the history of
his own psychological development. In *The Princess* he develops a way
of exploring contemporary problems which utilises his particular talent
for the creation of romantic landscape (Ida's college has the appearance
of the Palace of Art refurnished for practical use), without treachery to
his new awareness of the commonplace. But in his exploration of the
problem posed by Ida's ambitions and aspirations he presents, yet again,
the problem of his own situation. This time he comes to what appears
to be a practical solution.

His progress towards that solution is visible in the revisions and additions which he made to the poem after its first publication. He made two
important innovations in its structure: in 1848 he added the songs which
the ladies of the house party sing in the pauses of the story game, and,
three years later, he added to the main body of the poem the passages
which describe the 'weird seizures' of the Prince. Tennyson was quite
explicit about his reason for adding the songs. The public, he grumbled,
did not take the meaning of his extravaganza, and he put the songs in to
make it clear.[6] This use of songs to control and direct the reader's
attention was a device which Tennyson often used in a long poem, and
even in the first versions of *The Princess* the songs which Ida reads or
sings by the bedside of the wounded Prince have an obvious significance
both in the action of the story and in Ida's development. 'Come down,
O Maid' speaks for itself—it is a reproach to Ida for her stony and
remote ideals, and it invites her down from the mountain top of theory
to a present and fruitful good. This is yet another repetition of *The
Palace of Art* theme. Tennyson is still exhorting us to a humbler life in a
cottage in the vale:

And come, for Love is of the valley, come.

But if it is read in conjunction with Ida's other song, 'Now sleeps the crimson petal, now the white', 'Come down, O Maid' takes on another and fuller significance: it is not so much an address to an idealist as to a virgin. The images of virginity are all present in the poem, stars, snow and mountain tops, the 'height, the cold, the splendour of the hills'. The song emphasises the quality and barrenness in these images. Love, we are told, does not walk

> *With Death* and Morning on the silver horns,
> Nor wilt thou snare him in the white ravine,
> Nor find him dropt upon the firths of ice,

and the virgin heights, beautiful as they are, remain

> The monstrous ledges there to slope, and spill
> Their thousand wreaths of dangling water smoke,
> *That like a broken purpose waste in air.*

The simile of the broken purpose defines the intention of this description:

> So waste not thou; but come; for all the vales
> Await thee.

The waterfall wastes as the maiden wastes without love. Beautiful as the mountain is, it is the image of stagnation and waste and death. The characteristics of the valley on the other hand are fruitfulness and movement. Love goes

> hand in hand with Plenty in the maize,
> Or red with spirted purple of the vats.

The description of the valley, where the children call, and there is a 'moan of doves in immemorial elms', evokes the domestic, prosperous, English scene. It is meant to, and, by Tennyson's usual sleight of hand, the scene comes to stand for the rich peacefulness to which the virgin is invited. Even if the imagery itself, reinforced by a reference to *The Song of Songs* (Love is 'fox-like in the vines') did not give the poem this meaning, its association with the earlier song would. 'Now sleeps the crimson petal, now the white' is an erotic poem of the elaborately symbolic kind. In one image in particular it links up the marriage theme with the theme of the lady in the tower:

> Now folds the lily all her sweetness up,
> And slips into the bosom of the lake:
> So fold thyself, my dearest, thou, and slip
> Into my bosom and be lost in me.

This anticipates the end of *The Princess* when the Prince invites Ida to yield herself up, and means her not only to yield her virginity but her barren obstinacy. An earlier image puts it with felicity:

> Now lies the Earth all Danäe to the stars,
> And all thy heart lies open unto me.

The Princess herself has been a kind of Danäe, a virgin locked away from men in a tower, and here the virgin Danäe and the virgin Earth waiting for the fruitful embrace of Heaven are linked together. It is because this image is double that its significance quickens—the virgin Danäe is associated with Ida's remoteness, but the virgin Earth is linked with the fruitfulness which is to follow on the marriage of the Prince and the Princess, and which is illuminated later by the description of love in the valley. The Prince, with that faint priggishness which ruins him as a character, speaks of himself and Ida as 'yoked in all exercise of noble ends', but he has already put the matter a great deal better in an image which reflects the theme of the two songs:

> breathe upon my brows;
> In that fine air I tremble, all the past
> Melts mist-like into this bright hour, and this
> Is morn to more, and all the rich to-come
> *Reels, as the golden Autumn woodland reels*
> *Athwart the smoke of burning weeds.*

What is more, all this, the fruitfulness of the marriage, the dawn of new and better things, moves together in what is normally denied to Tennyson's poetry, an atmosphere of physical passion. Both the songs follow immediately on the passionate embrace of Ida and the Prince, and the Prince describes Ida as looking after this kiss like Venus

> when she came
> From barren deeps to conquer all with love;
> And down the streaming crystal dropt; and she
> Far-fleeted by the purple island-sides,
> Naked, a double light in air and wave,
> To meet her Graces, where they deck'd her out
> For worship without end;

It is a description with the faint luminosity of physical passion (Naked, a double light in air and wave), and it colours what follows. It also alters our imagination of Ida—no Amazonian woman, no severe leader to the truth remains. Danäe has come out of her tower.

There were other things in the earlier version of the poem which were meant to point to the symbolic value of the fruitful marriage, amongst them Psyche's child. Tennyson complained that no one saw the significance of the child, but this is not really surprising. Tennyson meant that Psyche's baby girl and her adventures in the break-up of Ida's college should be seen as the literal fulfilment of Ida's wish for women, that they should 'lose the child'. He wishes to indicate that in Ida's plan for the female sex there is a threat of barrenness, and also that in 'losing the child' women will lose the real, the defining qualities of the feminine nature. Between over-elaboration, sentimentality, and an erroneous metaphor he misses his purpose. Psyche's desire for her baby, Ida's yielding to the attraction of 'baby fingers, waxen touches' have a certain psychological reality (the outcry of the Virgin Queen, 'The Queen of Scots is lighter of a fair son, and I am but a barren stock', was not altogether provoked by dynastic grief). It is just possible too that Tennyson may have been right in supposing that care for children is the root of the feminine quality of compassion. But whatever truth there is in his conceptions of the feminine role is overlaid by the falseness and the fulsomeness of its expression:

> And half
> The sacred mother's bosom, panting, burst
> The laces toward her babe.

This fulsomeness is linked to an incurable domesticity.

Since no one took any notice of the child, Tennyson determined to hammer the moral at his readers and so inserted the series of lyrics sung by ladies of the house party. These are set at the beginning of the cantos; they set the tone and underlie the theme of each part of the narrative. The song which introduces the tourney is that sung by Lilia:

> Thy voice is heard thro' rolling drums,
>   That beat to battle where he stands;
> Thy face across his fancy comes,
>   And gives the battle to his hands:
> A moment, while the trumpets blow,
>   He sees his brood about thy knee;
> The next, like fire he meets the foe,
>   And strikes him dead for thine and thee.

This is followed after the battle by the other side of the picture:

> Home they brought her warrior dead:

In both lyrics the mind is directed to the bond between husband and wife in the children of the marriage. He sees '*his* brood about thy knee' and in the agony of the wife's bereavement,

> Rose a nurse of ninety years,
> Set *his* child upon her knee—
> Like summer tempest came her tears—
> 'Sweet *my* child, I live for thee.'

The dominating motif of the canto which follows this song is the thawing of Ida's iciness, in part by her response to the dangerous state of the Prince, but more insistently by her response to Psyche's appeal for her child. Cyril's speech puts the point:

> O fair and strong and terrible! Lioness
> That with your long locks play the Lion's mane!
> But Love and Nature, these are two more terrible
> And stronger. See, your foot is on our necks,
> We vanquish'd, you the Victor of your will.
> What would you more? give her the child! Remain
> *Orb'd in your isolation:*

To lose the child for Ida meant putting off the yoke of masculine domination, but the songs declare the grimmer meaning it had for Tennyson: to 'lose the child', either, that is, to put off womanly submissiveness, or to refuse the sacred duty of child-bearing, became for him a defiance of love and nature, and a loss of those powers of compassion and reconciliation which children give to the woman, and of courage which they give to the man. It is, in fact, to remain 'orb'd in isolation'.

Marriage, then, the relationship between man and woman, was fast becoming Tennyson's symbol of relationship with the world. It was his escape from isolation. The final revision of *The Princess* shows him certain of this issue. This revision was made after his marriage with Emily Sellwood in 1850, the year of the publication of *In Memoriam*, and the year in which Tennyson became Laureate. After his marriage with Miss Sellwood he said in his curiously unreticent manner, 'The peace of God came into my life before the altar when I wedded her'.[7] The revisions of *The Princess* reflect this conviction. For what he inserted into the poem at this point were the descriptions of the Prince's weird seizures, those states of being in which the Prince becomes uncertain of the reality of things:

> waking dreams were, more or less,
> An old and strange affection of the house.
> Myself too had weird seizures, Heaven knows what:
> On a sudden in the midst of men and day,
> And while I walk'd and talk'd as heretofore,
> I seem'd to move among a world of ghosts,
> And feel myself the shadow of a dream.

These seizures recur at crucial moments in the poem, and in the last stage of the story, when the Prince lies sick, his life is in danger, not from a wound, but from a deep trance in which he is aware of, but not concerned with, the outside world. The whole thing is very Tennysonian indeed. This, in fact, is the enchantment of the Lady of Shalott, the trance of the Sleeping Princess, and the Prince is restored to the world of real life by Ida's kiss. He is not, however, destroyed like the Lady of Shalott. On the contrary, Ida's love cures him of the weird seizures:

> lift thine eyes; my doubts are dead,
> My haunting sense of hollow shows: the change,
> This truthful change in thee has kill'd it.

Love, by establishing relationship, establishes the mind in its world. We may without hesitation suppose that Tennyson's marriage did precisely this—it stabilised the relationship he had been seeking between the inner and the outer world. The question remains: Did this new awareness of things as solid and stable blunt his perception of their mysteriousness? Is domesticity as ruinous as indulgence in morbidity? Whatever else this certainty did, at least it turned Tennyson into a public poet—not only, that is, into a Laureate, but a poet really concerned with the fabric of society as a subject for poetry. It is to the public poetry that we must now turn.

Chapter VI

The Laureate's Vocation

THE year 1850 was Tennyson's *annus mirabilis*. In it he published *In Memoriam*, married Miss Sellwood and became Poet Laureate. These events were not unconnected. Miss Sellwood's doubts about Tennyson's beliefs were quieted by the sentiments of *In Memoriam*: the poem made his marriage possible, and it also established his claim to the Laureateship. To later generations this claim rests on a simple fact. Tennyson was a better poet than Miss Barrett, or Leigh Hunt, or any of the other candidates proposed for the office. But in 1850 his poetic stature was not so obvious; in spite of the success of the 1842 *Poems* and of *The Princess* the public remembered the thunders of *The Quarterly* and had its doubts. *In Memoriam* changed that. The Victorians, and especially that most eminent of Victorians, Prince Albert, found in it their most articulate voice: the author had spoken for their deepest moods and concerns even before he was their Laureate. Prince Albert intervened: Mr Tennyson inherited Mr Wordsworth's official laurels.

The office of Laureate meant a great deal to Tennyson. It was, like his marriage, an element in his new psychological stability—a link which bound him to the world of affairs. To be the ceremonial voice of the State, the servant of its Servant, was to have status in the community, and what is more, a status, not merely as a person, but as a poet: there was no need to deny the inner voice or the solitary vision. As the Laureate, the Bard, the Licensed Prophet, he could be, and often was, as eccentric as he liked without severing himself from the body of society. The Laureateship was for him not so much an honour as a function, and a function which gave direction as well as public recognition to his inner sense of his own gifts and his own vocation. He was very serious about it:

> And here the Singer for his Art
> Not all in vain may plead
> 'The song that nerves a nation's heart,
> Is in itself a deed.'

This poem written in answer to a lady's complaint about Tennyson's militant patriotism, expresses something of his conception of his office.[1] Ceremonial Odes were well enough, and he was, in fact, startlingly successful as a ceremonial poet: the public poem in which accepted commonplaces must be uttered gravely, impersonally, and without undue sentimentality, was his peculiar province. But the composition of these poems could not and did not exhaust his sense of duty. He had, after all, been trained in the Romantic, the Wordsworthian school; had been accustomed to think of poets as 'the unacknowledged legislators of the world', men with sharpened perceptions of reality, and a message to their fellow men. The Bard, the Laureate, is the prophet as well as the priest of the community, the *Vates* who sees deep into the realities of the spiritual and moral life, and is capable of revealing to society the state of its own soul.

This sense of a public, prophet's duty, became, for good or ill, a major element in Tennyson's poetic life. After he became Laureate he rarely wrote private poetry. Some poems, *The Roses on the Terrace*, *The Voice and the Peak*, *Crossing the Bar*, stand out as the expression of personal emotion or reflection, but they stand out because of their rarity, and, significantly enough, they nearly all belong to the last phase of his development. This does not mean that he wrote with his eye perpetually on an audience: that is too simple an explanation of a complex situation. He seems rather, even in the most personal of insights or experience, to be conscious of public significance. This habit of mind sometimes leads him to absurdity, as in *The Human Cry* which was written partly as the conclusion of *De Profundis*, a poem which celebrates the birth of Hallam Tennyson, and partly to satisfy Jowett's desire for a Hegelian hymn to sing in Balliol College Chapel. But it also inspires some of his best work: in *Maud* and *Lucretius*, for example, his superb ability to display the disturbed mind is married to a sense of social disorder and its causes. This duality in method and apprehension is not a new thing: it is the natural development of those habits of thought and of technique which gave coherence to the *Poems* of 1842. The work which he did on that volume was almost a preparation for the Laureateship: it helped him to lay hold on the office as a vocation not a sinecure.

Tennyson recreated the Laureateship, and yet his fitness for it, his happiness in it were fortuitous. They were, almost, the accident of his temperament, rather than the product of a special talent or a particular training. For Tennyson was not really well placed to speak for his generation. Some schools of criticism require, what is virtually impossible, that a writer shall in feeling and expression reflect the shifts of mood and thought within the common life of his generation, and that he shall, at the same time, be capable of analysing and criticising that common life. The poet of an ideally integrated culture will and does transmit the rich, sensuous and spiritual awareness of his generation: there are in the writings of Homer, Virgil, Dante and Shakespeare energies which are not exclusively their own, which belong to the various societies in which they were born. But even poets of this stature do not transmit the full flavour of their periods: there were, for instance, qualities and complexities in the culture of Imperial Rome which are not felt either in the *Georgics*, or the *Aeneid*; qualities, say, of sophisticated barbarism of which Virgilian Latin is scarcely capable. For the more complex a society is the less it can be apprehended by a single mind however sensitive. And the society to which Tennyson was the official Laureate was very complex indeed. It was already highly articulated and specialist in the manner of modern cultures, but it retained the regional and hierarchical divisions of earlier generations. Tennyson's own life illustrates these divisions. He was the Parson's son, a member of that social grouping of which Jane Austen's novels make us pleasantly aware, the society of a 'few families', but his father's father was *nouveau riche*, a lawyer building a dynasty on the sudden prosperity of the fishing industry in Grimsby. When Tennyson moved away from his home world, to Cambridge, he found himself without realising it a member of the newest aristocracy of all: the arrogant aristocracy of middle class intellect which grew so powerful in Victoria's reign and beyond.[2] And though at a later stage he was to hob-nob with Viceroys and Prime Ministers; to be a guest at the house parties of the nobility, and to visit the Queen in the period of her seclusion, still these early worlds of pleasant country houses, and long intellectual discussions, were his milieu. In them he was in his way as secluded from the cruder energies of his age as Mr Podsnap's 'young person'.

It is revealing to compare his experience with that, say, of Wordsworth or of Dickens. By accident of environment Wordsworth touched on the quick of a life which was not that of his own class: he experienced almost first hand and responded to that vast change in the fabric of society which was first apparent in the altered rhythm of life in simple rural communities, the break-up of families as described in *The Female Vagrant* or in *Michael*, the pressure of changed economic conditions as shown in *The Last of the Flock* and *The Ruined Cottage*. He was fortunate too, and aware of his good fortune, in his experience in France: he had felt in his personal life the pulse not merely of local but of European change. Dickens again was lucky; he was born into an order which possessed no exact boundaries, the lower middle class of London and the Home Counties. The great gift which lower middle class life bestows, in a careless way, on its more intelligent members is a kind of negative capability, not so much the capacity to adapt, as the capacity to receive and reflect the colours of a variety of life. Dickens's social position provided him not with a place of rest but with a starting-point for exploration: it opened one way into the genteel drawing-rooms of those who had been successful in business or in the professions, the other into the warrens of London's slums and London's underworld. The accident of birth and family gave Dickens a wider range than that of any other writer of his time and he had, at the least, the sharpest eye for the mannerisms of that social complex we call Victorian.

Wordsworth and Dickens shared a good fortune; their early environment and experience gave them range. Tennyson's confined him. He spoke, to the last, with the strong Lincolnshire vowels of his youth;[3] the rural exclusiveness, the rural quiet remained with him until he died—at Aldworth where he had removed to avoid the influx of summer visitors to the Isle of Wight. This exclusiveness, innocent though it was, was a handicap. The pace of social change in the forty years of Tennyson's Laureateship was not as fast as it is in this century, but it was fast enough, and in some ways more radical than anything we have experienced since. The mere volume of social and political legislation gives us a superficial notion of the gradual metamorphosis of English life and culture throughout this period. Social legislation both reflects and creates social change, and the variety of the needs for which it catered in Victoria's reign shows something of the upheavals amongst her people. There were Factory Acts to regulate the new and growing industrial empires, and to control new conditions of work; Local

Government Acts to order the vast conurbations, no longer towns or
cities in any real sense, which industrial and commercial activity had
called into being; Railway Acts, Army Reforms, Reforms of the
Universities, Reforms of the Franchise to cater for a new political
consciousness, Education Acts to ensure literacy in the newly en-
franchised voter. The magnitude of the changes can be measured
perhaps by the Education Acts: when Tennyson became Laureate, the
larger proportion of the population could not read his poems, when he
died three generations of children had gone through the new Board
Schools: his successors would deal, for the first time, with a literate
nation. But it is not our business to discuss the Victorian achievement:
my point is that it is neither reasonable nor just to expect a poet of so
limited a social experience to apprehend or to express the full quality
of a culture in a state of such a rapid, manifold and varied change.

Yet Prince Albert was right. The new Laureate could and did, in spite of
his limitations, become the voice of a whole period and a phase of
culture. He was often at odds with the sentiments and opinions of his
contemporaries: the radical press attacked his royalist and patriotic
effusions; he himself described Englishmen as 'the most beastly self-
satisfied nation on earth', and he was often incapable of apprehending
the intellectual tone of men as far apart as Gladstone and D. G. Rossetti.
He does not represent the Victorian age because he understood it, or
was passively complacent either about its virtues or its follies, but because
his response to the mood and colour of the period is fuller and more
alive than that of any other contemporary poet. In spite of his want of
experience in the detail of Victorian life, his temperament and genius
were near to the quick of the era with all its aspirations and its absurdi-
ties. For in all the Victorian variety one thing was constant—change.
Under a solid front English society endured a continuing metamorphosis both in structure and purpose. Without being aware of the
details of change, and incapable of analysing its causes, Tennyson
responded, as he always had, to this fundamental instability in the
world around him. He has a kind of conditioned sensitiveness to
currents of thought and feeling, and to the unseen changes, which,
little by little, modified the ethos of the Victorian community:

> A ridge
> Of breaker issued from the belt, and still
> Grew with the growing note, and when the note
> Had reach'd a thunderous fullness, on those cliffs
> Broke . . . .

> Ever when it broke
> The statues, king or saint, or founder fell;
> Then from the gaps and chasms of ruin left
> Came men and women in dark clusters round,
> Some crying, 'Set them up! they shall not fall!'
> And others, 'Let them lie, for they have fall'n'.

This awareness of change in the fabric of society was for him a matter of feeling rather than of observation and reflection. It is, I would suggest, the virtue of his temperament: the melancholic turn of mind which in his youth made him too easily conscious of the darker places of the human mind, made him in his maturer years sensible of social realities which many of his more sanguine contemporaries could ignore. His personal position was secure: he was stable in the love and care of his wife and children but that quality of his spirit which turned to waste places, to seas, and to the vast distances of outer space, responded to the instability of his culture:

> That great wave
> Returning, while none mark'd it, on the crowd
> Broke, mixt with awful light, and show'd their eyes
> Glaring, and passionate looks, and swept away
> The men of flesh and blood, and men of stone,
> To the waste deeps together . . . .

When I see society vicious and the poor starving in great cities, I feel that it is a mighty wave of evil passing over the world, and that there will yet be some new and strange development which I shall not live to see. . . . You must not be surprised at anything that comes to pass in the next fifty years. All ages are ages of transition but this is an awful moment of transition.[4]

Matthew Arnold was also troubled by an awareness of dying order, and like Tennyson he expresses it in terms of the resistless movements of seas. But Tennyson possessed, again by virtue of his personal experience, what Arnold had lost, the will and the desire, 'to fight . . . and not to yield'. The Laureate's voice was meant to warn and to encourage, he receives and expresses the subconscious fears and doubts of his generation, but he also feels and presents their sense of vast achievement and their obstinate and sometimes irritating optimism. It is worth noting, however, that *Enoch Arden*, that poem most used by critics to demonstrate Tennyson's subservience to the values of his age, is a poem of which the central themes are death and exile, desolation and an unendurable solitude.

The dual character of Tennyson's Laureateship appears in the first volume he published as Laureate: *Maud and Other Poems. Maud* itself with its Carlylean denunciations of commercial corruption, is concerned with something a good deal more significant to Tennyson than the love affair of an unbalanced young man. The hero's despair is caused, in part, by a malaise in the social order . . . for which he constantly parades the evidence:

> Maud could be gracious too, no doubt,
> To a lord, a captain, a padded shape,
> *A bought commission, a waxen face,*
> *A rabbit mouth that is ever agape—*
> *Bought? what is it he cannot buy?*
> And therefore splenetic, personal, base,
> A wounded thing with a rancorous cry,
> At war with myself and a wretched race,
> Sick, sick to the heart of life, am I,

Maud's voice cuts across this sick despair:

> She is singing an air that is known to me,
> A passionate ballad gallant and gay,
> A martial song like a trumpet's call!
> Singing alone in the morning of life,
> In the happy morning of life and of May,
> Singing of men that in battle array,
> Ready in heart and ready in hand,
> March with banner and bugle and fife,
> To the death, for their native land.

Maud's song might, by its description, have been *The Charge of the Light Brigade* which is in the same volume. Tennyson's first Laureate poem, the magnificent *Ode on the Death of the Duke of Wellington*, is also in this volume. I do not use the word 'magnificent' as a superlative, but to suggest the quality of the poem; its realisation of the formal magnificence of a public occasion, its exaggeration of a dead, and rather crusty, soldier and politician into a public symbol:

> O fall'n at length that tower of strength
> Which stood four-square to all the winds that blew!

The Ode displays not merely Tennyson's sense of public order, but, like *The Charge of the Light Brigade*, his response to personal courage. It is personal courage and public duty which Maud's song expresses to the hero, and her celebration of these virtues is set against his justifiable sense of public corruption. So that in the 1854 volume we find, both in the major and in the minor poems, a significant combination: social corruption linked to personal despair; personal courage bound to and considered as the bastion of public order.

Maud and Other Poems was the first collection of Tennyson's poems to be published after he became Laureate, and it was perhaps more unpopular than any other of his books except the 1832 volume.[5] The criticism which it aroused may have caused Tennyson to modify his methods, but not his purpose. The double awareness of the Victorian world which appears in the *Maud* volume continues to be the *motif* of his work, and is best illustrated in the curious affair of *Locksley Hall Sixty Years After* and *On the Jubilee*. These are not distinguished poems, but they do display both Tennyson's own sense of his vocation and the extent to which, in the thirty years after *Maud*, he had impressed it on the public mind. At the time, the late eighties, when these two poems were composed Tennyson was very much disturbed and depressed by two deaths, that of his son Lionel, and that of Gordon at Khartoum. Lionel's death was the greater grief, but Gordon's was a public shock as well as a private sorrow. Gordon was a man of soldierly virtues, simple and single-minded to the point of fanaticism, and wanting in any kind of political sense. Tennyson liked him. The combination of personal courage with a naive, visionary personality was always attractive to him. His sense of the quality of Gordon's character increased the outrage which he, in common with most of the public, and the Queen herself, felt when Gordon was killed. The fact that Gordon, by his arrogant indifference to orders, was at least partially responsible for his own death did not cross Tennyson's mind. What he saw in the fall of Khartoum was the betrayal of national honour: his grief, combined with a sense of treachery at the heart of things, embitters the meditations of *Locksley Hall Sixty Years After*. In this poem the hero of the earlier *Locksley Hall*, now eighty, looks back on the past, and the ideals which he had expressed in his youth. Then, though disappointed in love, he cried:

> Not in vain the distance beacons. Forward, forward let us range,
> Let the great world spin for ever down the ringing grooves of
>   change.

> Thro' the shadow of the globe we sweep into the younger day;
> Better fifty years of Europe than a cycle of Cathay.

Mother-Age (for mine I knew not) help me as when life begun:
Rift the hills, and roll the waters, flash the lightnings, weigh
   the Sun.

O, I see the crescent promise of my spirit hath not set.
Ancient founts of inspiration well thro' all my fancy yet.

This was in the eighteen-forties, and the age of the young Victoria had
taken the lines as watchwords. Hope, life, and the dream of intellectual
and social progress are contained in them. Now, in the eighteen-
eighties, the old man is not at all sure that progress is a benefit to man:

'Forward' rang the voices then, and of the many mine was one.
Let us hush this cry of 'Forward' till ten thousand years have gone.

*   *   *

Forward then, but still remember how the course of Time will
   swerve,
Crook and turn upon itself in many a backward streaming curve.

His range of complaint against the 'Mother-Age' is most impressive.
Through his mouth Tennyson inveighs against worldliness and moral
corruption, the creeping ugliness of industrial civilisation, the degrada-
tion of the poor, and the loss of what he calls 'old political common
sense'. When the poem was published the public was shocked and
angry. This was not merely an indictment of the civilisation for which
it was responsible, but an indictment of what it considered its own
major virtue. Progress, the steady evolution of the bigger and better,
was the jewel in Victoria's crown. The Victorians could not understand Tennyson's mind: they had felt the fall of Khartoum, but by
making a convenient and perhaps justifiable scapegoat of Gladstone,
they had absolved themselves from any complicity in Gordon's
death, and got on with cataloguing, in preparation for the Queen's
Jubilee, their own very considerable achievements. These were the
evidence of that progress which Tennyson himself had taught them to
expect and praise: they were astonished to find that their official oracle
now despised the cry of 'Forward' which he had been among the first
to raise. But, though Tennyson seemed to have reneged on the Victorian
ideal, his influence and his prestige were such that *Locksley Hall Sixty
Years After* was considered as likely to be a blight on the public rejoicing.
Mr Gladstone at least felt obliged to write a considered critique of the
poem, reviewing the reforms of the fifty years of the Queen's reign,

and rebuking the Laureate's pessimism. 'Justice', said Mr Gladstone, 'does not require, nay rather, it forbids that the Jubilee of the Queen be marred by tragic notes.'[6]

Tennyson could not, as Sir Charles Tennyson rightly says, ignore the Prime Minister's hint. He was now, as the official Laureate, to compose the official Jubilee Ode: it was his business as the mouth of the people to translate the public sense of solid achievement into suitable ritual utterance. Prophetic duty had to be reconciled with public office. The Ode, however, is more remarkable for metrical ingenuity than the fire of holy conviction:

> You then joyfully, all of you,
> Set the mountain aflame to-night,
> Shoot your stars to the firmament,
> Deck your houses, illuminate
> All your towns for a festival,
> And in each let a multitude
> Loyal, each, to the heart of it,
> One full voice of allegiance,
> Hail the fair Ceremonial
> Of this year of her Jubilee.

The old man was not to be flattered out of his gloom:

> Are there thunders moaning in the distance?
> Are there spectres moving in the darkness?

He was sure, and on the whole he seems to have been right, that there were. Even if we do not allow for this sombre pizzicato in the bass part of *On the Jubilee*, the poem cannot be regarded as hypocritical in its praise of Victoria's reign. Tennyson praises the Queen herself at length: he is somewhat perfunctory in what he says of the wider achievements of her people:

> Fifty years of ever-broadening Commerce!
> Fifty years of ever-brightening Science!
> Fifty years of ever-widening Empire!

He did in fact believe that these things were achievements and admired them. What he did in *Locksley Hall Sixty Years After* was not so much to decry them as to express his sense of the threat to society which was implicit in the achievement itself. 'Broadening Commerce' and increasing wealth are real goods; but as Ruskin and Morris as well as

Tennyson and others reminded their generation they were paying a heavy price for prosperity in ugliness, and squalor, and human waste:

> Is it well that while we range with Science, glorying in the Time,
> City children soak and blacken soul and sense in city slime?
>
> There among the glooming alleys Progress halts on palsied feet,
> Crime and hunger cast our maidens by the thousand on the street.
>
> There the Master scrimps his haggard sempstress of her daily bread,
> There a single sordid attic holds the living and the dead.
>
> There the smouldering fire of fever creeps across the rotted floor,
> And the crowded couch of incest in the warrens of the poor.

From the high ground of present knowledge social historians can see and compare the misery of the eighteenth-century rural slum with that endured in urban slums of the nineteenth century: perhaps the Hanoverian peasant was worse off than the Victorian factory hand.[7] But the quality of misery is, in any age, absolute to those who suffer it and social evil is always social evil. The things that Tennyson described in *Locksley Hall Sixty Years After* were no less real than the massive achievements of the Victorians: his indictment is echoed, more quietly, through page after page of Royal Commissions and Enquiries: it was endorsed by the more sensitive of his contemporaries. But the facts were not facts of which his contemporaries wished to be reminded. For the family poet, the celebrator of the pure Galahad, the upright Arthur, to thrust the facts of overcrowding, incest and prostitution under the noses of their daughters was outrageous. But it was more than a threat to family modesty: it threatened the steadiness of life. The stability of the Victorian ethic depended on the obstinate refusal of the average Victorian liberal to examine the relations between political freedom and economic responsibility. The masters and mistresses of sweated sempstresses and tailors, the factory owners, still rebellious about factory inspectors, and adamant about trade unionists, the landlords opposing the new sanitation laws, could and did argue that the interference of governments with the natural workings of 'economic law' would be disastrous. But such a position is only possible to men and women of sensibility provided they are not reminded, as they were by a host of writers, Dickens, Mrs Gaskell, Kingsley, even Disraeli, that, in spite of the nation's blameless adherence to the laws of progress, many of its members were living in sub-human conditions. The force of *Locksley Hall Sixty Years After* lay not in its power as a poem (it is not a good poem) nor as a social document (its accusations are general, not particular) but quite simply in Tennyson's position. He was *the* poet: it was as if Mr Eliot, in his old age, had written a play about race riots or juvenile delinquency.

Tennyson's indignation at the plight of those among the crawling alleys does not lead him to any sympathy with popular movements. Compassion for the oppressed classes was one thing. Sympathy with their aspirations another:

> Envy wears the mask of Love, and, laughing sober fact to scorn,
> Cries to Weakest as to Strongest, 'Ye are equals, equal born.'
>
> Equal-born? O, yes, if yonder hill be level with the flat.
> Charm us, Orator, till the Lion look no larger than the Cat,
>
> Till the Cat thro' that mirage of over heated language loom
> Larger than the Lion,—Demos end in working its own doom.

These sentiments did not endear the Laureate to the radical movements, and to us *Locksley Hall Sixty Years After* looks like a curious mixture of the radical and the reactionary, with all the inconsistency of a burst of senile bad temper. But the impression is deceptive. Tennyson's social conscience worked in a different context from ours; to him both the evils suffered by the poor *and* the popular revolutionary movements were symptoms of a much deeper, a moral malaise in society. He meant what he said:

> Gone the cry of 'Forward, Forward', lost within a growing gloom;
> Lost, or only heard in silence from the silence of a tomb.
>
> Half the marvels of my morning, triumphs over time and space,
> Staled by frequence, shrunk by usage into commonest common-
> place!
>
> 'Forward' rang the voices then, and of the many mine was one.
> Let us hush this cry of 'Forward' till ten thousand years have gone.

The desire for progress had become an evil because, by their perpetual restlessness for some new thing, men made themselves the allies and agents of the inevitable change which threatened their security.

> Forward, backward, backward, forward, in the immeasurable sea,
> Sway'd by vaster ebbs and flows than can be known to you and me.

This is not a political attitude, but it is an attitude which makes a man sensitive to political currents. Tennyson's need for personal security is here translated into a need for the security of society. This is not what some critics consider it to be, a craving for the security of his own place and position in a particular society, a security obtained only by flattering the vicious emotional attitude of his own generation. It was society itself which needed to be stable, which needed to establish itself in the face of threats to its equilibrium.

Political and popular movements threatened it with a violent disintegration. The threat which Tennyson felt, the threat of Demos, of a violent and irrational populace, was bred in the blood of every cultivated early Victorian. Tennyson's generation had grown up in the shadow of the French Revolution; in spite of their young and eager sympathy with movements for intellectual and popular emancipation, they could not be altogether untroubled by the nightmare of the Terror which hung over their parents and grandparents, especially when they themselves glimpsed the real brutality of revolution. Kingsley's early and horrified experience of the Bristol Riots inhibited for years his compassion for the poorer classes. Tennyson's attitude to politics was never quite so liberal after he had witnessed some of the excesses of the Reform Bill Riots.[8] The fear of physical violence which would disintegrate the fabric of a known society inspired his fear of the 'Celtic Demos' which, for him, was almost a symbol of irrational politics allied with the forces of irrational change:

> Social Truth shall spread,
> And justice, ev'n tho' thrice again
> The red fool-fury of the Seine
> Should pile her barricades with dead.

> But ill for him that wears the crown,
> And him, the lazar, in his rags:
> They tremble, the sustaining crags;
> The spires of ice are toppled down,

> And molten up, and roar in flood;
> The fortress crashes from on high,
> The brute earth lightens to the sky,
> And the great Æon sinks in blood.

But disorder in the body politic was nothing beside the real threat to society. It is significant that *Locksley Hall Sixty Years After* had its origin in a mood of personal bereavement, and that it dwells once again on the moral and spiritual need for a belief in immortality:

> Truth, for Truth is Truth, he worshipt, being true as he was brave;
> Good, for Good is Good, he follow'd, yet he look'd beyond the grave,

>   *   *   *

> Truth for truth, and good for good! The Good, the True, the Pure, the Just
> Take the charm 'For ever' from them, and they crumble into dust.

The new shock of Lionel's death, and of Gordon's no doubt raised the old demon of mutability, and showed Tennyson again the abysm of the endless cycle of things. But it is always necessary to build a bastion against the dark. Tennyson, looking round, saw men at work to pull down the bastion, deliberately destroying the values which protected them from the nightmare of the meaningless:

> Bring the old dark ages back without the faith, without the hope,
> Break the State, the Church, the Throne, and roll their ruins down the slope.

> Authors—essayist, atheist, novelist, realist, rhymester, play your part,
> Paint the mortal shame of nature with the living hues of Art.

> Rip your brothers' vices open, strip your own foul passions bare;
> Down with Reticence, down with Reverence—forward—naked —let them stare.

>   *   *   *

> Do your best to charm the worst, to lower the rising race of men;
> Have we risen from out the beast, then back into the beast again?

He saw the malaise of his society as a moral not a political disease, or rather he saw political evil as the flower of moral disorder. The atheist and the scientist deny the eternal and ignore the human:

> Is it well that while we range with Science, glorying in the Time,
> City children soak and blacken soul and sense in city slime?

The loss of 'old political common sense' is, in his mind, bound up with the abandonment of certain standards of morality and personal integrity.

The individual, though he may not realise it, is in his pursuit of emancipation allied with the forces of change and decay.

A number of poems, *Lucretius*, *Northern Farmer, New Style*, even *Aylmer's Field* reflect and develop this theme, and the theme itself explains the mystery of the apparent conflict between Tennyson's awareness of a need to ameliorate social conditions at home, and his exaltation of the British People in World Affairs. Sir Charles Tennyson suggests that Tennyson was a progressive at home, and an imperialist abroad, but this, though a reasonable statement of the position in current terms, is not quite just to the situation as it was. Tennyson the liberal, and Tennyson the reactionary were by no means the contraries they appear to be, and Tennyson's Imperialism was perfectly consistent with his general attitude. Imperialism is to most of us the worn-out dream of a national superbia. But if it was a dream it was certainly not one of the visions current in Tennyson's youth. For though he lived on into the nineties, he was in fact an *early* Victorian; he was nearly thirty when Victoria came to the throne, and he grew up, and settled down in a period when India was still administered by a trading company, when *The Times* could urge the Government to give up the colonies because they were so expensive and statesmen at dinner parties sighed 'Would to God that Canada would go'. He was already an old man when Disraeli flattered the Queen into an Empress: the Jingoism which was born of colonial competition between the great European powers, and which, finally, disgraced and discredited itself in the South African wars, was the excitement of a later and more strident generation. Any comparison of Tennyson's imperialistic verse and that of Rudyard Kipling reveals, for instance, a difference of tone which is the fruit of a difference in generation and attitude. For in Tennyson's time the great Imperial question was not how to maintain the glory of the British Raj, not how to satisfy the fierce independence of colonial peoples without too much loss of prestige or harm to the colonials themselves, but how to shed the responsibility of the colonies cheaply and quickly.[9] Tennyson's Imperial vision was in fact born of the indignation he felt at the desire of some members of the public to be rid of Canada—a desire which seemed to him a betrayal. Canada, the true North, rather than India, was the emotional centre of his Imperialism and he thought of the Empire in terms not of the India Act but of the Durham Report. Mrs Tennyson notes in her diary:

> He has read and given me to read *Fraser's Magazine* with suggestive articles on colonial federation, and against the inclosure

of commons, against which he has always protested. A general Colonial Council for the purpose of defence sounds to us sensible. He advocated inter-colonial conferences in England; and was of the opinion that the foremost colonial ministers ought to be admitted to the Privy Council or to some other Imperial council, where they could have a voice in Imperial affairs . . . [10]

The Empire to Tennyson was a collection of other Englands bound to the Crown, to whom England herself had a responsibility. The famous passage about the Empire in *To the Queen* is not so much an assertion of England's right to rule as of her duty to protect:

> The loyal to their crown
> Are loyal to their own far sons, who love
> Our ocean-empire with her boundless homes
> *For ever-broadening England.*

He was attacking those who for reasons of economy wished to shake off and leave undefended the half-developed communities of Canada and Australasia:

> that true North, whereof we lately heard
> A strain to shame us, 'keep you to yourselves;
> So loyal is too costly! friends—your love
> Is but a burthen: loose the bond, and go'.
> Is this the tone of empire? here the faith
> That made us rulers?

But for all his insistence on the mightiness of England, the faith that made us rulers and so forth, his teaching that it is England's duty to defend the states dependent on her is not entirely disinterested. Later, when in one of his economy drives Gladstone reduced the size of the Navy, Tennyson assailed him in a tub-thumping poem called *The Fleet*:

> Our own fair isle, the lord of every sea—
> Her fuller franchise—what would that be worth—
>   Her ancient fame of Free—
>   Were she . . . a fallen state?

> Her dauntless army scatter'd, and so small,
>   *Her island-myriads fed from alien lands—*
> The fleet of England is her all-in-all;
>   Her fleet is in your hands,
>   And in her fleet her fate.

A note to the poem makes it clear that in Tennyson's mind the safety of the colonies, to be secured by a strong fleet, was intimately bound up with the safety of the Home Country, and that safety, as the poem says, is as much a matter of trade as of military security. The Empire was a source of English Glory, but also, and perhaps more importantly, it was a defensive alliance, a bastion for the stable order of things which meant so much to him.

This was, fundamentally, a realist and practical attitude to the Imperial situation as it existed in his own day, but it is based on the curious assumption that all England's overseas possessions were of the same type; the type represented by Canada and Australia where the population, being largely British in origin, have an emotional tie with the Home Country. The problem of binding alien races into a single allegiance was not one which had occurred to Tennyson; all the races and peoples under Victoria's umbrella were, to him, one happy and loyal family.

> To all the loyal hearts who long
> To keep our English Empire whole!
> To all our noble sons, the strong
> New England of the Southern Pole!
> To England under Indian skies,
> To those dark millions of her realm!
> To Canada whom we love and prize,
> Whatever statesman hold the helm.
> Hands all round!

There was for him no question of the 'white man's burden', or 'lesser breeds without the law'; citizens of the 'new Englands' were automatically Englishmen owning English loyalties. It is this conception of loyalty which lies behind such lines as these from *The Defence of Lucknow*:

> Had they been bold enough then, who can tell but the traitors had won?

> *   *   *

> Praise to our Indian brothers, and let the dark face have his due!
> Thanks to the kindly dark faces who fought with us, faithful and few,
> Fought with the bravest among us, and drove them, and smote them, and slew,
> That ever upon the topmost roof *our banner in India blew*.

Normally it is those who ally themselves with a foreign and conquering power against their own countrymen who are regarded as traitors, but Tennyson here takes it for granted that the natural bond of the Indian people is, like his, with the Mother Queen. Those who strive against it are not simply 'enemies', but 'traitors'. It is a curious point of view, and one which repels us. For the trouble with Tennyson's imperialist philosophy is that, however understandable, it is still a mystique, and a mystique which limits his sympathies. We cannot get away with a Mother Empress nor, I hope, with a vision of things in which all men, whatever their race and history, are to be made model Englishmen. Such a world would not be so much unethical as intolerably dull, and this is the real fault of the religion of the British Empire. Tennyson's version of it, with its conception of Federation of Nations in a near-feudal relationship with Victoria, is at once astonishingly modern and astonishingly belligerent and naive: behind it lies the need which dominates *Locksley Hall Sixty Years After*, the need to defend the society he knew from change, the personal need to extend into the wider world the social ties which upheld him at home.

His vision of Empire is accompanied by fear. Tennyson glorifies the greatness of England, but he is also terrified that she will not be great, that she will be left open and defenceless in the changes of the world. His anger with Gladstone, his fury at the Liberal Government's reluctance to be bothered with Imperial ambitions is almost hysterical, and it is a note of fear not complacency which runs through the flag-wagging poems of his later years. From the warrens of the poor and the threats to the fabric of society which he saw in violent democratic movements he turned to the Empire, to the vision of allegiance and alliance as a bulwark against the rising waters. If loyalty breaks, all breaks. The Queen, significantly called the Mother Queen, is the central rock to which he clings. This fear is the force which unites Imperialism and Liberalism in his work. It is a noticeable fact, and one which bears out this view of Tennyson's political attitude, that after *In Memoriam*, all his major works are concerned with some kind of failure. The *Idylls of the King* which he intended to be his crowning work, the presentation of his ideal, presents not the triumph but the corruption and collapse of that ideal. *Enoch Arden* turns to disappointment and death; *Sea Dreams*, in the allegory of the wife's dream, displays the continual collapse and fall of faiths and civilisations; *Despair* the complete collapse of a personality lost in the transition of society from an old faith to newer philosophies. Even the flag-wagging poems do not celebrate conquests.

12

They are either warnings to flee from the wrath to come like *The Fleet*, or exhortations to oppose it, as in *Riflemen Form*. What is celebrated is not the military success but the military operation that was very nearly a failure, the charge of the Light Brigade, the battle of *The Revenge*, and the defence of Lucknow. These incidents were not, in the ordinary sense of the word, triumphs; what Tennyson celebrates in them is the capacity of the human spirit to stand out against odds:

> Men will forget what we suffer and not what we do. We can
>   fight!
> But to be soldier all day and be sentinel all thro' the night—
> Ever the mine and assault, our sallies, their lying alarms,
> Bugles and drums in the darkness, and shoutings and soundings
>   to arms,
> Ever the labour of fifty that had to be done by five,
> Ever the marvel among us that one should be left alive.

*   *   *

> Thoughts of the breezes of May blowing over an English field,
> Cholera, scurvy, and fever, the wound that *would* not be heal'd.

*   *   *

> Grief for our perishing children, and never a moment for grief,
> Toil and ineffable weariness, faltering hopes of relief,
> Havelock baffled, or beaten, or butcher'd for all that we knew—

*   *   *

> But ever upon the topmost roof our banner of England blew.

Courage is really the major theme of the mature Tennyson, not only in the military poems, but also, say, in *Enoch Arden*, and in *Maud*, where what saves the hero is not so much the Crimean War as the capacity which he acquires, through the War, to resist the phantoms bred by his temperament. It is this courage which Tennyson offers as a hope to what he saw as a self-destroying society. The Imperial Dream is, in a way, the outward symbol of courage against odds.

II

Tennyson was neither a political philosopher nor a professional politician. As an undergraduate he was, like the rest of the Apostles, interested in movements for political and social reform, and as a member of the House of Lords, committed to neither party, he was able, later in his life, to play a part in crucial political battles.[11] But, in spite of a certain common sense, he was curiously unsophisticated about the political scene. He pestered Gladstone with letters full of high political moralising;[12] he bombarded 'cotton-spinners' with indignant poems, but he never understood the game of parliamentary manoeuvre, and had no more appreciation than most of his contemporaries of the relations of economics and politics. The fall of Khartoum is a case in point: there was a real political principle at stake in the Sudan crisis, which Tennyson quite failed to grasp. No doubt Gladstone mishandled the situation, no doubt he delayed when he should have acted, but still Gordon, a mere general, a military servant of the state, had disregarded his orders and in doing so had, willingly or unwillingly, forced the Government's hand in a matter of national policy. Tennyson would have had no sympathy with Gladstone's reluctance to interfere in Egypt, but he should have had the wit to see that Gordon's action involved the whole question of the subordination of the military to the civil power. But, in the wave of emotion after Khartoum, like the rest of England he forgot, or ignored, or simply failed to recognise the principles involved in the crisis. The truth is that with all his virtues Tennyson did not possess the gift of analysis which enables a skilled politician to discern the lines of principle or development in a confused situation. His capacities were intuitive rather than analytic or executive.

This did not of course prevent him from philosophising his intuitions or from adopting what may loosely be called a political programme. He has a social philosophy which is not unlike the personal philosophy which he works out in *In Memoriam*. Its centre is certainly the same: the concept of perpetual change controlled and directed by law:

> The old order changeth, yielding place to new,
> And God fulfils Himself in many ways.

I need hardly say that such a philosophy was both natural, and highly congenial to the Victorian mind. Older political philosophers, Hooker, say, or Burke, or even Rousseau assume that there are states of society which are in some way natural to man: they differ not about this fundamental assumption, but about what is 'natural'. The notion that forms of society are fluid, that they can and do change under the pressures of historical events is, *as a commonplace*, a nineteenth-century phenomenon, and it is in harmony with the intellectual tone of the

period. In the fifties and sixties Darwin's theory of the evolution of
the species challenged Lyell's theory of dynamic change as an explanation of physical and biological phenomena: the distinction between the
two theories was of the greatest importance scientifically but in the
popular mind Darwin's theories strengthened the emotional and psychological effects of Lyell's. Lyell thought in terms of process, of
continual changes in physical environment producing and destroying
species: Darwin thought in terms of continued evolution under the
pressure of a need to adapt to environment, and he conceived, as Lyell
never did, of a recognisable continuity in the development of a particular species. But both doctrines emphasise that physical and biological
life are in a state of constant change and development. We may suppose
that these scientists were subtly influenced by the intellectual temper
of their period, or that their ideas were taken over from biology and
geology into other fields of speculation, but whatever the explanation,
the concepts of process, evolution, progress begin to appear not only
in scientific work but in the discussion of literature, theology, constitutional history and certainly in political philosophy.

Tennyson himself was Hegelian by temperament rather than by
reading. He constantly interpreted life in terms of great cosmic changes:

> I said: 'When first the world began,
> Young Nature thro' five cycles ran,
>   And in the sixth she moulded man.'

> ⋆   ⋆   ⋆

> There rolls the deep where grew the tree.
>   O earth, what changes hast thou seen!
>   There where the long street roars, hath been
> The stillness of the central sea.

> The hills are shadows, and they flow
>   From form to form, and nothing stands;
>   They melt like mist, the solid lands,
> Like clouds they shape themselves and go.

Many a hearth upon our dark globe sighs after many a vanish'd face,
Many a planet by many a sun may roll with the dust of a vanish'd
        race.

But when he comes to consider changes in society his attitude varies. In
his youth, under the strong enchantment of the Romantic poets, he
saw change as the instrument of freedom:

Thus truth was multiplied on truth, the world
   Like one great garden show'd,
And thro' the wreaths of floating dark upcurl'd,
   Rare sunrise flow'd.

And Freedom rear'd in that august sunrise
   Her beautiful bold brow,
When rites and forms before his burning eyes
   Melted like snow.

Until the unfortunate affair of the Spanish Rising in 1830 his attitude
to politics was like that of all the young men of his set, Byronic,
Shelleyan, dominated by the vision of the millenium. But it is one
thing to dream of legendary poets scattering their words like sparks
among mankind, and dying, martyred in the cause of freedom, quite
another to find oneself or one's friends responsible for a useless and ill-
managed cloak and dagger rising in which other people are killed. It
is one thing to preach the millennium, another to watch the mobs and
the rick fires in Reform Bill and Corn Law riots. Tennyson's enthusiasm
for progress remained:

Not in vain the distance beacons. Forward, forward let us range,
Let the great world spin for ever down the ringing grooves of
   change.

His enthusiasm for revolution which had never been as strong, say, as
Sterling's or Arthur Hallam's, waned:

So let the change which comes be free
   To ingroove itself with that which flies,
   And work, a joint of state, that plies
Its office, moved with sympathy.

       ★   ★   ★

Of many changes, aptly join'd,
   Is bodied forth the second whole.
   Regard gradation, lest the soul
Of Discord race the rising wind;

A wind to puff your idol-fires,
   And heap their ashes on the head;
   To shame the boast so often made,
That we are wiser than our sires.

He thought he had found a way of reconciling progress with stability, at least that he saw and admired it in the British Constitution:

> It is the land that freemen till,
>   That sober-suited Freedom chose,
>   The land, where girt with friends or foes
> A man may speak the thing he will;
>
> A land of settled government,
>   A land of just and old renown,
>   *Where Freedom slowly broadens down*
> From precedent to precedent:

This has been described, with some justice, as Burke and water; Tennyson in later life described it as 'old political common sense', and he clung to it as a panacea in spite of his awareness of conditions in Victorian society which made it less than adequate. Like Burke, the younger Tennyson thought of freedom and power in political terms, in terms, that is, of active participation in government and in the absence of political or legal restraints on opinion. 'Freedom slowly broadening down/From precedent to precedent' implies a conception of political change within a settled constitutional social order. But the changes which took place in England in the nineteenth century were not so much political as social; they were changes, that is, in the organisation of daily life, rather than the structure of government. The problems which they created could not be solved by the application of 'old political common sense'. The extension of the franchise to ten-pound freeholders does not rid a country of sweat shops and enforced prostitution, nor does it deal with the sanitary problems of new cities, or provide the medical organisation to deal with epidemics. Political enfranchisement itself demanded other changes in the accepted order; the extension, for example, of the educational system, and a revision of the responsibilities of the various ranks and classes in society, a revision that Tennyson was, in his old age, to view with horror.

> He had a great horror of doctrinaire Socialism with its opposition to the Christian revelation and the old traditions of feudal chivalry. Some social democratic writings, he said, made him 'vomit mentally'. He saw clearly enough that a new social condition was coming to the world, but he longed for it to come by evolution *and under the guidance of those who had the benefit of political tradition and transmitted culture.*[13]

He was expressing this kind of view in 1885 nearly fifty years after the composition of 'You ask me why, tho' ill at ease', and he was still hankering for the broadening of freedom 'from precedent to precedent'. This is a persistence of view which shows both a remarkable innocence of mind and a complete inability to understand the political and social lessons of fifty years. It is significant that two years before this the Fabian Society was founded (this I suppose was the origin of the social democratic writing he so much disliked) and two years after, in the year of the Jubilee, the Independent Labour Party.

The reference to the traditions of feudal chivalry is important. Tennyson's approach to the problems of social reform is fundamentally paternalist. He was not ignorant of the sufferings of the poor: less ignorant or indifferent than many of his more liberal contemporaries, but for him the ideal of social relationships and social action is set out in the country house scenes in *The Princess*. The Master of the house is:

> A patron of some thirty charities,
> A pamphleteer on guano and on grain,
> A quarter-sessions chairman, abler none;

On the land of this excellent character the common people, happy and healthy, enjoy the gadgets of the mechanical and scientific age. Tennyson urges this (the scene he describes was probably an actual scene), as an example:

> Why should not these great Sirs
> Give up their parks a dozen times a year
> To let the people breathe?

Why not indeed? If this kind of thing was irrelevant in 1885, in 1845 when *The Princess* was published the appeal to feudal and chivalrous responsibilities was neither eccentric nor empty. Dizzy's Young England movement was founded on precisely these lines—and for all its romantic silliness that movement had the great virtue of reminding the wealthy and the privileged that power carries responsibilities. But England was no longer feudal England. Chivalry was outmoded as a political force. The Sir Walter Vivians of Tennyson's world were threatened by the rise of a new aristocracy:

> Sick, am I sick of a jealous dread?
> Was not one of the two at her side
> This new-made lord, whose splendour plucks
> The slavish hat from the villager's head?

Whose old grandfather has lately died,
Gone to a blacker pit, for whom
Grimy nakedness dragging his trucks
And laying his trams in a poison'd gloom
Wrought, till he crept from a gutted mine
Master of half a servile shire,
And left his coal all turn'd into gold
To a grandson, first of his noble line,
Rich in the grace all women desire,
Strong in the power that all men adore,
And simper and set their voices lower,
And soften as if to a girl, and hold
Awe-stricken breaths at a work divine,
Seeing his gewgaw castle shine,
New as his title, built last year,
There amid perky larches and pine,
And over the sullen-purple moor
(Look at it) pricking a cockney ear.

Maud's hero is here deploring what Tennyson and many of his
contemporaries conceived to be an outstanding feature of their history,
the rise of the manufacturer and the financier to positions of power and
influence. Some of them took Tennyson's view of this, some the view
displayed by Dickens in *Bleak House* where he makes the Dedlocks, the
representatives of the old aristocracy, inferior in personality and power
to the iron-master Rouncewell. Modern historians tell us that these
writers over-emphasised the shift of power, that the great landowning
families by virtue of their investments and the development of their
property, retained and increased their economic power, and that the
Industrial Revolution, so far from depressing the lot of millions,
improved their standard of living.[14] Well, this may be so (there has
rarely been a period in history when men have been the best judges of
their own situation), yet there can be no doubt that the Victorians were
troubled by a sense of change in their order, and that many of them
associated their forebodings with the rise and spread of industry, and
with the financial methods which were its corollary. Developing
industry requires capital, and encourages speculation. The great
solidity of the Victorian period was crossed and harried by financial
excitements, the Railway speculations of the forties, or Stock Exchange
bubbles of the sixties like the Sadleir scandal which Dickens utilised
and described in *Little Dorrit*.[15] Tennyson himself was infected and
influenced by the urge to invest in this or that speculative scheme. He

lost his own small fortune in the early forties by investing it in a project
for machine-made wood-carving, and in the fifties his capital was again
threatened by the rumoured failure of a joint stock bank. It is no
wonder that in *Sea Dreams* he writes with feeling of gimcrack financial
schemes:

> Small were his gains, and hard his work; besides
> Their slender household fortunes (for the man
> Had risk'd his little) like the little thrift,
> Trembled in perilous places o'er a deep:
> And oft, when sitting all alone, his face
> Would darken, as he cursed his credulousness,
> And that one unctuous mouth which lured him, rogue,
> To buy strange shares in some Peruvian mine.

In *Maud* the tragedy of the poem begins when the hero's father commits
suicide because 'a vast speculation had failed'. This poem, however,
shows that it was not fear of recurrent personal tragedy which made
Tennyson loathe speculation but a sense of its effect on social relations:

> Why do they prate of the blessings of Peace? we have made
> them a curse,
> Pickpockets, each hand lusting for all that is not its own;
> And lust of gain, in the spirit of Cain, is it better or worse
> Than the heart of the citizen hissing in war on his own hearthstone?
>
> But these are the days of advance, the works of the men of mind,
> When who but a fool would have faith in a tradesman's ware or
> his word?
> Is it peace or war? Civil war, as I think, and that of a kind
> The viler, as underhand, not openly bearing the sword.

*   *   *

> Peace sitting under her olive, and slurring the days gone by,
> When the poor are hovell'd and hustled together, each sex, like
> swine,
> When only the ledger lives, and when only not all men lie;
> Peace in her vineyard—yes!—but a company forges the wine.

This concentration of the 'golden age' on the commercial vitiates every
kind of human relationship, even the most personal,

> A Mammonite mother kills her babe for a burial fee.

Certainly it corrupts and changes the web of impersonal relationships on which the order of master and man, employer and employed, buyer and seller, is built:

> I keep but a man and a maid, ever ready to slander and steal;
> I know it, and smile a hard-set smile, like a stoic, or like
> A wiser epicurean, and let the world have its way:
> For nature is one with rapine, a harm no preacher can heal;
> The Mayfly is torn by the swallow, the sparrow spear'd by the shrike,
> And the whole little wood where I sit is a world of plunder and prey.

'Nature red in tooth and claw' has become the image of competitive society. The law of society, Tennyson suggests, is like that of the fierce struggle of primitive creatures to exist: 'Cheat, and be cheated or die'. He may indeed be taking a gloomy view: but he has laid his finger on a situation which many Victorians saw as new and as evil: the needs of their expanding economy had altogether destroyed the near-decayed web of allegiances and loyalties, between lord and tenant, craftsman and apprentice, master and servant, on which the older society was based, and replaced it with a link for which Carlyle found a name, 'the cash nexus'.

More modern thinking would not necessarily regard this as a bad thing: we are told that this progress of men in society is from status to contract, and in a historical perspective the destruction of an outworn feudal and paternalist system of relationships may seem inevitable and necessary. But to the casualties of the transition period historical necessity may prove no comfort: certainly it cannot excuse the indifference of contemporaries to their plight. Tennyson was not a political genius: he was no better equipped than the average Victorian to understand the vast complexity of the social and economic forces at work in his society, and had no notion of where they were tending. He only saw the breakdown of a relationship he found good, and he wished to restore it. He has no strictly political solution to offer for the troubles of his time; he falls back on personal and moral solutions. His guides in this were his friends F. D. Maurice and Thomas Carlyle. Carlyle and Maurice were themselves moral and not social philosophers, that is, their thinking turns not on questions about the nature of society and its activities, but on questions about the responsibility of individuals within complexes of social relationships. This is particularly true of

Carlyle to whose thinking *Maud* owes an obvious debt. Tennyson draws on *Past and Present* for the picture which he gives of commercialised society in his poem; it was in this work that Carlyle pressed on the public the fact that necessity drove the very poor to habitual infanticide; that they used the payments from the burial clubs to relieve financial pressure. Like Tennyson, he ridicules the blessings of peace:

> 'Violence', 'war', 'disorder': well, what is war and death itself, to such a perpetual life-in-death and 'peace, peace' where there is no peace.[16]

Carlyle, in spite of the turgidity of some of his prose, had a thoroughly realist view of what was happening to his society, although his solutions do not, in the light of subsequent history, recommend themselves to us. When he complains that the very poor kill their children to keep themselves at a subsistence level, he does not so much deplore their poverty as the fact that it appears to be no one's business to do anything about it. He prophesies against the indifference of the nation, the refusal of the rich to accept their responsibilities. This is the familiar Victorian complaint; Carlyle had the acumen to set his finger on the real weakness of a liberal capitalist society, the fact that the ethics of commercial competition recognise no natural obligations to the community as a whole. But he is not a Young Englander, he had the sense to see that the old order of things was dead. Though in the past the traditional aristocracy of Church and landed gentry had carried a real responsibility, now it had neither energy nor purpose. Plugson of Undershot, the industrialist, is a barbarian in a jungle of factories but there is more to him than to the huntin', shootin' remnants of the landed classes. It is axiomatic to Carlyle that these worn-out remains of older arrangements should be, or more importantly, would be, swept away. He has none of Tennyson's horror of revolution. 'Freedom slowly broadening down from precedent to precedent' was not his idea of a proper development of things. He looks for cataclysm as part of the nature of the universe:

> Your mob is a genuine outburst of Nature; issuing from and communicating with, the deepest deep of Nature. When so much goes grinning and grimacing, as a lifeless formality, and under the stiff buckrum no heart can be felt beating, here once more, if no where else, is a Sincerity and Reality.[17]

His revolutionary fervour is not propagandist: it is the recognition of fact rather than the encouragement of a course of action. The force which is behind things—the Everlasting Yea—will, in times of decay, reassert itself and raise up a new and energetic order. This chimes in well with the biological theories of the period, and would be congenial to Tennyson, even though he shrank from actual catastrophe:

> The old order changeth, yielding place to new.

Carlyle has been called mystical, but he is about as mystical in his thinking as Marx or Shaw. The *Everlasting Yea* is the force which, driving through history, compels men not to contemplate but to do. Work, says Carlyle, is the end. There are things to be done, and men will be raised up to do them. They have no choice in the matter and can afford neither pity for themselves nor laxity with others. Carlyle may be a revolutionary, but he is profoundly anti-democratic. His idea of order is essentially one of submission; everyone is bound to serve the great force of things incarnate in those individuals whose evident power is renewing man's life. Power, by which one means the energy of a personality rather than the means of control and direction a man may possess, was Carlyle's god—hence his glorification of Cromwell and Mahomet, and Frederick of Prussia. Only such persons have the inborn right to control and direct, and our business is to recognise and serve them. They must not serve themselves; their great virtue is to have the courage to lead because, as with Samson of Bury, the responsibility of leadership has been laid upon them. The people— the others—must be led to fulfil themselves by these makers of history.

It is necessary, in order to deal with the responsibilities arising in the development of industrial society, that the men of energy who were forming it, the Plugsons of Undershot, should take up their burden. Carlyle's exemplars display, and he knew it, the moral defects of crude power, but his principle is more important than his examples. Nothing, he says, can be done unless men have the courage to be what they are, and to take up the duties which destiny has laid on them, undiverted by conventions, respectabilities or fears of presumption. Echoes of this are very evident in Tennyson's admirations and his contempts:

> Plowmen, Shepherds, have I found, and more than once, and
>   still could find,
> Sons of God, and kings of men in utter nobleness of mind,
>
> Truthful, trustful, looking upwards to the practised hustings-liar;
> So the Higher wields the Lower, while the Lower is the Higher.

Here and there a cotter's babe is royal-born by right divine;
Here and there my lord is lower than his oxen or his swine.

And obviously it is at the back of his patriotic feelings:

> Pray God our greatness may not fail
> Through craven fears of being great.

Yet the influence of Carlyle on his verse is more than the mere echo of Carlyle's dedicated belligerence. It is deeply absorbed into his thinking, but is tempered partly by Burke, partly by the curiously similar but gentler doctrines of the Rev. F. D. Maurice. Maurice's famous 'Christian Socialism' was not of a kind which would appeal, say, to the *New Statesman*; he was a collectivist rather than a socialist with a strong belief in the virtues of co-operative enterprise. He had set his mind against the prevailing and Utilitarian conception of a society based on the interplay of economic interests. In this he is at one with Carlyle, but he is, as Carlyle was not, a Christian, and a disciple of Coleridge. He conceives of the force of righteousness, not as driving men from outside, but as indwelling in the souls of men where it struggles with the forces of evil. He is in no sense an evolutionist, for he clearly believes that the righteous God is and was and will be, and the nature of his relationship with men is unchanged. His convictions about God drive him to realise the responsibility of one man to another:

> If God presents Himself to us as the Father of a family, it is not necessary for the knowledge of Him that we should force ourselves to forget our relations to each other, and to think of ourselves as alone in the world. And, though as I have admitted and asserted, the sense of sin is essentially the sense of solitude, isolation, distinct individual responsibility, I do not know whether that sense, in all its painfulness and agony, ever comes to a man more fully than when he recollects how he has broken the silken cords which bind him to his fellows; how he has made himself alone by not confessing that he was a brother, a son, a citizen.[18]

Because men are born into a created order which exists in the mind of God, and into a relationship with Him, they are born into a network of relationships, for God is a God of many not of one. There are bonds between men which subsist independently of the individual's recognition of them, and which lay on him a whole series of duties. The awareness of these bonds leads Maurice to conceive of the social order itself as 'the Kingdom of Christ', and it is this which is the foundation of that theology of society which is his peculiar legacy to Anglicanism. It is also the foundation of a position less easily justifiable. Maurice has a strong sense not only of the family but of the nation as the unit of God's order, and the instrument of his will. This to him is biblical. The dispensation of God towards the world in Scripture is conceived of in terms of nationality: each people has its own special function. Maurice also thinks biblically about war. God roused up Assyria to be a scourge for the sons of Israel, and in the same way the warfare of modern nations may be an instrument of God's justice and a means of establishing his purpose. Like Carlyle, Maurice recognises the place of the dedicated individual in carrying out God's purposes. As he says, in a sermon on the death of Wellington which recalls Tennyson's *Ode on the Death of the Duke of Wellington*:

> A military chief, then, who brought into the transactions of civil life the manly sense which had governed him in the camp, who would suffer no pettiness of party or of individual feeling to stand in the way of that which was to be carried out, who looked facts in the face, making his own opinions bow to them, who taught with few words that there is an order among men which they must obey, or suffer, may well be thought to have worked more in the spirit of this text—to have done more that the sword shall be turned into the ploughshare—than those who set one against the other, and who would make the state of peace unlike that of war only in being more heartless, contentious, inhuman.[19]

It is fair to say, as we did of Carlyle, that this approach to social questions is not propagandist: Maurice was anything but belligerent. He presents a philosophy of history, not an incitement to violence. War may be evil, but in a fallen world God's will is worked out even by the vices of men. At the same time the man who wrote this about Wellington must be, and was, profoundly anti-democratic. God's order for England was not a people's order but one which is hierarchical in structure and constitution.

These then were the views of Tennyson's friends. He did not of course take them over wholesale, for he could not, like Carlyle, find exhilaration in cataclysm, and he showed no signs of grasping Maurice's theology of history. Besides he had views of his own. But their views were congenial to him: they helped him to frame a social philosophy from a mere collection of attitudes, and helped him, too, in his earnest attempts to warn the Victorians of the disease in their body politic.

III

Maud is Tennyson's first attempt to represent the state of society, and it is also his central political poem. Yet the critics normally treat it as the history of a neurotic. It is that, certainly, and it exhibits all Tennyson's skill in the presentation of morbid psychological states. But we shall miss the whole point of it if we fail to recognise how explicitly the hero's neurosis is linked with a corruption in society. The man is wrecked or nearly wrecked, by the unnatural state of a community given over to the ethics of the catch-phrase 'Damn you Jack, I'm alright'. The young man is sick with the disease of his age, the inability to find reason or purpose in anything, and his state reflects Tennyson's in *In Memoriam*, except that it is marked by a refusal to see or accept any kind of social responsibility:

> For the drift of the Maker is dark, an Isis hid by the veil.
> Who knows the ways of the world, how God will bring them
>   about?
> Our planet is one, the suns are many, the world is wide.
> Shall I weep if a Poland fall? shall I shriek if a Hungary fail?
> Or an infant civilisation be ruled with rod or with knout?
> *I* have not made the world, and He that made it will guide.

The disease is a direct result of the social situation analysed by Carlyle. The desire for cash has already ruined the bonds between men, between, for instance, the hero's father and Maud's for Maud's father made money out of the speculation which bankrupted the hero's family.

Brooding on this, and the fact that it seems no more than a common example of the normal state of society, Maud's hero damns the entire human race. 'We men are a little breed.' But the voice of Maud breaks in on his cynicism and apathy:

> Singing alone in the morning of life,
> In the happy morning of life and of May,
> Singing of men that in battle array,
> Ready in heart and ready in hand,
> March with banner and bugle and fife
> To the death, for their native land.

Maud's song, whatever it was, specifically contradicts his mood. The 'little breed' are capable of sacrifice and of courage. His cure begins. He falls in love, and love restores relationship; puts a value not only on the thing beloved but on the whole world:

But now shine on, and what care I,
Who in this stormy gulf have found a pearl
The countercharm of space and hollow sky,
And do accept my madness, and would die
To save from some slight shame one simple girl.

Would die; for sullen-seeming Death may give
More life to Love than is or ever was
In our low world, where yet 'tis sweet to live.
Let no one ask me how it came to pass;
It seems that I am happy, that to me
A livelier emerald twinkles in the grass,
A purer sapphire melts into the sea.

It is true that personal stability may be regained by love, but what has
that to do with the social order? Much: for Maud's lover approaches
his duties to society in a new mood because of her love. We are
outraged when Maud,

seem'd to divide in a dream from a band of the blest,
And spoke of a hope for the world in the coming wars—
'And in that hope, dear soul, let trouble have rest,
Knowing I tarry for thee,' and pointed to Mars
As he glow'd like a ruddy shield on the Lion's breast.

Our judgment is too hasty. Before falling in love the hero would not
weep 'if a Hungary fail', now, in the context of the Crimean War, he is
ready to take up his duties to the infant and distant civilisation 'ruled
with rod or with knout'. For Tennyson and his generation the Czar
of all the Russias was the symbol of despotism, and though many
saw the Crimean War as a political and military blunder, costly in
money and suffering, many saw it as a fight against Tyranny. Maud's
hero learns to serve something outside himself. In doing so he sets an
example. Tennyson is not glorifying war *quâ* war, but war as a remedy
for what he thought a worse disease. No more, he says, shall,

Britain's one sole God be the millionaire:
No more shall commerce be all in all, and Peace
Pipe on her pastoral hill a languid note,
And watch her harvest ripen, her herd increase,

Commerce, the lust of gain, encourages the internecine conflict, the
want of social relationship which the feud between the family of Maud
and her lover, which ends in actual murder, typifies and illustrates. But

Maud's voice has called her lover to something better. War, at any rate, imposes a sense of relationship: a sense that sacrifice and loyalty are more important than the making of money:

> I trust if an enemy's fleet came yonder round by the hill,
> And the rushing battle-bolt sang from the three-decker out of the foam,
> That the smooth-faced snubnosed rogue would leap from his counter and till,
> And strike, if he could, were it but with his cheating yardwand, home—

Maud was Tennyson's first venture as a Laureate, and it met with little success. This was partly because the public were expecting another *In Memoriam* and were disconcerted to find a passionate love-story; partly because Tennyson's attacks on the accepted position were too open. His reference to the 'broad-brimmed hawker of holy things' was generally taken as a hit at John Bright and gave offence. It was certainly a hit at the Manchester School—'cotton-spinners' were Tennyson's symbolic villains—and the plain truth was that the public, uneasy about the management of the Crimean War, could not be sure that the cotton-spinners were not right and Tennyson wrong. *Maud* was his last attempt to put across his social theories in a direct manner. Afterwards his methods were more oblique. 'I tried in my *Idylls*', the old man said in a later discussion of social problems, 'to teach men the need of an ideal, but I feel sometimes as if my life had been a very useless life'. The need to correct was strong in him, and not only the *Idylls* but the rest of his long life's work was directed to the making of mirrors in which the Victorian public could see itself and be ashamed. He falls back on the apparently innocuous, novelettish love-story which he did so well. *Maud* itself is such a story but there the social context, the social cause of the disaster was too explicit; elsewhere his growing tact led him to shift the centre of interest from the social to the personal. As we saw he always thought of the marriage bond as the archetype and model for social relationship. Already, in the 1842 volume, he had shown his resentment that this vitally personal relationship should be replaced by marriage made, as it were, on the market:

> They wedded her to sixty thousand pounds,
> To lands in Kent and messuages in York,
> And slight Sir Robert with his watery smile
> And educated whisker.

13

In his later work marriage-marketing typifies the corruption of a social order by competition. He returns to it in *The Wreck, Northern Farmer, New Style, The Flight* and *Aylmer's Field*. In *The Wreck* the husband was:

> All day long far-off in the cloud of the city, and there
> Lost, head and heart, in the chances of dividend, consol, and share—
> And at home if I sought for a kindly caress, being woman and
> weak,
> His formal kiss fell chill as a flake of snow on the cheek.

Finance has eaten the heart out of love. In *Aylmer's Field* the personal tragedy is explicitly, if incidentally, held up as a warning. The girl who pines to death for love is represented as fulfilling the old social responsibilities: she cares for her father's tenants, and arouses their loyalties and their love. But she is the last of her race, and her parents, in breaking off her love-affair, from pride of position, break the tradition of generations, they

> broke the bond which they desired to break,
> *Which else had link'd their race with times to come—*

The parents' pride is dangerous: it may provoke people to break the social bond in disorder and revolution. The story takes place in the period of the French Revolution; and Tennyson's warning is fierce:

> out yonder—earth
> Lightens from her own central hell—O there
> The red fruit of an old idolatry—
> The heads of chiefs and princes fall so fast,
> They cling together in the ghastly sack—
> The land all shambles—naked marriages
> Flash from the bridge, and ever-murder'd France,
> By shores that darken with the gathering wolf,
> Runs in a river of blood to the sick sea.
> Is this a time to madden madness then?
> Was this a time for these to flaunt their pride?

The text of the funeral sermon, 'Your house is left unto you desolate', is a warning against the pride which chooses barrenness rather than love.

Aylmer's Field is in the *Enoch Arden* volume, which is very much concerned with solitude and society. The old problem which Tennyson treated in *The Palace of Art* reasserts itself in a context not personal but social. Arden, when wrecked on the island, is isolated from his own kind, shut in the limits of his own being. When he is picked up he is found to have lost the use of human speech, and cannot communicate with his fellows. We are faced with a real problem of lost relationship. But Arden is not at the mercy of his solitude even when he returns and finds the natural bonds of marriage broken in his long absence:

> He was not all unhappy. His resolve
> Upbore him, and firm faith, and evermore
> Prayer from a living source within the will,
> And beating up thro' all the bitter world,
> Like fountains of sweet water in the sea,
> Kept him a living soul.

Faith, courage and action control the demons of the mind which beset him on the desert island. The Victorians would accept this view of the case. The surface morality of the poem belonged to their personal code: submission to Providence is the rule in every evil circumstance. But this is not all. Certainly submission to God is expressed in the words and thoughts of the untaught fisherman, but what moves us in the poem, and it does move us in spite of the superficial sentimentalities of the little wife and the dying child, is the spectacle of a man of Arden's moral stature shut out from the society natural to him. In the scene where he gazes through the window at Philip and his children, the merest suspension of our embarrassed mockery will show us that we have here a familiar and ancient symbol, light and life within the house, darkness outside, and the spirits wailing round the home they cannot enter. But Arden is not a spirit, and not evil; the anguish of the poem lies in his dignity as a human being. I do not believe that this poem is a mere sentimental story. It is set at the beginning of a volume in which the other poems, *Aylmer's Field* and *Sea Dreams*, present stories as embodiments (or rather reminders) of the theme of the cash nexus as a threat to society: they show the dark side. *Arden* is surely the counter-poem: the reminder of nobility in the humblest, and the anguish of a man cut off from the human bond.

After this Tennyson was ready to present his ideal in what he intended as his major work, *Idylls of the King*. This is commonly regarded as an allegory of the moral life of the individual. Tennyson asks the Queen to 'accept this old imperfect tale/New-old, and shadowing sense at war with soul', but this account of his theme was later than his original conception of the poem. The first *Idylls* published were not allegorical at all but exemplary, and they were, in fact, subtitled *The True and the*

False, Enid and Elaine being presented as types of true love, Guinevere and Vivien of the false. It was in the *Holy Grail* volume that the 'sense and soul' symbolism began to appear, and it was not really explicit until Tennyson had finished the extremely elaborate allegory of *Gareth and Lynette*. His purpose, in fact, revealed itself to him over twenty or so years of work, and the theme of the earlier poems is much less subtle. Arthur complains in *Guinevere* of the destruction of his kingdom by the sin of his Queen:

> But I was first of all the kings who drew
> The knighthood-errant of this realm and all
> The realms together under me, their Head,
> In that fair Order of my Table Round,
> A glorious company, the flower of men,
> To serve as model for the mighty world,
> And be the fair beginning of a time.
>
> *   *   *
>
> And all this throve before I wedded thee,
> Believing, 'lo mine helpmate, one to feel
> My purpose and rejoicing in my joy.'
> Then came thy shameful sin with Launcelot;
> Then came the sin of Tristram and Isolt;
> Then others, following these my mightiest knights,
> And drawing foul ensample from fair names,
> Sinn'd also, till the loathsome opposite
> Of all my heart had destined did obtain,
> And all thro' thee!

We need not suppose, in accordance with the allegory, that in this passage the rational soul addresses the sensuous soul *de haut en bas*: Guinevere is Guinevere, an adulterous woman, and for Tennyson marriage, as in *The Princess*, is a union of energies which is to revivify the world. The breaking of the marriage-bond undoes and destroys all this. The tinny nobility of Arthur's endurance of personal injury has always jarred on the sensitive reader, but there is nothing tinny about his anguish for his kingdom:

> The children born of thee are sword and fire,
> Red ruin, and the breaking up of laws,
> The craft of kindred and the Godless hosts
> Of heathen swarming o'er the Northern sea.

The poem wakes up; its imaginative centre is here. All four of the earliest Idylls dwell exclusively on the effects of Guinevere's adultery: because of her liaison with Lancelot, Geraint's relationship with his wife is threatened, Vivien is given her opportunity to corrupt the court and does corrupt the wisdom of Merlin, and Elaine is destroyed. It would not, then, be unjust to Tennyson's purpose to forget, for the moment, that Arthur can be viewed as a symbol of the soul of man, and to treat him as the king, the leader, the maker of the Table Round which 'was an image of the mighty world'. The whole set of *Idylls* then becomes a representation of the growth and destruction of social order.

Arthur bears all the marks of a Christianised, but recognisably Carlylean hero. He is a king from nowhere, not king by recognisable right of birth, but by right of the power in him, the power laid upon him, which makes the knights acclaim and follow him:

> The King will follow Christ, and we the King
> In whom high God hath breathed a secret thing.

He is a new power in the world and sweeps aside (as Carlyle's heroes sweep aside) old formulas and outworn prerogatives: he proves himself by overcoming heathen disorder, and by conquering the effete remnant of Rome. Gareth answers the objections to his claim by reiterating that this is he,

> who swept the dust of ruin'd Rome
> From off the threshold of the realm, and crush'd
> The Idolaters and made the people free?
> Who should be King save him who makes us free?

The strong man's strength is his inalienable right to leadership. But it is a leadership laid on him as a task and a duty, not as a privilege, and Arthur preaches to others the Carlylean doctrine of active work which he himself follows. Neither he nor they have the right to leave the allotted task to follow their own advantage, or even so high and holy a thing as the Grail:

> The King must guard
> That which he rules, and is but as the hind
> To whom a space of land is given to plow.
> Who may not wander from the allotted field
> Before his work be done.

The final mark of his Carlyleanism is his absolutism. Arthur leads, and what he achieves, and what his knights achieve is gained by their personal allegiance to himself. He

> Bound them by so strait vows to his own self,
> That when they rose, knighted from kneeling, some
> Were pale as at the passing of a ghost,
> Some flush'd, and others dazed, as one who wakes
> Half-blinded at the coming of a light.

They vow:

> To reverence the King, as if he were
> Their conscience, and their conscience as their King.

This is a good deal more than feudal; Arthur's knights are not simply his liege-men; they are men dedicated, through him, to the purpose which he serves. It is important here to remember that Arthur has the status of a symbolic as well as of an actual being: Tennyson is not advocating personal dictatorship. Arthur fulfils the divine purpose of order. He is the symbol of the human spirit, and like it, is no more than an agent.

As an agent he is committed to the establishment of moral and civil discipline and order. Tennyson is not really so interested in Carlyle's doctrine of leadership as he is in Carlyle's doctrine of work; the fulfilling of the tasks laid on man by the Everlasting Yea:

> And Arthur and his knighthood for a space
> Were all one will, and thro' that strength the King
> Drew in the petty princedoms under him,
> Fought, and in twelve great battles overcame
> The heathen hordes, *and made a realm and reign'd.*

The making of Arthur's realm shifts us from Carlyle to Maurice. Carlyle began his *Heroes and Hero Worship* with Odin because Odin was a cult-hero, one who first began human society, and was afterwards worshipped as a god. For the mythologists of Tennyson's day, as Tennyson knew, Arthur of Britain also belonged to this category.[20] But as Arthur was Christianised by Tennyson, so was his work. He establishes a just order:

> He rooted out the slothful officer,
> Or guilty, which for bribe had wink'd at wrong,
> And in their chairs set up a stronger race
> With hearts and hands, and sent a thousand men
> To till the wastes, and moving everywhere
> Clear'd the dark places and let in the law.

This work is not achieved by external means alone. The order of the land reflects the inward purity which Arthur requires of the Round Table. His knights swear:

> To break the heathen and uphold the Christ,
> To ride abroad redressing human wrongs,
> To speak no slander, no, nor listen to it
> To honour his own word as if his God's.

Edryn, son of Nud (who was so unheroic in the earlier versions of Arthurian legend as to carry off Queen Guinevere in a fit of love) is held up to Geraint as an example of one who has overcome himself, and Geraint is meant to feel that though he has cleared out the odd bandit stronghold, he has not really fulfilled Arthur's purpose. Arthur's ideal knight is not the pure Galahad, but Gareth who begins life with a determination to take up the work before him:

> Man am I grown, a man's work must I do.
> Follow the deer? follow the Christ, the King,
> Live pure, speak true, right wrong, follow the King—
> Else, wherefore born?

In setting out on a quest to free the innocent, Gareth overcomes four knights, of the Morning Star, the Noon, the Evening Star and Night. Here the moral allegory and the social meaning are very closely knit. These knights are honest-to-God villains, threatening the weak (whom it is the business of rulers to protect), but at the same time they represent the temptations of youth, of middle life, of age, and finally the terrors of death which Gareth must meet and overcome in order to follow the King. The corollary of this close relationship between individual goodness and peace and justice in society is the proposition that individual sin corrupts the state. The whole poem is meant to exemplify this. The Table was destroyed by the adultery of Guinevere and Lancelot.

Carlyle has little or no concern with righteousness; power, for him, excludes the normal moral sanctions. Maurice, on the other hand, is acutely concerned with the nation not only as a social but as a moral entity, and sees a distinct relationship between the evil in the heart and the weakness in the nation. Adultery, idolatry, self-righteousness, he says, 'eat up the land because they are eating up the hearts of those that dwell in it'. This is not the indignation of those who call down war and pestilence because the village has played cards on Sunday, but something a great deal more fundamental:

When the great men insisted on burdens being carried through the gates on the Sabbath-day, they were robbing the poor man of rights which God had claimed for him: they showed that they did not believe that He who was the common judge of prince and peasant, was in the midst of them. This want of brotherly feeling, this unbelief and godlessness, would assuredly bring destruction upon that land, for in them lie the seeds of destruction for all lands.[21]

The sin of Lancelot and Guinevere is a more personal sin, perhaps, than this, but the principle is the same. Relationship is destroyed: not only the relationship between Arthur and his wife, but that between him and his friend. The loyalty which binds the knights to Arthur, and in the strength of which he is able to fulfil his work of pacifying the kingdom, is deliberately broken, and the kingdom falls. The abominable wreckage which Tennyson makes of Malory's story of Balin and Balan is only justified by the fact that in this Idyll he establishes a direct relationship between adultery and brother-murder, and shows how the sin which eats up the heart of Guinevere and her lover eats up the land; the betrayal of relationship destroys relationship.

Tennyson created in the *Idylls* a mirror for the society of his times. We are presented with an ideal king, a warrior for Christ, throwing back the forces of barbarism, and ruling with justice, followed by a people labouring together to procure order and righteousness. There can be little doubt that this was his ideal for the British Empire. This in fact is what he revered in Gordon, who had the terrible zeal of the military missionary, and in Wellington. But the *Idylls* actually indicate not Tennyson's ideal for the Victorians, but his condemnation of them. Arthur's kingdom was destroyed by solid selfishness, as Tennyson feared his own generation were destroying their own law and freedom. We are not able to regard the *Idylls* with that enthusiasm which caused Lady Tennyson to see *Guinevere* as the noblest poem in the language, but we cannot altogether dismiss them. The question is, do they express an understanding of things which is really mediated to us through the poetry, or merely a didactic system easily detached from it? Did Tennyson really grasp and communicate what he intended to communicate? And this is a question not about Tennyson's beliefs but about the substance of the poetry itself.

Chapter VII

The Laureate's Art

THE one real loathing of Tennyson's later life was the group of writers that he called the 'Fleshly School'. 'L'Art pour l'Art' was an abomination to him: a symptom, in literature, of the general corruption of society. He had not the historical sense, nor perhaps the conceit, to see how much the work of these poets, on both sides of the Channel, derived from him,[1] and would have been distressed to find himself admired by later generations for precisely those qualities which he detested in Swinburne and others, the qualities, that is, of morbid sensitivity, and of a technical virtuosity unrelated or irrelevant to the content of his work. Their admiration is very odd. The manipulation of syllabic sounds and verbal images is not in itself 'art', and to praise a poet as an artist while dismissing his poem as meaningless is to damn with a paradox. Tennyson never intended to write pure poetry: the Laureate's art was united to the Laureate's purpose, and it presupposes the view of things which we outlined in the last chapter. He desired to hold a mirror up to society; to communicate what he conceived to be its state, its needs and the remedy for its ills.

As we have seen, his explicit intention was to move the public to a moral end. 'I tried in my *Idylls* to teach men the need of the ideal.' Today we hate 'poetry that has a palpable design on us', and to have said this of Tennyson is, to a more modern view than his, to condemn him. For whatever else we desire of poets one requirement is clear: that they shall not teach. The end of Art is nowadays felt to be defeated when the poet comes to the work of creation with a blue-print of

moral truths. The truths may be true enough, but they are not felt
to run with the grain of the poem. At times Tennyson certainly demonstrates this objectionable incongruity between theme and medium.
When Sir Thomas Bertram in *Mansfield Park* provides for his erring
daughter but refuses to receive her into his family, there is a fitness in
his refusal which leads us to forget the difference between our moral
code and Jane Austen's. But when Arthur harangues the sinful
Guinevere on the iniquity of receiving an adulteress back into the home,
we quarrel with Tennyson's morality, though his point is the same.
There is no *fitness* in it; it is a piece of moral stucco plastered on to the
main building without relationship either to line or material. To put the
contradiction in the most obvious way: this is a Warrior King,
presented with every trapping of mystery and pomp, the 'Dragon of
the great Pendragonship' on his helmet, addressing a fugitive Queen in
a convent of white Nuns. But his words are the words of a preacher
in a new pitch-pine pulpit. Arthur's passionate denunciation of
Guinevere is a different matter:

> The children born of thee are sword and fire,
> Red ruin, and the breaking up of laws.

This has the moral and aesthetic fitness of Sir Thomas Bertram's
treatment of Maria. It may be unjust, wrongheaded, or simply mistaken,
but it belongs to Arthur, and his *mores*. This is what Tennyson saw, not
what he felt ought to be seen, in the Arthurian kingdom which he had
made the mirror of his own society, and it runs with the grain of experience. But though it is fair to object to a moral unnaturally grafted on
to a poem, or even to suppose that there are kinds of moral statement
which it would be better not to attempt in poetry, to extend this
objection to every poetical statement of moral ideas is ludicrous. It
means, of course, the dismissal from poetry of explicit moral statement
and reflection, and a disregard for those forms of art which deal with
the direct statement of belief. Tennyson, the earlier Tennyson that is, is
principally a poet of symbol and evocation, his methods of communication are indirect. But even of the earlier Tennyson this was not
altogether true, and the Laureate has two methods, that of direct
approach, and that of evocative image, with which to approach his
task of infusing the public mind with an awareness of public virtue.

The Laureate/Teacher is by nature, and in the best and most limited
sense of the word, a rhetorician. He is concerned with the communication of clearly defined ideas and sentiments, and his peculiar care is

with forms and colours, with the recognised skills and devices of verbal
art when it is used to capture attention, to state, and to convince.
Laureate poems proper, the official celebrations of public events, are
necessarily rhetorical; the pleasure of them is not in the startling
brilliance or profundity of their thought, but in the skill of their
expression. If, for instance, *The Ode on the Jubilee* has any interest at all
it lies, not in originality of sentiment, but in complexity of form. This
is the least that can be said about rhetoric; its skills *can* be used to other
ends. They can be used to induce in the reader a passionate response to
ideas or sentiments. We may distrust this: there is no doubt, however,
that it requires considerable skill and is often the concomitant of
similar passion in the rhetorician. The broken opening of Cicero's
Catiline oration, or the verbal dexterity of the best passages of
Churchill's war-time broadcasts (the repetition, the alliteration of the
invasion passage, We will . . . . We will . . . , for example) makes its
impression on the listener, but no one will deny to Cicero the sense of
outrage, or to Churchill the sense of determination. This kind of verbal
management can, at its best, enlarge for the reader or the hearer an
imaginative apprehension of the ideas or sentiments expressed.
Tennyson's *Ode on the Death of the Duke of Wellington* is a case in point.
Technically the poem is a *tour de force*. The recapture in the metre of the
rhythm and jerk of the dead march of the funeral guard integrates the
public praise with the public mourning in a manner which robs both
of the conventional:

> Who is he that cometh, like an honour'd guest,
> With banner and with music, with soldier and with priest,
> With a nation weeping, and breaking on my rest?
> Mighty Seaman, this is he
> Was great by land as thou by sea.
> Thine island loves thee well, thou famous man,
> The greatest sailor since our world began
> Now, to the roll of muffled drums,
> To thee the greatest soldier comes;
> For this is he
> Was great by land as thou by sea.

The caesura in these lines has to be given the full value, and the broad
syllables given the heaviness with which Tennyson, with the Lincolnshire broadness echoing in his head, endowed them. Then the solemnity
of the poem makes its impact almost entirely through the sound. The
total effect of it is like that of Wordsworth's *Happy Warrior*, to enlarge

the mind's awareness of the soldier or sailor as the willing instrument of
certain moral powers:

> The long self-sacrifice of life is o'er.
> The great World-victor's victor will be seen no more.

Perhaps for a balanced view of Wellington—*Old Hookey*—as a historical
character, we should remember his stiff-necked Toryism and take
Byron's testimony as well as Tennyson's:

> You have obtained great pensions and much praise.
> Glory like yours should any dare gainsay,
> Humanity would rise and thunder 'Nay' . . . .
>
> Though Britain owes (and pays you too) so much
> Yet Europe doubtless owes you greatly more:
> You have restored Legitimacy's crutch,
> And prop not quite so certain as before;
> The Spanish, and the French as well as Dutch
> Have seen and felt how strongly you *restore*.

We should perhaps, but we do not; momentarily we accept Tennyson's
view. But Wellington himself is not really the figure which dominates
the mind. What possesses it is an awareness of the great soldier as public
hero and as public servant, and for this ideal Wellington is, for the
moment, the convenient symbol. The emotional force of that symbol is
felt in the rhetoric: it is the shifts of sound and images within the poem
which evoke a responsive mood in the reader.

This evocation of mood is accompanied in the Wellington Ode by
clear and direct statements about Wellington himself, and about the
moral values for which he stood. These were explicit in Tennyson's
mind and he uses his metrical skill to 'put them across' in poems which
were not, officially, Laureate poems. But the simple range of explicit
moral teaching which Tennyson presents to the public in poems like
Will, or *Wages* does not exhaust either his moral or his social apprehension. There remains his extraordinary sensitiveness to the moral and
intellectual climate of his period and his capacity to communicate it.
This sensitiveness is oddly inarticulate in terms of rational statement;
that is, Tennyson seems unable to formulate it in terms which could
satisfy the analytic reason, though he is able to recreate for the reader
the feeling and quality of certain situations. In the Epilogue to the
Idylls of the King he says of his own work,

> accept this old imperfect tale,
> New-old, and shadowing Sense at war with Soul
> Ideal manhood closed in real man,
> Rather than that gray king, whose name, a ghost,
> Streams like a cloud, man-shaped, from mountain peak.
> And cleaves to cairn and cromlech still,

Nothing could better indicate the differences in his work. There is the explicit statement of a moral idea: 'ideal manhood closed in real man', and there is, in the description of the 'gray king', the imaginative recreation of a particular atmosphere in the folk-lore of Arthur. Arthurian folk-lore has no moral significance, but in poems such as *Rizpah*, or *Despair* the same apprehension, the same capacity to find the evocative description is at work on situations essentially moral, essentially a part of the web of human relations. In reading them the reader becomes aware, as Tennyson was, of the individual agony which throws doubt both on common assumptions, and on the accepted ordering of society. The old woman in *Rizpah* has been collecting the bones of her son from the gibbet, to bury them, and now on her death-bed will not listen to the exhortations of the pious visitor to think of his sins:

> I came into court to the Judge, and the lawyers. I told them my tale,
> God's own truth, —but they kill'd him, they kill'd him for robbing
>   the mail.
> They hang'd him in chains for a show—we had always borne a good
>   name—
> To be hang'd for a thief—and then put away—isn't that enough
>   shame?
> Dust to dust—low down—let us hide! but they set him so high
> *That all the ships of the world could stare at him, passing by.*
> God 'ill pardon the hell black ravens and horrible fowls of the air,
> But not the black heart of the lawyers who kill'd him and hang'd
>   him there.

The 'black heart', and the 'hell black raven' have something of the overstated quality of melodrama, though they are in character with a woman of limited vocabulary, and of course they cannot be considered in isolation. What gives the passage its tone is the creeping horror of meiosis in 'horrible fowls of the air', for these we remember are the birds of prey which picked the criminal's bones. Similarly the extraordinary universalising of the emotion with 'all the ships of the world', though it remains within the simple resources of the peasant woman, brings home the all-absorbing, the world-embracing quality of her despair. Everyone is aware of the shame: 'All the ships of the world could stare at him passing by.' And this despair is the work of lawyers: it is the law itself, we are made to see in the story, which turns a boyish escapade into a tragedy. The art here remains like that of the *Ode on the Death of the Duke of Wellington*, an art of persuasion, but its success depends on causing the reader's apprehension to chime with the poet's, not on the striking statement of particular sentiments.

II

His official poetry is, of course, direct in its approach, but when it is called 'direct' this does not imply that it has the kind of simplicity, even informality, characteristic, say of Wordsworth, or Burns or even of Donne. This belongs if not exactly to 'private' poetry, at least to poets talking on their private occasions, and Tennyson is speaking on those which were public. Battles, Jubilees, Public Exhibitions, the births, deaths and marriages of Princes, are subjects in which a personal concern is, at the very least, irrelevant. Our attitude to these things has changed a good deal: whether from the want of privacy in great urban areas, or whether from other social and psychological causes, the purely private and personal has come to be immensely valued, so that, on the one hand, there are now large numbers of people who shrink with distaste from the public beanfeast of a Victory, or a Coronation, and, on the other, a vast mass whose interest in a state occasion is an interest in the 'personal angle', or in the back-stairs gossip of celebrity. But the state occasion for the Victorian was something in which he was implicated not as a private person, but as a citizen. This limits what can be said, and the official poet could deal in little but generalities. This was a handicap but he had the advantage of a body of common sentiment to which he could make a direct appeal. The good Laureate is a ritualist. His poetry is part of the ceremony of public life; in a sense he can help to create it by imposing on domestic occasions, like the marriage of royalty, a certain dignity and solemnity. His business is to generalise and formalise in such a way that the particular occasion is stripped of individual eccentricities and set in the perspective of a common order.

The private conceit and the oblique image are out of place in such poetry. The poet is obliged to make a direct appeal to the body of sentiments common to him and his public, without which, indeed, no really common ritual is possible. In such cases the 'stock response' is not a dishonest device, but the proper medium of expression. We do not speak of the 'intellectual impurity' of a fanfare of trumpets at a Coronation, or the 'dishonesty' of the Lord Mayor's scarlet, or a Priest's vestments. Tennyson's major problem, however, was that, although there was a body of common sentiment, there was no available poetic convention in which to express it. The late eighteenth century had exhausted the conventions of public writing bequeathed to it by Milton and Dryden, while the idiom of the Romantic poets was, as Arnold pointed out, primarily designed for the expression of private and personal emotion. Tennyson's Laureate verse is not, then, the verse of a complacent poet working in an outworn convention, but the vigorous creation of new forms for a new national consciousness not unlike that of the Elizabethan age. The emphasis in this poetry is not on image and conceit, but on movement and diction. This does not mean that Tennyson employs a 'poetic diction'; the substratum of his Laureate verse is not an elaborate and specialised language only used in poetry, but 'a selection of the language really used by men'. This is particularly true of those Laureate poems which are concerned not with ceremonial but with dramatic occasions:

> For Scarlett and Scarlett's three hundred were riding by
> When the points of the Russian lances arose in the sky;
> And he call'd, 'Left wheel into line!', and they wheel'd and obey'd.
> Then he look'd at the host that had halted he knew not why,
> And he turn'd half round, and he bade the trumpeter sound
> To the charge, and he rode on ahead, as he waved his blade
> To the gallant three hundred whose glory will never die—
> 'Follow,' and up the hill, up the hill, up the hill,
> Follow'd the Heavy Brigade.

This, but for the reversal in the last two lines, is almost a classic example of the Wordsworthian dictum that the language of poetry does not differ from that of prose, except by the superaddition of metre. The reversion and repetition of the last two lines, which are not those of prose, produce their effect, at least in part, by contrast with the extreme normality of the rhythm and idiom of the first half of the stanza. Though the diction of the *Idylls* is often elaborate, artificial and over-wrought, the language of the Laureate poems, and indeed of many of the other poems of the period is unexpectedly plain and natural.

However, though fundamentally a natural diction, it is stiff at times and formal, as it has to be to meet Tennyson's purposes. He is obliged to pay public compliments, to declare that such and such an event has or is about to happen. For instance, he had to inform a public, already sufficiently aware of the fact, that Queen Victoria had reigned fifty years:

> Fifty times the rose has flower'd and faded,
> Fifty times the golden harvest fallen,
> Since our Queen assumed the globe, the sceptre.

This is not mere pompous emptiness. 'Queen Victoria has reigned fifty years' is a newspaper statement of fact; a piece of information, imparted and docketed for the use of the future historian. Here the developed kenning, the repetition, and the heavy alliteration call attention to the fact as something out of the ordinary, as having significance. The alliteration on the *f*, for example, makes for a concentration on the length of time which is taken up later:

> Henry's fifty years are all in shadow,
> Gray with distance Edward's fifty summers,
> Ev'n her Grandsire's fifty half forgotten.

It is not a question simply of any fifty years, but of something special about this particular half century; its achievement is an occasion for public rejoicing. The poem itself is not distinguished, but it affords a clear example of Tennyson's making poetic ceremonial out of plain fact by the use of rhetorical skills. The ceremonial quality is imparted to his poems by every device of art; the kenning, the descriptive identification,

> Sea-Kings' daughter from over the sea,

and the elaborate personification sometimes combined with it,

> He, on whom from both her open hands
> Lavish Honour shower'd all her stars,
> And affluent Fortune emptied all her horn.

At times the formal conceit is continued throughout a poem. But Tennyson, for the most part, avoids the thinness of texture which normally results from these devices; the passage quoted had a certain emblematic quality:

> Fifty times the rose has flower'd and faded,
> Fifty times the golden harvest fallen,
> Since our Queen assumed the globe, the sceptre.

The rose, the golden harvest, the sceptre, are not used as images in the passage: it is a fact that real, non-symbolic roses have flowered and faded fifty times since Victoria came to the throne. Nevertheless all these things are, in other contexts, used symbolically and they are meant to carry the associations which they have within particular systems of symbols into the atmosphere of this poem. Much of the Imperial effect achieved by Tennyson in his Laureate work depends on this use of quasi-symbolic vocabulary. A group of words, gold, rejoice, mourn, glorious, jubilant, imperial and so on, appear over and over again . . . partly because of their sound value (many of them are heavy poly-syllables, or long-vowelled, weighty words) but more often because of their associations. The Wellington Ode has this:

> Let the bell be toll'd:
> And a reverent people behold
> The towering car, the sable steeds:
> Bright let it be within its blazon'd deeds,
> Dark in its funeral fold.
> Let the bell be toll'd:
> And a deeper knell in the heart be knoll'd;
> And the sound of the sorrowing anthem roll'd
> Thro' the dome of the golden cross;
> And the volleying cannon thunder his loss;
> He knew their voices of old.

This has the heavy sorrowing words, knoll, and bell, and toll, and sable, dark, and funeral fold, and the bright military words, reminiscent of action and glory . . . steeds, golden, blazon'd deeds, anthems and volleying cannon. They are general terms enough and belong to the generalised mood of a state funeral. There is sufficient of the particular, in the reference to St Paul's dome, where Wellington was buried, to fix the mood to a particular instance. Elsewhere this trick of aligning the familiar with the exotic is used to produce particular effects:

> The golden news along the steppes is blown,
> And at thy name the Tartar tents are stirr'd;
> Elburz and all the Caucasus have heard;
> And all the sultry palms of India known,
> Alexandrovna.
> The voices of our universal sea
> On capes of Afric as on cliffs of Kent,
> The Maoris, and that Isle of Continent,
> And loyal pines of Canada murmur thee,
> Marie Alexandrovna!

Here we have the Miltonic use of the rolling lists of names used to
suggest, as they do suggest, the romance of a union between two great
empires. The cliffs of Kent, the familiar, the near, the very nearly symbolic, serve as a local centre for the global movement of the poem. And
just as the familiar name of Kent draws the far Tartar hordes into the
perspective of an English scene, so by an opposite but complementary
technique Tennyson gives the dowdily familiar a dignity by placing it
in other contexts:

> lo! the giant aisles,
> Rich in model and design;
> Harvest-tool and husbandry,
> Loom and wheel and enginery,
> Secrets of the sullen mine,
> Steel and gold, and corn and wine,
> Fabric rough, or fairy-fine,
> Sunny tokens of the Line,
> Polar marvels, and a feast
> Of wonder, out of West and East.

After 'secrets of the sullen mine' 'Steel and gold' cease to be the names
of metals used in industrial processes and assume their poetic associations; so do 'harvest' and 'husbandry' and 'corn and wine', words
which carry the weight of a near-biblical prosperity. Victorian
commerce is made to take on a borrowed glamour, and its ordinary
materials are coerced by the diction into a ritual of industry—not indeed
by any special quality of the images used, but simply by a manipulation
of the penumbra of associations which words derive from centuries of
use. Nor is it fair to object that this kind of glamour is inappropriate:
the Victorian felt, as we do not, the amazement of a world-wide
commerce. Though his prosperity was not as simple a matter as that of
the patriarchs, basically all human prosperity is the same and may be
expressed in the time-worn symbols of increase.

The success of these poems depends very largely on the movements
of the verse. The poem we are considering, the *Ode sung at the Opening
of the International Exhibition*, moves, unexpectedly, in the rhythms of
Comus's invitation to the revellers:

Steel and gold, and corn and wine,	Meanwhile welcome joy and feast
Fabric rough, or fairy-fine,	Midnight shout and revelry,
Sunny tokens of the Line,	Tipsy dance and jollity.
Polar marvels, and a feast	Braid your locks with rosy twine,
Of wonder, out of West and East,	Dropping odours dropping wine.

It would not, at first sight, seem likely that the rhythms of a Bacchic revel were suitable for an International Exhibition, an Earl's Court bean-feast. But in writing these everlasting *Odes* Tennyson had a very difficult task, and here he has to turn a catalogue of industrial and scientific products into poetry. The dance rhythm directs attention away from the mere multiplication of exhibits to that excitement which many people feel in the contemplation of a great variety of goods and artefacts, an excitement to which the Victorians were especially prone. This pleased, child-at-a-pantomime excitement is not simply the product of the metre used. The metre is trochaic, the line is octo-syllabic, but lines of eight syllables arranged in trochees do not necessarily produce a dancing mood. Patmore once committed himself to a rash statement that certain metres possess a natural solemnity or a natural lightness. Tennyson, thereupon, sent him examples of his solemn metre used lightly, and his light metre used solemnly. And his comment was just. A good prosodist is a man who handles his metres flexibly to his own purposes, not one who uses them to a pattern. The point about the rhythm of the verse quoted is not that Tennyson used Milton's metre, but that his verse here moves in Milton's movement. And this is a much more complex business than the achievement of a correct scansion.

In most English verse there is a kind of counterpoint in which the rhythms of the reading voice are superimposed on the regularity of the metre. It is this which accounts for the extraordinary variety in the movement of English blank verse. The five metrical stresses in a regular ten-syllable iambic verse need not coincide with the emphasis of the speaking voice, and the stressed syllables do not necessarily receive equal weight when the verse is read. Some variations are produced by strictly metrical devices, by reversing a foot, by elision, or syncopation; others depend on diction. Variations in stress value are the result, say, of length of syllable, or of devices like alliteration and assonance which modify the emphasis placed on a particular syllable, and even, simply, of the meaning and value of the word or syllable stressed. The famous 'conversational' blank verse of the Romantic poets was created by the manipulation of these stress values. The scansion of *Tintern Abbey*, for instance, is basically regular:

> Five years have passed, five summers and the length
>
> Of five long winters, and again I hear

Those waters rólling from their móuntain stréams
With á soft ínland múrmur.

It is clear, however, that these lines would be said with a movement like this:

Five years have passed,   five summers and the length

Of five long winters,   and again I hear

Those waters   rolling from their mountain streams

With a soft inland murmur.

In the first line of this the stress on 'and' is not as heavy as the stress on 'length', or on 'passed', simply because 'and' is a conjunction and not very important, and the length of these syllables helps with the repetition of *five* (twice in an unstressed position), to give a movement to the line which is complementary to the metrical pace. What Wordsworth does here is to adapt the verse paragraph of the Miltonic Epic to the movements of normal speech. The unit of sound in 'conversational' verse is still the paragraph, not the line, but while there is a continuity of rhythm from line to line as in the epic, the stresses are muted and the rhythmic pattern evened out. This produces a verse of which the movement is discursive and unemphatic though still strictly controlled by metre. Tennyson himself used this technique in the conversation piece which opens the first version of *Morte d'Arthur* but it is not in itself suitable for formal poetry. In the Laureate poems where there is an obvious need for a strong swinging line, the muted iambs of *Tintern Abbey* and *This Lime Tree Bower my Prison* would clearly be out of place. Instead Tennyson adapts the methods I have described to his own purposes. He uses the non-colloquial rhythms, trochaic, dactylic, anapaestic. But although these strong stress rhythms are appropriate to dramatic public occasions, they can be enormously monotonous. Their beat is so very regular, so very intrusive. Tennyson develops, and it is one of the triumphs of his prosody, a technique like that of Romantic blank verse, a method, that is, of breaking the severe regularity of these metres by counterpointing other rhythms across them. These are not necessarily the rhythms of speech; the reasons which prohibit the use of colloquial blank verse in formal poetry operate here; but they are allied to speech rhythms, they suggest not the movement of conversation but perhaps the movement of oratory. The normal scansion of the lines quoted from the *Ode sung at the Opening of the International Exhibition* is:

> Steel and gold, and corn and wine,
> Fabric rough, or fairy-fine,
> Sunny tokens of the Line,
> Polar marvels, and a feast
> Of wonder, out of West and East.

The movement of the line in recitation is this:

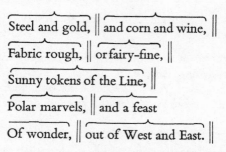

> Steel and gold, ‖ and corn and wine, ‖
> Fabric rough, ‖ or fairy-fine, ‖
> Sunny tokens of the Line, ‖
> Polar marvels, ‖ and a feast
> Of wonder, ‖ out of West and East. ‖

This is certainly not a speech rhythm, but it is a rhythm which accommodates the voice and allows its normal cadence to be heard through the metrical beat. Tennyson achieves this variation in part by using the pause as an element in rhythm, in part by the shift of this caesura, and in part, though this is not as evident in this passage as in some other poems, by variations in the strength of the stress. Again in the line:

> Fabric rough, or fairy-fine,

he makes use of alliteration as a reinforcement to the metrical stress, a trick picked up perhaps from his experiments with Old English prosody in his translation of *The Battle of Brunanburh*. In *On the Jubilee of Queen Victoria*, where the metre is in some verses quantitative,[2] we find that, in normal speech, the long syllable of the metrical foot would be stressed and it is often alliterated:

> X   X   X
> Fifty times the rose has flower'd and faded,

It is, in fact, Tennyson's vigorous and flexible use of all the verbal elements, quantity, sound, stress, in a line of verse which enables him to attain such a variety of movement in the use of standard metres. The normal pattern, for instance, of *The Defence of Lucknow* is this:

$$\text{X}\cup\cup \mid \text{X}\cup\cup \mid \text{X}\cup\cup \mid \text{X}\cup\cup \mid \text{X}\cup\cup \parallel$$

It is a falling rhythm. But this is what Tennyson does with it:

> Men will forget what we súffer ‖ and not what we dó. ‖ We can fight!
>
> But to be sóldier all day ‖ and be séntinel all thro' the night—
> Ever the mine and assault, ‖ our sallies, ‖ their lying alarms,
>
> Bugles and drúms in the dárkness, ‖ and shóutings ‖ and soúndings to arms.

The basic metre of these lines is regular, the movement is built upon them, by shift and variety of emphasis. Even in so late a poem as *Locksley Hall Sixty Years After* with its unmalleable trochaic metre, there is an enormous variety in the movement of the single lines:

She that holds ‖ the diamond necklace dearer than the golden ring, ‖

She the worldling ‖ born of worldlings ‖ —father, mother—‖

be content, ‖

Chaos, Cosmos! Cosmos, Chaos! ‖ who can tell how all will end?

Read the world's wide annals, ‖ you, ‖ and take their wisdom for

your friend.

This use of metre can be very easily adapted both to ceremonial occasional verse and to dramatic. Its flexibility permits the funereal pace of the Wellington Ode, and the lighter pace of the *Welcome to Alexandra*:

> Rush to the roof, sudden rocket, and higher
> Melt into stars for the land's desire!
> Roll and rejoice, jubilant voice,
> Roll as a ground-swell dash'd on the strand,
> Roar as the sea when he welcomes the land,
> And welcome her, welcome the land's desire.

At the same time it permits the colour of the living voice to appear through dramatic poetry, as in *The Defence of Lucknow* where the movement of the verse allows for, and expresses, the immediacy of the passion.

Tennyson's remarkable skill in the handling of sounds and metres has led us into an injustice in praising him. His technique, we say, is always superb, but it is often out of line with his diction, or with the melodrama of his sentiments. Now there is always a danger of melodrama in public poetry: first because public affairs, public occasions invariably loom larger than they are, secondly because there is always in them an element of abstraction. Weddings and coronations and crises are, in their public aspects, affairs of general symbols, general words: they are not things happening to a person, but to that monstrous conceptual creature, the community, the mass. The great difficulty in writing about them is to keep the general words somehow linked to the personal and the particular. Melodrama happens when the expression of an emotion soars away, like a balloon, from its anchor in actual human feelings, and it is more likely to happen when the feelings are, in any case, generalised and public. Tennyson's metrical skill was a method of keeping his language fastened to the reality of his subject, and where he is over-violent or melodramatic it is, often, his skill which fails him:

> Tho' niggard throats of Manchester may bawl,
> What England was, shall her true sons forget?
> We are not cotton spinners all,
> But some love England and her honour yet.

There is here a useless cacophony of vowel sounds, *man, may, bawl, all,* of which Tennyson at his best was incapable. And when we feel a melodramatic violence in the indignation of *Maud,* or *Locksley Hall Sixty Years After* it is not because the metrical technique masks the crudity of the diction but because it brings it into strong relief:

> Is it well that while we range with Science, glorying in the Time,
> Cíty chíldren soak and blacken soul and sense in cíty slime?

Tennyson himself complained that he hated a hissing line, and this offen-
sive regularity, with the emphases both of the reading voice and of the
metre falling heavily and monotonously on an alliterated *s* sound, may
show no crude mistakes in scansion but it is not altogether what we, and
certainly Tennyson, would call 'perfect' technique. But in his best
verse, diction, image and metre move together in a way which makes
technical skill the instrument of feeling, *A Welcome to Alexandra* is a
case in point. The poem is not a major poem, but it is successful in its
purpose. It was written to celebrate the marriage of Alexandra of
Denmark with the Prince of Wales. Tennyson is really concerned with
celebration:

> Welcome her, welcome her, all that is ours!
> Warble, O bugle, and trumpet, blare!
> Flags, flutter out upon turrets and towers!
> Flames, on the windy headland flare!
> Utter your jubilee, steeple and spire!
> Clash, ye bells, in the merry March air!
> Flash, ye cities, in rivers of fire!
> Rush to the roof, sudden rocket, and higher
> Melt into stars for the land's desire!

The material of the poem lies in the activities of public rejoicing:
activities which are in themselves recognisably symbolic, and which
Tennyson treats as an almost anthropomorphic yearning of the land
itself for Alexandra. But it is the management of the verbal patterning
which is impressive here. The mind is left with a sense of vivid detail
caught in the actual sound and movement of the words:

> Warble, O bugle, and trumpet, blare.

The remarkable thing is that the sound conveys not only aural but visual
detail:

> Flash, ye cities, in rivers of fire!
> Rush to the roof, sudden rocket, and higher
> Melt into stars for the land's desire!

The half-rhyme of 'flash' and 'rush', the quickened pace of 'sudden
rocket', the spillover of the lines from 'higher' to 'melt', with the
consequent slowing and flattening down of the movement, suggest
very vividly the uprush of fireworks, and their quiet fall. But this
accumulation of the detail of public festival is not merely for the detail's
sake. Moving together in the metrical swing the words themselves,

'clash', 'flash', 'rush', 'flutter', 'warble', 'blare', the 'merry March air', though precise in meaning, produce an effect of exhilaration, of a land half drunk with rejoicing. The poem is certainly concerned to pay compliment to the Princess of Wales, but it is also concerned with a royal marriage as a public event. All Tennyson's sense of the Queen as a symbol of the common life, all his awareness of the marriage bond as the archetype of social relationship are caught up with and infuse the verse with a personal delight.

This engagement of Tennyson's emotions in the event he is celebrating is often inspired by a great leader or a great act of courage. The strength of the movement in *The Charge of the Light Brigade*, the *Revenge* and *The Defence of Lucknow* springs from his response to genuine courage. The metrical virtuosity of *The Revenge* is the concomitant of an extreme plainness of narrative, enlivened now and then by the revealing detail,

> And a pinnace, *like a flutter'd bird*, came flying from far away.

The poem is almost naked of images, but once and again there is an image which rises so naturally from the narrative as not to be recognised as an image:

> Thousands of their seamen made mock at the mad little craft
> Running on and on, till delay'd
> By their mountain-like San Philip that, of fifteen hundred tons,
> And up-shadowing high above us with her yawning tiers of guns,
> Took the breath from our sails, and we stay'd.
>
> And while now the great San Philip hung above us like a cloud
> Whence the thunder bolt will fall
> Long and loud,
> Four galleons drew away
> From the Spanish fleet that day,
> And two upon the larboard and two upon the starboard lay,
> And the battle-thunder broke from them all.

The inhibiting presence of the San Philip is felt through the mountain and the *yawning* tiers of guns, and the *cloud* and it is remarkable how this last image is beautifully extended so as to carry the narrative forward:

> And the battle-thunder broke from them all.

The shift of the verse-movement underlines the effect of these images, for while never losing the effect of narrative it follows the movements of the emotion. The lengthened line,

And up-shadowing high above us with her yawning tiers of guns,
Took the breath from our sails . . . .

with the drag in the long syllables of 'shadowing' and 'yawning' drags
out the breath like the suffocating bulk of the San Philip itself, while the
abrupt end of the line with the heavy beat on the last syllable matches
metrically the full stop of the Revenge:

> . . . and we stay'd.

The full beat in the line often falls so as to reinforce the impact of
sudden action:

> And the battle-thunder broke from them all

In other poems as well it falls so as to bring home the revealing detail:

> Flash'd all their sabres bare,
>
> Flash'd as they turned in air.

The odds and the excitement of battle are in the verse itself, which seems
to flex like a muscle to the poet's almost sensual awareness of the event.

It might well be agreed that, of its kind, the Laureate poetry is good:
that it does capture the sense of particular occasions. But is this enough?
Can the occasional poet ever present anything of universal significance?
Except for the kind of historical accident which made the Great
Exhibition of 1851 a symbol of the mid-Victorian age, occasions of
this kind are incidents of a momentary importance. Tennyson lifts them
out of this bondage to date by emphasising the communal and Imperial
elements, but even he can do little more than this. The other kind of
occasion has more potentiality. In the Wellington Ode, as we have
already seen, Tennyson generalises the Duke's achievements until they
come to stand for the mythical leader dedicated to his community, and
this is his normal method; to strip down an achievement to its essentials
was his way of revealing its importance. The Charge of the Light Brigade
was an act of courage performed in particular circumstances and
producing not only admiration but a sickened anger at waste and
military stupidity. Later, it had its effect in the abolition of the purchase
system in the staffing of the army.[3] Tennyson gives it the simplicity of a
ballad:

> 'Forward the Light Brigade!'
> Was there a man dismay'd?
> Not tho' the soldier knew
> Someone had blunder'd:

And though it is now hackneyed it still has a ballad's effect. The particular event described becomes, through the poem, very nearly archetypal. Similar and even more disastrous military mistakes, redeemed by similar and even greater military courage are half-forgotten. There were no poems about the landings at Gallipoli, or the Dieppe Raid and these have half-faded from the public memory. *The Charge of the Light Brigade* stands as it were for them:

> Not tho' the soldier knew
> Someone had blunder'd.

The phrase is very nearly an epigram of national contempt. But there is something more here. Earlier on, I said that Tennyson did not celebrate victories, only magnificent defeats and defiances, the Revenge running under the guns of the San Philip, the English flag streaming on the fortress of Lucknow. It is not patriotism which they display (though after all a love of the local is a universal passion) but the sense of weakness pitting itself bravely against immitigable disaster:

> Storm'd at with shot and shell,
> Boldly they rode and well,
> Into the jaws of Death,
> Into the mouth of Hell
> Rode the six hundred.

This emerges from the movement as well as the content of the poems. The slow march and muffled drums for Wellington move in the rhythms of that poem, as the excitement of the charge (they said the poem moved like the thunder of the horse-hooves) does in *The Charge of the Light Brigade*. But what is more important is the masculinity and tension of the movement in these poems. This is neither neurosis nor hysteria, but courage against odds:

> Plunged in the battery-smoke
> Right thro' the line they broke;
> Cossack and Russian
> Reel'd from the sabre-stroke
> Shatter'd and sunder'd.
> Then they rode back, but not,
> Not the six hundred.

III

In these occasional poems Tennyson sums up all he wanted to say in
the *Idylls of the King*. For in these he presents the everlasting struggle to
maintain dignity and order in the face of attacking forces, and with
this the ideal of loyalty and service: all that the Arthurian epic was to
represent to the Victorians. Arthur, in a way, was no more than a
glorified Wellington. Tennyson's need to do it again arises partly from
the deafness and blindness of the public, partly from his perverse
attachment to the myth of Arthur. He had always intended to write
the Arthurian poem, and he did.[4] The failure of this enormous work,
for in spite of individual felicities and insights it is *as a whole* a failure,
is due to the incompatibility of his purpose and the medium in which
he is trying to express it. He tries to force on Arthur the role of the
noble soldier wearing duty's iron crown:

> Not once nor twice in our rough island-story,
> The path of duty was the way to glory.

It is a role which Wellington, despite his very obvious faults, was able
to sustain: devotion to duty after all was part of his character. Arthur,
of course, could not. Prophetically, in the Prologue to *Morte d'Arthur*
Tennyson dreamt of him 'like a modern gentleman/Of stateliest port',
and it is this kind of dignity which he attempts to thrust on the gray king
of the Arthurian legend. Unfortunately, Arthur and his court had, in
the course of centuries, acquired certain well-defined characteristics
not altogether consonant with Tennyson's moral purpose. There is a
yet graver flaw in the work. The *Morte d'Arthur* (later *The Passing of
Arthur*), the earliest written of the *Idylls*, was written at the time of
Hallam's death, and the tale of Arthur's disappearance from this world
with its implied doubt about his fate—was he really dead, was he gone
to Avilion to heal his wounds?—was a true medium for Tennyson's
mood of bereavement, and his doubts about immortality. The action
of the story is capable of carrying just this emotional significance. Since
what was in question was a personal mood, the fantasy involved is not,
as we saw earlier, very much out of place. But, in the later *Idylls*,
Tennyson is trying to turn a fantasy into a myth: he wanted desperately
to make the legend of Arthur the type and symbol of public life in the
nineteenth century. Such an attempt was bound to fail: Tennyson's
associations with Arthur were precisely personal and not public, and
Arthur himself was too remote to carry real meaning to the Victorians.
The project drooped under its own artificiality.

Tennyson had every excuse for the experiment. The Victorians had become mediaeval-minded. Scott, Tennyson's own early work, Pugin, the Pre-Raphaelites and perhaps the extraordinary starvation of the senses produced by a combination of industrialism and evangelical respectability, created a strong public taste for the glamour of the Middle Ages. Almost anything would be swallowed if sweetened with a little chivalry, and an odd monk or knight. Morris's *Defence of Guenevere*, Arnold's *Tristram and Iseult*, Swinburne's *Tristram of Lyonnesse*, Rossetti's *Ballads*, and a good many other poems, were, after all, habituating the public to 'the Romance of Illicit Passion' and did not provoke the routine 'shame' of their own moral code. On the other hand Hawker's *San Graal*, with its extraordinary opening:

> Ho, for the San Graal, vanished vase of heaven
> That held like Christ's own heart an hin of blood,

and the delicate, enamelled modulations of Christina Rossetti, to say nothing of *The Blessed Damosel*, with its Pre-Raphaelite angels in albs and embroidered vestments, were overlaying the blighted imagination of Protestant dissent with the mediaeval trappings of a more colourful religion. After all, Tennyson had more or less invented the Arthurian poem which his contemporaries found so useful: there was no apparent reason why he should not use it and the fashion for mediaevalising, to his own ends. Besides, as we have seen, he had already developed a technique of presenting states of mind through the narrative lyric. The method he was now to use in putting across 'the need of an ideal' was, in a sense, only an extension of the method of his early poetry.

We can treat at least the first four *Idylls of the King*, the first in time that is, the set called 'The False and the True', as poems of *The Princess* pattern. These are exemplar stories meant to illustrate some virtue or quality of normal life—they are rather like Victorian narrative paintings, and like them suffer the same minute attention to detail, the same overpainting. The flowers and thorns around the door in Holman Hunt's picture of *The Light of the World* are Tennysonian in meticulous detail, in that attention to reality which produces a strong impression of unreality. Tennyson's message, about the true and the false wife, was meant to emerge from the main story, as Hunt's was to emerge from the whole picture, but in both a lavishness of detail is embroidered on to the main theme. Actual description is elaborated beyond any reasonable need:

> Then rode Geraint into the castle court,
> His charger trampling many a prickly star
> Of sprouted thistle on the broken stones.
> He look'd and saw that all was ruinous.
> Here stood a shatter'd archway plumed with fern;
> And here had fall'n a great part of a tower,
> Whole, like a crag that tumbles from the cliff,
> And like a crag was gay with wilding flowers:
> And high above a piece of turret stair,
> Worn by the feet that now were silent, wound
> Bare to the sun, and monstrous ivy-stems
> Claspt the gray walls with hairy-fibred arms,
> And suck'd the joining of the stones, and look'd
> A knot, beneath of snakes, aloft, a grove . . .

Then again Tennyson is meticulous in his images: Geraint, looking at Enid, to observe her reactions, eyes her,

> As careful robins eye the delver's toil:

Elaine, kissed, 'slips like water to the floor'; Mordred hates Sir Lancelot for some injury, and

> ever after, the small violence done
> Rankled in him and ruffled all his heart,
> As the sharp wind that ruffles all day long
> A little bitter pool about a stone
> On the bare coast.

This extraordinary attention to the minutiae of the natural world was, for his own public, one of Tennyson's major achievements. That magpie-minded generation saw it as his *art* and art, is a proper term for these descriptions since they are certainly produced by the highly skilled manipulation of language. As mere bits of isolated 'word-painting' they show the accuracy of Tennyson's eye and have a kind of charm, and often real beauty. But most of them are versified observation unrelated to the main action, and they tend to impart a curious gloss and shimmer to the surface of the poems, a gloss which in the long run dulls their appeal. Tennyson's models are partly to blame. The Arthurian story runs to detail, especially in *Mabinogion*, in which catalogues of detail are regarded as evidences of the bard's skill; while the rules of epic prescribe the elaborate 'epic simile' of which the purpose sometimes seems to be to get as far from the action as possible.

But these inorganic digressions are out of line with Tennyson's intention; they distract from his meaning and force him to the inartistic
device of explicit moral homily. What is really happening in the poem
takes place *under* the lapidary work.

The *Idylls of the King* were composed over a very long period of time;
from *Morte d'Arthur* to *Balin and Balan* there is a gap of forty years,
though the main body of the poems was considered and composed
through the fifties and sixties. A deeper reading of them shows
Tennyson learning to adapt this enamelled descriptive work to his
purpose. In *Geraint and Enid* the image of the robin watching the delver
for the worms is repeated, rather clumsily, along with other motifs, like
that of Enid's dress of faded silk, at the points in the poem where the
situation changes, and it becomes a kind of comment on the action.
One mention of the robin or the silk dress recalls another: the developments in the situation are emphasised and interpreted by the repetition.
We saw that Tennyson used this method in *In Memoriam*, and fairly
early in his composition of the *Idylls* he returned to it as a means of
developing his theme. Merlin's riddling underlines the mysteriousness
of Arthur; the songs of Vivien, Gawaine, and Tristram, like the songs
in *The Princess*, make explicit an underlying theme, and the blazons in
the walls at Camelot begin to carry meaning. In these and other
descriptions Tennyson builds up, parallel with the story, with the
actual events of the poems, a commentary on their significance. This
clearly is the right use for his elaborate descriptions. It was easy enough
in the mediaeval setting of the poem to transfer the weight of the detail
to heraldic descriptions, to the blazons of shields, the windows in the
great hall of Camelot, the symbolic carving on the gates of the city.
Nor is it possible to complain that these descriptions are inorganic.
Though connected with the action, they do not and are not meant to
belong to it; they are, as it were, mirrors in which it is repeated and
revealed for what it is. *Gareth and Lynette*, which combines the ancient
legend of Beaumains with a full-length allegory on the life of man, has
a good many of these descriptive passages and nearly all of them have
a double meaning. Gareth, for instance, overcomes the knight of the
Sun, who is a real enough enemy, but who also represents ambition
and avarice, the temptations of middle age:

> So when they touch'd the second river loop,
> Huge on a huge red horse, and all in mail
> Burnish'd to blinding, shone the Noonday Sun
> Beyond a ranging shallow. As if the flower,

That blows a globe of after arrowlets,
Ten thousand-fold had grown, flash'd the fierce shield,
All sun;

The complicated symbolism of the high noon of day and of life, and
the splendours of wealth are integrated in this evocation of brightness.
The round shield and the round sun are brought together and the
shining coin comes to mind by the implications of the description.
Mutatis mutandis this integration is also present in the descriptions of
Arthur's Hall and of Camelot. Here we come up against something else.
This is the description of Camelot in *The Holy Grail* when the knights
return from the quest to find it half ruined:

> 'O, when we reach'd
> The city, our horses stumbling as they trode
> On heaps of ruin, hornless unicorns,
> Crack'd basilisks, and splinter'd cockatrices,
> And shatter'd talbots, which had left the stones
> Raw, that they fell from, brought us to the hall.'

This description, compared with that of Geraint's arrival at the ruined
castle of Earl Yniol, is incomplete, and fanciful, but it suggests and
threatens and has the real quality of ruin:

> shatter'd talbots, which had left the stones
> Raw, that they fell from,

At first the reader does not recognise the strange beasts as those of
carving; 'hornless unicorns', 'cracked basilisks' suggest a ruin beyond
the merely physical, and impress the mind with the ominous sense of
foredoom that hangs over Arthur's kingdom—an impression the
stronger for the memory of those passages in which the splendour of
Camelot is described. Tennyson has returned to his earlier skill—the
suggestion of spiritual states and moods by the evocation of physical
imagery. He uses this skill even in the earlier *Idylls*. Merlin in *Vivien*
feels the ominous threat of coming disaster:

> So dark a forethought roll'd about his brain,
> As on a dull day in an Ocean cave
> The blind wave feeling round his long sea-hall
> In silence:

But such images are isolated, no more than descriptive evocations of
incidental states of mind. In the later *Idylls* Tennyson knew his own

mind. Now he still wants to suggest states of mind, but also to demonstrate the context in which these mental states belong. The long descriptive passages in *The Holy Grail* and *Pelleas and Ettarre* and *The Last Tournament* make us share in the subjective states of the various characters:

> when he saw
> High up in heaven the hall that Merlin built,
> Blackening against the dead-green stripes of even,
> 'Black nest of rats,' he groan'd, 'ye build too high'.

This manner of seeing the great hall against the heaven, with its emphasis on a sickening black and green, a 'dead-green,' evokes the ugly and the menacing, and makes us know the disillusion of Pelleas, as in *The Holy Grail* we know the desolation of Percivale, but this sense of disillusion and desolation is the medium of our knowledge of the fall of Arthur's kingdom, and all that it means. The last long battle in the mist is the most famous of all these evocations:

> Then rose the King and moved his host by night,
> And ever push'd Sir Modred, league by league,
> Back to the sunset bound of Lyonnesse—
> A land of old upheaven from the abyss
> By fire, to sink into the abyss again;
> Where fragments of forgotten peoples dwelt,
> And the long mountains ended in a coast
> Of ever shifting sand, and far away
> The phantom circle of a moaning sea.
> There the pursuer could pursue no more,
> And he that fled no further fly the King;
> And there, that day when the great light of heaven
> Burn'd at his lowest in the rolling year,
> On the waste sand by the waste sea they closed.
> Nor ever yet had Arthur fought a fight
> Like this, last, dim, weird battle of the west.
> A deathwhite mist slept over sand and sea:
> Whereof the chill, to him who breathed it, drew
> Down with his blood, till all his heart was cold
> With formless fear; and ev'n on Arthur fell
> Confusion, since he saw not whom he fought.
> For friend and foe were shadows in the mist,
> And friend slew friend not knowing whom he slew;
> And some had visions out of golden youth,

And some beheld the faces of old ghosts
Look in upon the battle; and in the mist

★   ★   ★

Shield-breakings, and the clash of brands, the crash
Of battle-axes on shatter'd helms, and shrieks
After the Christ, of those who falling down
Look'd up for heaven and only saw the mist.

This is the bewilderment in the mind of Arthur and the loss of Logres,
but it stands for the cold chill of the heart, and the chaos which falls on
the world with the loss of familiar order and familiar values.

From the accumulation of these descriptions, from songs, and visions
and emblematic devices, certain significances of the *Idylls* begin to
emerge. The songs, for instance, catch up the shifts and changes of the
natural world. Lynette's songs mark the passage of Gareth's success
with addresses to the sun and moon; Tristram's songs, and Vivien's,
emphasise the relationship of love and natural forces:

'Free love—free field—we love but while we may:
The woods are hush'd, their music is no more:
The leaf is dead, the yearning past away:
New leaf, new life, the days of frost are o'er.'

And more than these, which express the peculiar personalities of the
singers, there is the riddling of Merlin about Arthur:

'Rain, sun, and rain! and the free blossom blows:
Sun, rain, and sun! and where is he who knows?
From the great deep to the great deep he goes.'

for this represents Arthur himself as associated with weather, and
growth, and the cycles of the seasons. The *mythagogues* of Tennyson's
youth had made Arthur a sun god, a fertility cult hero,[5] and it is possible
that Tennyson may be recalling this facet of his hero's character. At
any rate, this emphasis, in the various songs, on the natural world is in
accordance with the general plan of the *Idylls* in which the events move
through the four seasons of the year. A symbolism of natural forces
moves through the poem, woods, and waters, storm and mist. Other
symbols are thrown up in much the same manner, historical symbols
like that of the White Horse, which Tennyson attaches to the invading
heathen; a symbolism of jewels like that of the diamonds which flashed
like a shower of light across the body of the dead Elaine, or the rubies

of 'dead innocence' which Tristram fastened round the neck of Queen Isolt:

> Before him fled the face of Queen Isolt
> With ruby-circled neck,

Then again there are the much greater symbols, the mysterious city of Camelot, the desert of desolation in *The Holy Grail*, the sea from which Arthur comes and to which he returns. All these things carry an atmosphere with them and infuse the *Idylls of the King* with a brooding suggestion of some meaning greater than that of the immediate action. Tennyson's overt purpose was to present an ideal, but the ideal has many elements. There is, for instance, a sense of history. The Heathen of the White Horse were really the heathen Saxons, whom the shadowy Romano-British chieftains, Arthur's prototypes, defied; but through the struggle between them and Arthur, defined in the opposing symbols of the Cross and the White Horse, Tennyson presents what to his Victorian mind was the major significance of history, the victory of civilisation over primitive chaos. This notion of history was, of course, the offspring of ideas of process and evolution, and it is characteristically moral, being bound up with the idea of 'working out the brute' in the individual. The building of Camelot, wrought by the Lady of the Lake, is never finished, and yet was finished from the beginning, for it represents the making of the human soul. Arthur's kingdom is an extension of Camelot, the world of sense commanded by the soul.[6]

All this, however, the vision of society led by a hero mysteriously come from the unknown, and of the world of sense commanded by a spiritual power arising from the deep, is crossed and threatened by natural forces. Sometimes, as in Lynette's song, or in the opening of *Guinevere*, they rejoice with the ideal. Sometimes, as in the songs of Vivien, and Tristram, though neutral in themselves, they can be used by sinful men, and threaten to corrupt right order.

> This fire of Heaven,
> This old sun-worship, boy, will rise again,
> And beat the cross to earth, and break the King
> And all his Table.

In the last analysis, the natural order itself, being subject to decay, undermines the achievement of Arthur. Reasons are given for the break-up of Logres—Merlin's surrendering his wisdom to the mere sensuality of Vivien, Lancelot's betrayal of honour to sensuality—but the imagery of the creeping year which runs all through the poem suggests that, to Tennyson, the mere fact of being in time ensures a downfall of the ideal itself.

This welding together of themes so that one image stands for all deepens the significance of all the semi-narrative, semi-dramatic poems of Tennyson's middle and later period. The complex imagery of *Maud*, in many ways the crowning achievement of his life, like the imagery of the *Idylls*, binds together the story of a neurotic individual with the theme of a society ruined by its own structure. The hero's father went to his death when the wind

> like a broken worldling wail'd,
> And the flying gold of the ruin'd woodland drove thro' the air.

The deliberate and near-metaphysical link of analogy made here between the state of man and the state of the natural world is sustained throughout the poem. The man and the maid, ever ready to slander and steal, were, we saw, juxtaposed with the animal strife of the woodlands, but Maud, the beautiful Maud, is constantly described and discussed in an elaborate symbolism of the lily and the rose.[7] The blush of joy in her betrothal is diffused until the whole world is flushed with pleasure in it:

> Till the red man dance
> By his red cedar-tree,
> And the red man's babe
> Leap, beyond the sea.

The lover's joy in Maud extends not merely through space but through time:

> There is none like her, none.
> Nor will be when our summers have deceased.
> O, art thou sighing for Lebanon
> In the long breeze that streams to thy delicious East,
> Sighing for Lebanon,
> Dark cedar, tho' thy limbs have here increased,
> Upon a pastoral slope as fair,
> And looking to the South, and fed
> With honey'd rain and delicate air,
> And haunted by the starry head
> Of her whose gentle will has changed my fate,
> And made my life a perfumed altar-flame;

And over whom thy darkness must have spread
With such delight as theirs of old, thy great
Forefathers of the thornless garden, there
Shadowing the snow-limb'd Eve from whom she came.

This imagery helps the poem to achieve a universality of which the hero's tale is, by itself, incapable. The introspection of the neurotic young man is set into a context, and the sixteen-year-old Maud—the daughter of Eve, the rose of roses—becomes all the women with whom young men are in love. In a lesser way this is true of the lesser poems. The *motif* of the dreams, for instance, lifts *Sea Dreams* from the realm of the sentimental to something which is well beyond sentimentality, and indeed rather frightening. The clerk dreams, properly enough, of bankruptcy, of a fleet of glass ships sailing across concealed rocks. This dream is a comment both on his own foolishness and on the foolhardy hopes and speculations of Victorian society. His wife, however, dreams of the crash of civilisations. Both dreams are wrought out of the sea sounds:

> the great ridge drew,
> Lessening to the lessening music, back,
> And past into the belt and swell'd again
> Slowly to music: ever when it broke
> The statues, king or saint, or founder fell;
> Then from the gaps and chasms of ruin left
> Came men and women in dark clusters round,
> Some crying, 'Set them up! they shall not fall!'
> And others, 'Let them lie, for they have fall'n.'
> And still they strove and wrangled: and she grieved
> In her strange dream, she knew not why, to find
> Their wildest wailings never out of tune
> With that sweet note; and ever as their shrieks
> Ran highest up the gamut, that great wave
> Returning, while none mark'd it, on the crowd
> Broke, mixt with awful light, and show'd their eyes
> Glaring, and passionate looks, and swept away
> The men of flesh and blood and men of stone,
> To the waste deeps together.

It is the old Tennysonian theme of the inevitability of change, tinged with the wife's memories of the cliff walk, and a strange sadness which finds the collapse of things both in the image of the sweet music, and in the destroying wave. The same kind of significance is built up in

Enoch Arden without a dream. Here we return to the meanings of *The Palace of Art*; it is the desolation of the isolated soul which is evoked by the images:

> No sail from day to day, but every day
> The sunrise broken into scarlet shafts
> Among the palms and ferns and precipices;
> The blaze upon the waters to the east;
> The blaze upon his island overhead;
> The blaze upon the waters to the west;
> Then the great stars that globed themselves in Heaven,
> The hollower-bellowing ocean, and again
> The scarlet shafts of sunrise—but no sail.

Enoch Arden has been too contemptuously dismissed as another example of Tennyson's abandonment of himself to public tastes and conventions, but, when we look into it, it appears as another meditation on the individual isolated from his society, and, like the *Idylls of the King*, a study in heroic failure. But it is not, like the *Idylls*, removed from the context of normal life. It is easy to laugh at the phrases about 'his own little wife', or Tennyson's meticulous concern with the shelves in the parlour, but domestic and private life, the sphere of the shelves in the parlour, is after all one context in which social relations are worked out. I am not at all sure that the juxtaposition of the tropical beauty and solitude of the island, and the life of daily work in the village is not in itself a conception capable of greater poetry than Tennyson was able to give it at that period. There is, at least, a psychological truth in Enoch's apathy when the spring of his endeavour was broken which is only disguised by the unfortunate semi-Miltonic movement of the blank verse lines:

> Yet since he did but labour for himself,
> Work without hope, there was *not life in it*
> *Whereby the man could live*; and as the year
> Roll'd itself round again *to meet the day*
> *When Enoch had return'd*, a languor came
> Upon him, gentle sickness, *gradually*
> *Weakening the man*, till he could do no more,
> But kept the house, his chair, and last his bed.

Enoch Arden is a failure as a poem only because Tennyson is using a Tennysonian method for a subject which demanded a Wordsworthian treatment.

This is a mistake which Tennyson does not make in the Lincolnshire pieces or in the great ballad poems, *Rizpah* and *Despair*, which present, through the sufferings of individuals under particular circumstances, the sufferings common to flesh. The imagery in these poems is not developed as a commentary on the situation but simply as a means of displaying the situation itself. The poems are nakedly vivid in their presentation:

Nay, but I am not claiming your pity: I know you of old—
Small pity for those that have ranged from the *narrow warmth of your fold,*

*   *   *

And Doubt is the lord of this dunghill and crows to the sun and the moon,

Flesh of my flesh was gone, but bone of my bone was left—
I stole them all from the lawyers—and you, will you call it a theft?—
My baby, the bones that had suck'd me, the bones that had laughed and had cried—
Theirs? O, no! they are mine—not theirs—they had moved in my side.

As Eliot says, it is the enormous variety of Tennyson's art which secures his position, but the resources of that art are directed to the exploration of a single yet inclusive problem, the problem of the soul that endures the anguish of being in a crumbling world, and has only the defence of its own courage and the companionship of others.

Chapter VIII

The Ancient Sage

THE old age of a Romantic poet is a spectacle rarer and more interesting than the stereotype of poetical youth. Tennyson lives up to expectation: in the midst of the dinner parties, the audiences with the Queen, and the visits of the great and the good to Farringford and Aldworth he had developed a routine of eccentricity. There was the retirement to the summer-house to compose, the pipes and the port and the reading aloud after dinner, the cloak, the sombrero, which Gladstone was so afraid Tennyson would wear in the House of Lords; there was the occasional legendary remark. The morbidity of Tennyson's youth had mellowed to a privileged grumpiness, and all the aged poet would admit of his youthful melancholy, the dark demon in the blood, was a tendency to gout. Age itself had freed him from the burden of youth, the tendency to identify itself with its own emotions. The hero of *Locksley Hall Sixty Years After* does not repent or renounce his earlier passions; he observes them with a distant curiosity:

> Gone the fires of youth, the follies, furies, curses, passionate tears,
> Gone like fires and floods and earthquakes of the planet's dawning
>   years.
>
> Fires that shook me once, but now to silent ashes fall'n away.
> Cold upon the dead volcano sleeps the gleam of dying day.
>
> Gone the tyrant of my youth, and mute below the chancel stones,
> All his virtues—I forgive them—black in white above his bones.

Fires fallen away to silent ashes is the image of what we commonly expect from the old, but the calm of Tennyson's age was not the calm of a want of energy. *Locksley Hall Sixty Years After* views the tumult of youth through the spectacles of an old man's anger, an anger of a different kind from that which inspired the first *Locksley Hall*. In the earlier poem Amy's lover was shaken with personal bitterness about a personal injury; grown to be an old man and a grandfather, he directs his rage against social disorders many of which did not influence his own life in any way. He is so old that the evils of society no longer touch him personally, but for that reason his judgments on it are fiercer. Though more violent in denunciation in his age, he is more impersonal.

And the curious thing about the aged Tennyson is his impersonality. The detachment of age is sometimes no more than a sedative producing the after-dinner sleep of senile decay, but Tennyson is inquisitive; in his detachment he turns to consider his own past, to consider it more-over as something outside himself. Impersonality becomes a virtue informing the observation of his own emotional and spiritual history. *Merlin and the Gleam, To Edward Fitzgerald, The Roses on the Terrace* all look back in tranquillity and see past experience as completed experience, as something having reality and significance apart from those who suffered or acted in the events and emotions described. Nothing is happening now, nothing is to happen, except death, nothing remains for the old man but to reflect on, to understand and to give shape to his own experience. For the most part Tennyson's later work is a long and continued meditation on the meanings found in the passing of time, a meditation which is sometimes expressed in reflective poems or in the shaping of a story, sometimes in direct reference to his own life in poems about himself and his friends. He did not indeed limit his meditation to his own past. That persistent sense of his vocation which found ful-filment in the Laureateship led him to undertake a monumental and public meditation on England's past, on the history of that empire and civilisation of which he believed himself to be the appointed voice. For of course it was the Laureateship which turned him into a dramatist. Drama is the most public form of literature, dramatic poetry is part of the English heritage, English history is part of England's glory—it follows that the vocation of reviving the historical poetical drama falls to the serious Laureate. Tennyson had little or no talent for drama, and a very considerable genius as a lyric poet, so, not unnaturally, the dramas upon which he pinned his hopes of reviving the glories of the Elizabeth-ans are unread and unacted, while the lyrics of his last period include some of the best known and the finest of his work. But the inspiration behind both lyric and drama is the same—these poems are meditations on reality, and especially upon the reality revealed by the pattern of past experience.

It is important to recognise that there is a common element in the poetry of Tennyson's last period, since to recognise it delivers us from a misjudgment, a misinterpretation of the last poems most persuasively argued by Mr Johnson in *The Alien Vision of Victorian Poetry*. Mr Johnson makes a sharp division between the dramas and the lyrics of Tennyson's last period, and for him this distinction is the final proof of a division between Tennyson's public and his private personality. Lyric represents the personal, drama the public poet. The argument is very convincing, and yet one cannot in the end recognise this Jekyll and Hyde mentality in a poet who, when he knew he was dying, and in the very act of receiving the Last Sacrament, murmured a line from one of his own plays.[1] Many things could be said about this: it is incongruous, it is self-conscious (except that Tennyson was never self-conscious), but certainly it does not display a man in whom the public and the private mind are irrevocably divided. The incident is indicative only, and not a piece of conclusive evidence of Tennyson's own attitude to relations of the public and the private in poetry. But to my mind the poetry itself does not display Mr Johnson's sharp antithesis. Tennyson's history plays all represent moments in the struggle, as seen through the Victorian historical imagination, of England against the domination of the Roman Church. It is not considered as a religious struggle—Tennyson was not a rampant Protestant—but as a political one. The model for these plays is Shakespeare's *King John* and in them Tennyson conceives of Rome not as a spiritual authority but as a foreign power interfering with the liberties of the true-born Englishman. The real patriotism of the nation, and its spirit, appear in its bucking against this foreign domination and shaking off the yoke of Papal power. But the incidents in which Tennyson displays this saga of the Empire and the Papacy turn not on triumph, but once again on heroic failure. Two of the plays, *Harold* and *Becket*, are worthless; the third, and the first composed, *Queen Mary*, though rambling and tediously Shakespearian, leaves on the mind the image not of Rome, or of England, but of the unfortunate Mary. She, and Harold, and Becket, though their position is obscured by the complications of unreal love plots, stand as examples of the old order yielding place to new. *This*, I think, is what Tennyson is apprehending in the

course of English history. In *Sea Dreams* the clerk's wife dreams of the
crash of faiths and civilisations into the roaring floods. The Saxon
kingdom of Harold, the Church of Mary, are examples of this unend-
ing process; they topple into the sea of time with heaven knows what
anguish to the individuals caught up in this destruction. This theme is
not exclusively public, nor is it exclusively personal; it is the theme, as
we have seen, of nearly all Tennyson's maturer poetry, and is in fact
the point at which his public and private preoccupations meet.

In the later lyrics Tennyson still concerns himself with the old order
which has yielded, or must yield place to new, but now the transience
of things is viewed with an inner tranquillity:

> Sunset and evening star,
>   And one clear call for me!
> And may there be no moaning of the bar,
>   When I put out to sea,
>
> But such a tide as moving seems asleep,
>   Too full for sound and foam,
> When that which drew from out the boundless deep
>   Turns again home.
>
> Twilight and evening bell,
>   And after that the dark!
> And may there be no sadness of farewell,
>   When I embark.

The root of this tranquillity was a gift which Tennyson longed to
impart to his generation. For when modern critics speak of Tennyson's
later verse as peculiarly 'personal', what they have in mind is not
Owd Roa or *Romney's Remorse*, but the mystical passages of poems like
The Higher Pantheism, and *The Ancient Sage*, although in these poems
Tennyson does not necessarily speak in his own person. Their view of
these lyrics as essentially private is based on two premises, first that any
religious emotions expressed in poetry are inevitably personal and
therefore private; second that a concern for public order is necessarily
political or social, that it will be directed towards the organisation and
the institutions of society, not to the individual dispositions of citizens.
But Tennyson did not share these assumptions. As we saw in the last
chapters his concern with society is not of a social crusader's kind. For
him the corrupt condition of a community reflected the corrupt
condition of the human heart. When he speaks of a mystical reality he

is not retiring into an ivory tower of religious emotion. On the contrary, the mystical reflections bear, and are meant to bear, directly on the state of the common weal. In writing poems about his mystical intuitions Tennyson set out to combat the materialism which he saw as the root of social evil, and these poems are not less but more didactic than *Enoch Arden* and the *Idylls of the King*. The Ancient Sage in combating the agnostic hedonism of his companion discusses, like St John in Browning's *A Death in the Desert*, problems not of the Ancient but of the Victorian world:

> Wherefore thou be wise,
> Cleave ever to the sunnier side of doubt,
> And cling to Faith beyond the forms of Faith!

Unlike Browning, however, Tennyson sees the intellectual problem in a social and moral context.

His apprehension of the relations between the intellectual, the moral, and the social is very vivid indeed. *Locksley Hall Sixty Years After* rages not so much against the political behaviour of the age as against the thoughts and attitudes which produced it. In *In Memoriam* Tennyson looked to see the deliverance of moral man from his animal ancestry:

> Arise and fly
> The reeling Faun, the sensual feast;
> Move upward, working out the beast
> And let the ape and tiger die.

This deliverance was the purpose and meaning of history but in his own age men seemed determined to return to brutality and disorder:

> Tumble Nature heel o'er head, and, yelling with the yelling street,
> Set the feet above the brain and swear the brain is in the feet.

*   *   *

> Do your best to charm the worst, to lower the rising race of men;
> Have we risen from the beast, then back into the beast again?

Arthur's kingdom reclaimed from the wolf 'reels back into the beast and is no more'. What all this meant to Tennyson is I think better seen, and is certainly better expressed in *Lucretius*. Lucretius pursues the calm of reason:

> The sober majesties
> Of settled, sweet, Epicurean life.

But the potion which Lucilla gave him,

> Confused the chemic labour of the blood,
> And tickling the brute brain within the man's
> Made havock among those tender cells, and check'd
> His power to shape:

Tennyson here implies a physical explanation of the visions which beset Lucretius, but the image of the brute brain 'tickled', an image of touch, evokes an awareness of sensuality increased by Lucretius's own description of his state:

> it seems some unseen monster lays
> His vast and filthy hands upon my will,
> Wrenching it backward into his;

I do not think we can avoid the sense of struggle and the sense of loathing in the imagination of great hands 'wrenching' the sage from his contemplation. The beautiful clarity and order of the Lucretian world falls back into chaos at the touch of an 'animal vileness' over which wisdom has no control. Tennyson is not only concerned with the moral confusion of Lucretius as an individual. The poet's state of mind after drinking the potion is specifically related to civil disturbance. In dreaming Lucretius says he

> thought that all the blood by Sylla shed
> Came driving rainlike down again on earth,
> And where it dash'd the reddening meadow, sprang
> No dragon warriors from Cadmean teeth,
> For these I thought my dream would show to me,
> But girls, Hetairai, curious in their art,
> Hired animalisms, vile as those that made
> The mulberry-faced Dictator's orgies worse
> Than aught they fable of the quiet Gods.

The breaking of order in republican Rome is not then to be associated with military power (there are no 'dragon warriors from Cadmean teeth') but with corrupting orgies in which the cruelty of Sulla is shockingly allied with his lust. Later on in the poem Lucretius, on the point of suicide, remembers that his name is one with that of Lucretia,

> Whose death-blow struck the dateless doom of kings,
> When, brooking not the Tarquin in her veins,
> She made her blood in sight of Collatine
> And all his peers, flushing the guiltless air,

Spout from the maiden fountain in her heart.
And from it sprang the Commonwealth, which breaks
As I am breaking now!

Again there is an image of falling blood, again a reminder of lust, Lucretia and Sulla, the beginning and the end of the Roman Republic whose fall symbolises and is symbolised by the downfall of Lucretius. Chastity, the integrity which dies to preserve itself, and represents the control of man's reason over his bestial ancestry begins the City; animal vileness, the lust which disintegrates even the philosopher's calm, destroys it.

Lucretius, of course, was Tennyson's answer to the 'Fleshly School', intended first to show what a chaste-minded poet could do if he chose to handle 'fleshly' subjects, and secondly to show in its true colours the sensuality which Swinburne and Rossetti glorified. The poem is like *Ulysses* in that it uses a classical story to present Tennyson's apprehension of an immediate situation, but unlike it in that it is completely objective; the situation is outside the range of Tennyson's personal concerns. There is a note of detachment in his vision; the nightmares of Lucretius are set against an imagination of the life of the gods

> who haunt
> The lucid interspace of world and world,
> Where never creeps a cloud, or moves a wind,
> Nor ever falls the least white star of snow,
> Nor ever lowest roll of thunder moans,
> Nor sound of human sorrow mounts to mar
> Their sacred everlasting calm!

The same contrast appears in *Vastness*:

> Raving politics, never at rest—as this poor earth's pale history
>   runs,—
> What is it all but a trouble of ants in the gleam of a million
>   million of suns?

This sense of the unimportance of human confusion is not altogether pleasant. The glance of 'Astronomy and Geology, terrible Muses' shrivels, Tennyson says, the laurels of the poet, and it was astronomy and geology that, setting man against the vastness of time and space, desolated the Victorian imagination. But in the contemplation of vastness the poet sees time's tragedies in perspective. Those things that matter survive the catastrophes of nature as well as the catastrophes of history. This Tennyson felt even in *Locksley Hall Sixty Years After*:

Forward, let the stormy moment fly and mingle with the Past.
I that loathed, have come to love him. Love will conquer at the last.

This sense of a central stillness, of balance while the world rages and
passes, and civil order is threatened by moral corruption, is the theme
of Tennyson's later, more personal poems. It is also his remedy for the
evils of his time, the remedy which Lucretius missed.

This quietness of mind is clearly related to the experience we discussed
when dealing with *In Memoriam*:

What is all if we end but in being our own corpse-coffins at last,
Swallow'd in Vastness, lost in Silence, drown'd in the deeps of a
meaningless Past?

What but a murmur of gnats in the gloom, or a moment's anger
of bees in their hive?
Peace, let it be! for I loved him, and love him for ever: the dead
are not dead but alive.

The certainty of Tennyson's later years is less of 'a conversion experience' than that of *In Memoriam*, it is much more a bread-and-butter
affair nourishing the business of daily life, and it does not yield to
shifts of mood or fortune. In the long brooding on his past of which
Merlin and the Gleam is an example he had found an understanding of
his mystical intuitions and is able to present what he conceives to be the
reality of things, independently of his peculiar experience of it. The
Ancient Sage speaks plain without symbol or evocation:

The days and hours are ever glancing by,
And seem to flicker past thro' sun and shade,
Or short, or long, as Pleasure leads, or Pain;
But with the Nameless is nor Day nor Hour;
Tho' we, thin minds, who creep from thought to thought,
Break into 'Thens' and 'Whens' the Eternal Now:
This double seeming of the single world!—

In age the old man, Tennyson, or his proxy the Sage, confronts the
shape of reality behind the double consciousness to which he had always
been subject. The world of the senses passes, and passes away,

'What Power but the Years that make
And break the vase of clay,
And stir the sleeping earth, and wake
The bloom that fades away?'

Yet under all the fleeting things of time there is a permanence,

> Speak to Him thou for He hears, and Spirit with Spirit can meet—
> Closer is He than breathing, and nearer than hands and feet.

What the poet now concerns himself with is not the inexplicable co-existence of the mutable and the eternal, but their real relationship. A newer and a fuller knowledge of this seems to dawn on him in the *Idylls of the King*. Speaking of spiritual certainty in *In Memoriam* Tennyson says,

> I found Him not in world or sun,
>   Or eagle's wing, or insect's eye;

he relies on the interior witness to spiritual reality, the 'truths in manhood darkly joined', the heart which stands up and answers 'I have felt'. But King Arthur says:

> I found Him in the shining of the stars,
> I mark'd Him in the flowering of His fields,
> But in His ways with men I find Him not.
> I waged His wars, and now I pass and die.

For Arthur the very workings of the natural world are a witness to the reality of the supernatural, yet his faith continues even when the workings of creation appear to deny it. In *In Memoriam* Tennyson described two kinds of experience, an awareness of the fleeting, reasonless world, the

> ever-breaking shore
> That tumbled in the Godless deep.

and a communion with the dead and with God which cancelled out the hopelessness of his situation. There was doubt, and there was certainty, but the two were disparate, incompatible moods aligned to incompatible accounts of the universe. If the universe were as irrational as the death of Arthur Hallam made it seem, then there was no God, but if the mood of mystical experience could be taken as a guarantee, then there was a God, and a meaning in existence. But in the *Idylls of the King* the sense of bewilderment and confusion could and did coexist with an absolute conviction of the reality of divine things. Arthur has no doubt whatever about the being of God, but this does not cure his sense of the irrationality of the world; it aggravates it:

> Why is all around us here
> As if some lesser god had made the world,
> But had not force to shape it as he would,
> Till the High God behold it from beyond.

This attitude to faith is much more solid and serious. Reality is not sought only in a curious trance of consciousness, only, that is, in the solitude of the mind, but also in the outer world. In *Flower in the Crannied Wall* it is the mystery of material existence, not the mystery of self-conscious identity which leads Tennyson to consider the reason of things:

> I hold you here, root and all, in my hand,
> Little flower—but *if* I could understand
> What you are, root and all, and all in all,
> I should know what God and man is.

For if this attitude to faith is more solid and serious it is also subject to a harsher questioning. The tranquillity of mind which Tennyson attained was not by any means a facile ignorance of evil. *Flower in the Crannied Wall* ends with a movement towards curiosity, 'If I could understand', and the 'if' is here the expression of a suspended mind, the mind that is lost in the innocence of wonder. But other and less tolerable *ifs* troubled the old poet. There was indeed a certainty in his experience but it was a certainty which, like his own Arthur, he was bound to find in conflict with the facts of his world, and which he was forced to probe, not to settle his own doubts but to understand those which corrupted his age. The period of *Flower in the Crannied Wall* was the period in which Tennyson in common with the eminent of his generation belonged to the famous Metaphysical Society,[2] where it was possible to hear Manning matched with Huxley, and where Tennyson would have every opportunity of hearing the arguments of a newer and more materialistic unbelief than that which troubled his own youth. *Vastness, The Higher Pantheism, The Voice and the Peak* and *The Ancient Sage* were his answers to the ponderous sceptics of that society, and to the scientific scepticism which they promoted. Just as in *Lucretius* he attempted a moral counterblast to the materialist, so in this group of religious poems he attempts to deploy his own experience to meet and to counter the metaphysical arguments of the sceptic.

The purpose of these poems is not to express his own pure wonder in the contemplation of reality, though their mood suggests it. The experience Tennyson describes is not to stand for itself, and it follows that it is no longer sufficient for Tennyson to state his feeling as he does in *In Memoriam*; he must understand and explain it. He refuses, for instance, to identify the reality which he seeks and feels with the being of the outer world:

> Earth, these solid stars, this weight of body and limb,
>   Are they not sign and symbol of thy division from Him?

On the other hand he came to believe that the existence of the created world is rooted in the existence of God who is

> The Abysm of all Abysms, beneath, within
> The blue of sky and sea, the green of earth,
> And in the million-millionth of a grain . . .

We become aware of the presence of God through and in the natural world, but the natural world cannot satisfy, or express, or fulfil the plenitude of His being. All the time the poet is obscurely conscious of

> A deep below the deep,
>   And a height beyond the height!
> Our hearing is not hearing,
>   And our seeing is not sight.

This is a view of the relationship between God and the Creation which Tennyson might have found in a number of writers, in St Augustine for instance. But he is sublimely unaware that he is taking up a classical position. The odd thing is that he presents both in *The Higher Pantheism* and in *The Ancient Sage* a theory about the indwelling of God in creation which was not implicit in the mystical experiences which he describes in *In Memoriam* and elsewhere. Nowhere does he describe himself as aware of the immanence of God, and he does not, like Wordsworth, contemplate the intense reality of nature until, drawn into it, he sees 'into the life of things'. On the contrary he describes himself as reaching the reality of God by leaving behind all earthly things; indeed the Ancient Sage describes himself as finding a communion with the infinite through a self-induced loss of identity:

> More than once when I
> Sat all alone, revolving in myself
> The word that is the symbol of myself,
> The mortal limit of the Self was loosed,
> And passed into the Nameless, as a cloud
> Melts into Heaven. I touch'd my limbs, the limbs

Were strange, not mine—and yet no shade of doubt,
But utter clearness, and thro' loss of Self
The gain of such large life as match'd with ours
Were Sun to spark—

This of course is a statement of experience; Tennyson used to tell his friends that by repeating his own name he could induce a state of trance like that described here, and there are descriptions of a mental state not dissimilar to this in his juvenilia.[3] The experience is not incompatible with the Sage's assertions about the Eternal Now which underlies the fleeting forms of time. But the idea of a Being sustaining the being of the outer world is not necessarily contained in the experience of inward trance. That so much of Tennyson's later poetry connects the two suggests, at least, that he was seeking to supply a theology which would validate or at least explain his personal experience.

Tennyson himself had not a theological or a philosophical mind. Though much revered by the Apostles and later by the Metaphysical Society he was really without that power of rational analysis which they so admired. But it is safe to say that he had an enormous capacity for receiving ideas, especially those which were in line with his experience, and, as it were, brooding them into life and shape. The ideas expressed in these religious poems can, I think, be traced to F. D. Maurice, who was not given to sharp analysis, but whose approach to Christianity supplies a link between direct religious experience of the kind Tennyson describes, and the explanation of the world which Tennyson thinks compatible with this experience. Maurice, who was Tennyson's friend, and in some respects his spiritual guide, had a new approach to Christianity, an apologetic peculiarly calculated to irritate both Christians and non-Christians, for he believed that all religions and nearly all philosophies were, viewed in a proper light, no more than a witness to the revelation of God implanted in, indeed integral to, the soul of man. Jews, Muslims, Pagans, Quakers and Deists may all be regarded as cryptotrinitarians, for their faiths, properly considered, display some part of the truth of Christianity, and, if followed to their logical conclusions, must bring the believer to the full possession of the Catholic faith. The arguments by which, in *The Kingdom of Christ* and *The Religions of the World*, Maurice unravels the threads which bind all sects into the true Church are very ingenious, and sometimes convincing. The root of his conviction is a belief about the nature of

man: all men, he held, are by the very fact of existence rooted in the
Word of God; they derive their being from their union with the
Second Person of the Trinity, in His capacity as the Word of Creation,
and in Christ they are united with His Father. It is this fundamental
union with Christ, not the processes of reason, which brings a man to
the possession of the truth. But Maurice had better speak for himself.
One of his *Theological Essays* is devoted to 'the sense of righteousness in
man', that is, to that conviction of integrity which Job claimed before
the Lord, and which, Maurice says, most men feel in themselves. We
should accept he declares,

> That Christ is in every man, the source of all light that ever
> visits him, the root of all the righteous thoughts and acts that
> he is ever able to conceive or do.[4]

And this is the explanation of that inward righteousness:

> We apply the principle to those facts, when we say boldly to
> the man who declares that he has a righteousness which no one
> shall remove from him—'That is true. You have such a right-
> eousness. It is deeper than all the iniquity which is in you. It lies
> at the very ground of your existence. And this righteousness
> dwells not merely in a law which is condemning you, it dwells
> in a Person in whom you may trust. The righteous Lord of man
> is with you, not in some heaven to which you must ascend
> that you may bring Him down, in some Hell to which you
> must dive that you may raise Him up, but nigh you, at your
> heart.
> The principle is expressed again when we say, 'You maintain
> that the pain you are suffering is not good but ill—a sign of
> wrong and disorder. You say it is a bondage from which you
> must seek deliverance . . . .'
>   Even so. Hold fast that conviction. Let no man, divine or
> layman, rob you of it. Pain is a sign and witness of disorder,
> the consequence of disorder. It is mockery to say otherwise.
> You describe it rightly; it is a bondage, the sign that a tyrant
> has in some way intruded himself into this earth of ours. But
> you are permitted to suffer the consequence of that intrusion,
> just that you may attain to the knowledge of another fact—
> that there is a Redeemer, that He lives, that He is the stronger.
> The righteous King of your heart whom you have felt to be so
> near you, *so one with you, that you could hardly help identifying
> Him with yourself,* even while you confessed that you were so
> evil, He is the Redeemer as well as the Lord of you and of man.

Believe that He is so. Ask to understand the way in which He has proved Himself so. *You will find that God, not we, has been teaching you of Him*, that He has been talking with you in the whirlwind, while we were darkening counsel by words without knowledge.[5]

This is very near of course to Tennyson:

Speak to Him thou for He hears, and Spirit with Spirit can meet—
Closer is He than breathing, and nearer than hands and feet.

But Maurice's language is so rhetorical, so much more the dramatic language of appeal than that of sober analysis, that it is perhaps difficult to take this as a statement of what he really believed rather than as a metaphor, rather like Tennyson's own metaphors. Still, this conviction of an inner righteousness possessed because the soul of man is rooted in 'a Person not a law' is perfectly sober. Maurice regards this inner witness as the answer, for instance, to the rationalism of Strauss's *Das Leben Jesu*. Man's own nature proclaims his need for, and his co-inherence with his Redeemer:

. . . It becomes a necessity—not of my traditional faith, or of my fears, but—of my inmost spirit, that I should find some One whom I did not create, some One who is not subject to my accidents and changes, some One in whom I may rest for life and death. Who is this? What name have you for Him? I say it is the Christ, whose name I was taught to pronounce in my childhood; the Righteous one, the Redeemer in whom Job, and David, and the Prophets trusted, *the ground of all that is true*, in you, and me, and every man; . . . the Light that lighteth every man who cometh into the world. Apart from Him, I feel that there dwells in me no good thing; but I am sure that I am not apart from Him, nor are you, nor is any man.[6]

All this finds echoes in Tennyson, early, in *In Memoriam*:

If e'er when faith had fall'n asleep,
  I heard a voice, 'believe no more'
  And heard an ever-breaking shore
That tumbled in the Godless deep;

A warmth within the breast would melt
  The freezing reason's colder part,
  And like a man in wrath the heart,
Stood up and answer'd, 'I have felt.'

No, like a child in doubt and fear:
But that blind clamour made me wise;
Then was I as a child that cries,
But, crying, knows his father near;

And what I am beheld again
What is, and no man understands;
And out of darkness came the hands
That reach thro' nature, moulding men.

There is indeed reason to suppose that this and other parts of *In Memoriam* display those influences by which Maurice drew Tennyson, in the latter half of the forties, nearer to orthodox Christianity. But the Maurician doctrine is much clearer in the later poems. In *The Ancient Sage* for instance:

If thou would'st hear the Nameless, and wilt dive
Into the Temple-cave of thine own self,
There, brooding by the central altar, thou
May'st haply learn the Nameless hath a voice,
By which thou wilt abide, if thou be wise,
As if thou knewest, tho' thou canst not know.

It is worth remarking that the Ancient Sage, like Maurice, is here attempting to counter the agnosticism of his companion by appealing to an inner witness.

Like Maurice, Tennyson contrasts the knowledge which comes from human reasoning and is like 'the swallow on the lake',

That sees and stirs the surface-shadow there
But never yet hath dipt into the abysm,

with the communion with reality inherent in human consciousness. To know the real, they believed, was of the nature of man. For Maurice, 'the Real' included the facts of Christianity. In this he is Coleridgean. In a moment of expansion Coleridge had said that he would have been a Christian before the birth of Christ, and by this he meant that the truth of Christian theism is inherent, and discernible, in the very nature of the universe and of man. This is Maurice's position, and Maurice owed much to Coleridge. But Maurice also believed that the truths which men feel to exist, and after which they struggle, are declared to them in the life and death of Christ, and announced in Holy Scripture. The historical revelation completes and makes plain the natural revelation. Maurice's approach to religion is, for all his metaphysics, fundamentally that of a biblical Christian, and it is also fundamentally historical. God had chosen one nation in which to announce Himself and His Salvation, and this pattern is repeated and modified in the histories of the several nations through whose growth and history God shows forth and fulfils His divine purpose.[7]

This approach to religion was likely to be congenial to Tennyson, for it combines his own sense of design in history, of movement towards the 'one divine event to which the whole creation moves', and an explanation of those mystical intuitions of reality which disturbed and established his conscience. Indeed it is sometimes difficult to see where Tennyson's thinking runs parallel to Maurice's, and where it is derived from it. He had been associated with Maurice in his Cambridge days; he was a member of Maurice's congregation in the Temple in 1847 and 1848. On the other hand, Maurice, in dedicating his major and most controversial work, *Theological Essays*, to Tennyson in 1853 acknowledges a debt to him and demonstrates it by illustrating his argument from *In Memoriam*. In a sense the two men complemented each other. For Maurice, though he had a subtlety of mind, and an imaginative sympathy with the Coleridgean tradition which Tennyson himself lacked, wanted Tennyson's gift of a direct experience of reality. Tennyson had reason to be grateful to him not for the conviction that there was something 'far more deeply interfused' in the fabric of the universe, but for a doctrine which validated his own experience:

> And mine in his was wound, and whirl'd
> About empyreal heights of thought,
> And came on that which is, and caught
> The deep pulsations of the world.

Maurice is arguing that this kind of experience belongs to the nature of things; that there is something in the consciousness of man which brings him into the orbit of 'that which is'. He can experience reality because there is a direct relationship between the human mind and its divine original, and this experience is the witness of truth:

> like a man in wrath the heart
> Stood up and answer'd 'I have felt'.

If this doctrine of Maurice's validates Tennyson's experience, it also explains it, and in explaining it shifts the centre of attention from the individual's consciousness of reality to the nature of the cosmos. Maurice has a theology, not a mere psychology. He argues that the

Logos, the Divine Word, underlies all material existence, but that as Incarnate Godhead, it is united in a special way with the nature of man. It is because of the union of the human and the divine in Christ that men are capable of the intuitions of the real which Tennyson describes. What Maurice asserts in a confused, shifting and never quite definite manner, is that Divine Being, the Eternal and Immutable, underlies and sustains the phenomenal and the transient.

Maurice's doctrines were viewed with suspicion in his own time. His Professorship at King's College was taken away from him because he was said not to believe in the eternal punishment of the damned.[8] What the controversy really turned on was the definition of the word eternity. Maurice refused to think of eternity as everlasting time. Eternity he said was a mode of God's existence, not an infinite succession of moments, but a state of being unconditioned by the limits of time.[9] God does not live from moment to moment as we do, He simply is. To Him, all times, places, and persons are simultaneously present, and when the Christian is promised eternal life what the promise means is not that he will go on living through aeons of time, but that he will be made able by his relationship with God to share this quality of the divine life. It follows that Hell cannot in its own nature be eternal, for eternity is a quality belonging to Godhead. But it is the principle, not the precise theological issue which concerns us here. For this is Tennyson's contrast; a contrast between the 'thens and whens' of time and the 'Eternal Now'. Maurice goes further. The Incarnation of God in Christ has, he says, made this state of eternal life present in every man, and every man who will can lay hold of it, even though the succession of time to which men are subject in this world obscures the eternal present.

This doctrine, though it offended bishops, would serve Tennyson as a bond between the occasional awareness of That which Is and which is outside time, and the opposite experience, his continuing consciousness of the flux of things. It is not only consonant with his experience: it mitigates the contradictions in it. But by the time Tennyson came to write *The Ancient Sage* which is his fullest expression of this view of the world, he was no longer concerned with his own moods of doubt. Doubt is expressed in the poem by a second figure: the principal voice speaks peace and security. The companion to whom the Sage expounds his doctrine represents the doubts and despairs of the age, materialist hedonism combined with a weary agnosticism, and his tone is quite different from that of the Tennyson of *Supposed Confessions*, and *The Two Voices*. It is the tone of the young men of the seventies and eighties.

It reflects both the tough-minded agnosticism of Huxley, Tyndall, and
the Metaphysical Society and the corruption of the imagination, that
mal de siècle, which the uncertainty of the period bred in its young men.
The disciple does not believe in anything but the material world:

> 'How far thro' all the bloom and brake
>   That nightingale is heard!
> What power but the bird's could make
>   This music in the bird?'

but his unbelief does not release him from anxiety. On the contrary he
is imprisoned by the transient: the world is darkened by its own
purposelessness. There is an everlasting succession of change; there is
grief and there is joy, but even these pass:

> 'But vain the tears for darken'd years
>   As laughter over wine,
> And vain the laughter as the tears,
>   O brother, mine or thine,
>
> For all that laugh, and all that weep
>   And all that breathe are one
> Slight ripple on the boundless deep
>   That moves, and all is gone.'

This mood of the disciple's is a combination of scientific scepticism and
fin de siècle gloom but it is also coloured by the intolerable sense of a
widening impersonal universe which Tennyson expresses in *Vastness*
and *Parnassus*. In a sense the growth of scientific knowledge in the
Victorian era did not so much alter the ideas or doctrines of men; it
revolutionised their imagination of the world. Men came to see
themselves as too little, too unimportant, to be of value in the great
expanse of things.

If we think of the companion's attitudes as lying within the sphere
of metaphysics, then the Ancient Sage's reply to him appears as a
refusal to face the point at issue:

> nothing worthy proving can be proven,
> Nor yet disproven: wherefore be thou wise,
> Cleave ever to the sunnier side of doubt,
> And cling to Faith beyond the forms of Faith!

But it is the disease of the agnostic imagination, not the confident
assertions of intellectual scepticism which Tennyson is combating. The

Ancient Sage attempts to alter his companion's vision of things; he
puts before him a picture of reality different from and opposed to the
bleak scientific diagrams which at that period were replacing the religious account of the universe. Science concerns itself only with material
phenomena, with what passes away:

> Knowledge is a swallow on the lake
> That sees and stirs the surface-shadow there
> And never yet hath dipt into the abysm.

It cannot and it does not touch on the permanent reality which underlies
the changing world, and which Tennyson evokes in *The Voice and the
Peak*:

> Not raised for ever and ever,
>   But when their cycle is o'er,
> The valley, the voice, the peak, the star
>   Pass, and are found no more.
>
> The Peak is high and flush'd
>   At his highest with sunrise fire;
> The Peak is high, and the stars are high,
>   And the thought of a man is higher.
>
> A deep below the deep,
>   And a height beyond the height!
> Our hearing is not hearing,
>   And our seeing is not sight.

How strongly this sense of a deep below the deep had touched and held
Tennyson's own imagination can be reckoned by his constant return to
the image of a boundless sea, or of deep water disturbed by transient
ripples and afterwards returning to rest and repose. More than any
other poet Tennyson responds to the wonder of the immeasurable:
astronomical distances, aeons of time, the visible but unmeasured
height of the peak and the stars, the unfathomed quietness of seas and
lakes, all of these impress on him the mysteriousness of the world,
mysteriousness which consists perhaps of a quality apprehended at the
heart of creatures, which he transfers to the more obviously transient
of things—for instance to the flower in the crannied wall. It is this
imagination of creation as holding at its heart a central quietness and
power which for him holds back the floodwaters of doubt, and which
he tries to communicate to the young men of his period. He explains

it in the terms we have already discussed; this mysteriousness arises from the Nameless Power who sustains the world in being:

> And if the Nameless should withdraw from all
> Thy frailty counts most real, all thy world
> Might vanish like thy shadow in the dark.

The companion complains indeed that the material world, though beautiful, is nothing but itself: the Nameless does not discover himself to the watcher. The Sage's answer to this sad aestheticism is significant:

> If thou would'st hear the Nameless, and wilt dive
> Into the Temple-cave of thine own self,
> There, brooding by the central altar, thou
> May'st haply learn the Nameless hath a voice,

He asserts in fact that the divine existence which sustains the world comes to be known at the centre of each individual consciousness. This assertion is certainly consonant with Maurice's belief that the Divine Word is inherent in the nature of man, and it reflects too the assertions of a number of mystical writers of whom Tennyson had probably never heard. This way of stating his experience brings together Tennyson's apprehension of the mysteriousness of the world with his realisation of the mysteriousness of the self. That mystery which the Ancient Sage perceives in the wonder of creation he seeks in his own being, and by contemplating the mysteriousness of his own identity breaks away from the limits of finite being.

Although all this is a matter of personal experience, not of philosophical theory, the *Ancient Sage* is not a personal poem: it is an attempt to put a case, to counter the arguments of the materialist unbeliever. The poet asserts not merely that he himself has felt the presence of God, but that a true imagination of reality cannot fail to perceive this presence in the visible universe and in the heart of man. He puts this case for moral and social rather than for doctrinal reasons. He believed rather naively, that free-thinking led inevitably to immorality of the grossest kind. In *The Promise of May*, Tennyson's only modern play, the hero's free-thinking leads him to the selfish seduction and betrayal of a young girl. The companion in *The Ancient Sage* is of the same moral type as this hero; he is ravaged in mind and body by a despairing debauchery. The Sage sets the doctrine of the Nameless before him as an incentive to moral and social virtue:

Let be thy wail and help thy fellow men,
And make thy gold thy vassal not thy king,
And fling free alms into the beggar's bowl,
And send the day into the darken'd heart;
Nor list for guerdon in the voice of men,
A dying echo from a falling wall;
Nor care—for Hunger hath the Evil Eye—
To vex the noon with fiery gems, or fold
Thy presence in the silk of sumptuous looms;

Why should the companion do all this? Because then,

thou may'st—beyond
A hundred ever-rising mountain lines,
And past the range of Night and Shadow—see
The high-heaven dawn of more than mortal day
Strike on the Mount of Vision!

Tennyson, in fact, offers his own personal vision as the reward of socially useful behaviour. There is no separation of the personal and the social here, but a close and incongruous marriage. Yet Tennyson is not necessarily mistaken in supposing that there is a natural affinity between moral conduct and the individual experience of God. His fatal error lies in his misunderstanding of the relationship between the spiritual and the moral, and his failure to comprehend it can be easily traced.

He knew, and knew from the beginning that whatever mysterious reality appeared to men through nature, or in their own consciousness, was seen as a thing infinitely desirable. This is clear as early as *Ulysses*:

Yet all experience is an arch wherethro'
Gleams that untravell'd world, whose margin fades
For ever and for ever when I move.

From somewhere beyond this world man is beckoned by some blessedness, some inexplicable longing which it is both anguish and joy to follow:

A whisper from his dawn of life? a breath
From some fair dawn beyond the doors of death
Far—far—away?

All life is an endeavour to follow and find this. But why is it, or should it be an endeavour? Tennyson identifies the object of this sweet desire with the Abysm below Abysms, but it cannot be reached except, as the Sage reaches it, by the dissolution of identity:

Dark is the world to thee: thyself art the reason why;
For is He not all but that which has power to feel 'I am I'?

Glory about thee, without thee; and thou fulfillest thy doom
Making Him broken gleams, and a stifled splendour and gloom.

Self is the barrier between the soul and its original, and underneath all
Tennyson's later poetry lies the doctrine which is expressed in his
persistent use of the image of the sea as the origin and end of life:

'Sun, rain, and sun! and where is he who knows?
From the great deep to the great deep he goes.'

The soul of man arises from the unknown deeps of divine being, and
returns at last to be reabsorbed as waterdrops by the great depth of the
ocean. The deep from which the soul comes is not, however, outside
time but within it:

Out of the deep, my child, out of the deep,
From that true world within the world we see,
Whereof our world is but the bounding shore—

The being of the individual is here and now related to the immanent
being of God, the Infinite One

Who made thee unconceivably Thyself
Out of His whole World-self and all in all—

It is the soul's individual being which keeps it from full communion
with the Divine Power, and its return to the World Self is conditioned
by that which defines its identity, its power of separate choice:

Live thou! and of the grain and husk, the grape
And ivyberry choose; and still depart
From death to death thro' life and life, and find
Nearer and ever nearer Him, who wrought
Not Matter, nor the finite-infinite,
But this main-miracle that thou are thou.

It is this sense of the return to God by means of endeavour in a mortal
identity which makes Tennyson's rather dreary moral exhortations
intelligible. He had already the perfect image for the yearning and
struggle of the soul after the divine presence which it already possessed
—the image of the voyager over dark seas which he had used consistently from his boyhood, and to which he returns in the last poems, in
The Voyage of Maeldune and *Merlin and the Gleam*. The sense of struggle

against the darkness of identity which at once reveals, and hides, the depth below depth of being discovered to the soul in mystical trance, is sufficiently expressed in the battle of the Mariners against the elements, while the sea itself is a potent and protean image for the mysteriousness of that being: nowhere more so than in Tennyson's most famous description of the soul's return to its beginnings:

> Sunset and evening star,
>   And one clear call for me!
> And may there be no moaning of the bar,
>   When I put out to sea,
>
> But such a tide as moving seems asleep,
>   Too full for sound or foam,
> When that which drew from out the boundless deep
>   Turns again home.

But this theme of the voyage over the sea, though not in itself moral, had always lent itself to moral exploitation. *Ulysses*, Tennyson said, expressed his need to go on more than anything in *In Memoriam*, although the *raison d'être* of *Ulysses* is clearly not endeavour but search:

> It may be we shall touch the Happy Isles,
> And see the great Achilles, whom we knew.

But in *Merlin and the Gleam*, in which Tennyson came to treat his own life under the figure of a pursuit of the 'gleam', the poem's emphasis is not on the yearning after the gleam, or what it symbolises, but on the overcoming of the difficulties of life:

> Once at the croak of a Raven who crost it,
> A barbarous people,
> Blind to the magic,
> And deaf to the melody,
> Snarl'd at and curs'd me.
> A demon vext me,
> The light retreated,
> The landskip darken'd,
> The melody deaden'd,
> The Master whisper'd,
> 'Follow the Gleam.'

The poem is, like *The Ancient Sage*, a work of moral exhortation. Merlin addresses the young Mariners and tries to induce them to follow his own ideal. In *The Voyage of Maeldune* the emphasis on conduct is still more marked. Maeldune and his mariners visit in their wanderings many islands each of which represents a particular temptation, and when they come to the end of their journey they find that the purpose which inspired it, the purpose of revenge, has disappeared from their hearts.

This is, of course, very proper but it is a very long way from that sense of overwhelming desire which colours 'Tears, idle tears' or 'Far, far away'. And it is less fruitful poetically. One of the troubles is that Tennyson has confused the pursuit of this desire with his notion of human progress towards

> That one far-off divine event,
> To which the whole creation moves;

another difficulty is that, because of this confusion of progress and desire, he comes to regard individual being as a barrier to the soul's communion with its original, and to identify individual being with physical being. What keeps man from God is his animal nature, and to return to God he needs to slough it off:

> Move upward, working out the beast
> And let the ape and tiger die.

He conceives of the soul and body of man as having different destinies. The position is clear in *By an Evolutionist*:

> The Lord let the house of a brute to the soul of a man,
> And the man said 'Am I your debtor?'
> And the Lord—'Not yet: but make it as clean as you can,
> And then I will let you a better.'

The suggestion is that the higher destiny of man is a reward for the control, even the suppression of his animal nature, and there is in the later Tennyson a very strong tendency to identify the physical, or the animal in man with moral corruption. Arthur's kingdom, because of the betrayal of Lancelot 'falls back into the beast, and is no more', Lucretius speaks of an 'animal vileness', and the potion which he drinks tickles 'the brute brain within the man's', while the apprehension of the Sage's disciple is warped by his debaucheries. This relegation of evil to material nature is a kind of Manichaeism which, while it is consistent with and indeed probably derives from his evolutionary theories, is thoroughly inconsistent with his immanentist theology. For it is the Divine Being which holds the material world in existence:

And if the Nameless should withdraw from all
   Thy frailty counts most real, all thy world
Might vanish like thy shadow in the dark.

It is besides at odds with his own apprehension and imagination of the
world:

O follow, leaping blood,
   The season's lure!
O heart, look down and up
   Serene, secure,
Warm as the crocus cup,
   Like snowdrops, pure!

Past, Future glimpse and fade
   Thro' some slight spell,
A gleam from yonder vale,
   Some far blue fell,
And sympathies, how frail,
   In sound and smell!

⋆   ⋆   ⋆

For now the Heavenly Power
   Makes all things new,
And thaws the cold, and fills
   The flower with dew;
The blackbirds have their wills,
   The poets too.

Where a poet's imagination and his doctrine are so far apart there must
somewhere be a failure in poetic power.

It is not, then, unreasonable to ascribe some of the weakness of
Tennyson's later work to this intellectual incoherence. Some of the
weakness is quite simply a matter of age. At seventy or eighty few poets
write with the vigour of youth, and none with its sensuous power. But
in one respect at least there is no failure of power. The old man's
imagination had grown into its vision of a central peace:

All night I heard the voice
   Rave over the rocky bar,
But thou wert silent in heaven,
   Above thee glided the star.

Hast thou no voice, O Peak,
   That standest high above all?
'I am the voice of the Peak,
   I roar and rave for I fall.'

A thousand voices go
   To North, South, East, and West;
They leave the heights and are troubled,
   And moan and sink to their rest.

The fields are fair beside them,
   The chestnut towers in his bloom;
But they—they feel the desire of the deep—
   Fall, and follow their doom.

The deep has power on the height,
   And the height has power on the deep;
They are raised for ever and ever,
   And sink again to sleep.'

Not raised for ever and ever,
   But when their cycle is o'er,
The valley, the voice, the peak, the star
   Pass and are found no more.

The Peak is high and flush'd
   At its highest with sunrise fire;
The Peak is high, and the stars are high,
   And the thought of a man is higher.

Though fretted by a generation so obstinate in following strange gods, Tennyson seemed to grow more and more into an unmoved quiet of mind. The very last poems are nearly all about the past, or about death, and some, the many written on the deaths of his friends, are about both. There is a quality in them, as in *The Roses on the Terrace*, or the elegiac verses on Edward Fitzgerald, which is totally alien to any modern imagination, for it includes not merely a quietness of mind about death, but also that extraordinary urbanity which all through Tennyson's life coloured and arose from his genius for friendship:

   The tolling of his funeral bell
      Broke on my Pagan Paradise,
   And mixt the dream of classic times,
      And all the phantoms of the dream,

> With present grief, and made the rhymes,
>   That miss'd his living welcome, seem
> Like would-be guests an hour too late,
>   Who down the highway moving on
> With easy laughter find the gate
>   Is bolted, and the master gone.
> Gone into darkness, that full light
>   Of friendship! past, in sleep, away
> By night, into the deeper night.
>   The deeper night? A clearer day
> Than our poor twilight dawn on earth—

This is not perhaps the Shakespearian calm, though like Shakespeare's it includes a sense of fruitful relationship, and of sacrifice to the gods of the hearth and the pasture, for, unlike Shakespeare's, it remembers no past guilt, and carries no sense of a redeemed and renewed life. The peculiarity indeed of Tennyson's life and poetry is, in spite of its conflicts, in spite of its concern with the moral, a curious innocence. Tennyson does not approach the tragic resolution because, although he knew the tragic disaster, he had never realised the tragic guilt. It is perhaps this that always we seem to miss in his poetry, perhaps this which in spite of his range and his skill makes him seem at times less than the really great.

Chapter IX

Evaluation

IN his essay on minor poetry Mr Eliot demonstrates how difficult it is to categorise poets, and how subtle are the considerations which must 'govern our estimate of their work.'[1] But in his judgment of Tennyson he recognises at least one entirely objective criterion by which we can determine a poet's status: it is the variety of Tennyson's achievement, he says, which makes him a great poet.[2] It is difficult to dissent from this: certainly Tennyson cannot be regarded as anything but a major poet. But greatness in poetry has its varieties and its degrees, and when we come to consider Tennyson's work something seems lacking in it, some element of vitality, or significance which we find and respond to in the works of other poets who are commonly called great. The reader of Tennyson, however much he admires or enjoys him, is left with a sense of a potentiality which remains in much, though not all, of his work, only half fulfilled. It is time now to consider this incompleteness in Tennyson's achievement.

The 'evaluation' of Tennyson's poetry is not, properly speaking, within the immediate scope of this kind of study, the function of which is historical rather than critical. But criticism of Tennyson has always moved within the context of a historical judgment, and is therefore liable to be modified by any change in our attitude to his period, or by any shift in our understanding of it. He wrote, it is said, in such a way because he lived in a society having particular assumptions and particular mores, and in so far as this is true of any poet in any period, it must be true of Tennyson who was not magically exempt from the common lot.

But condemnation of that society, of the Victorian frame of mind, is liable to be extended to any poet considered as typically Victorian. Moreover the critical problem in Tennyson's case is always seen as one involving in a special way the relationship of the poet and his contemporary audience: Tennyson is felt to have responded to the demands of that audience in a manner which compromised his private vision, and those demands, or what are supposed to be those demands, have always been a relevant factor in the criticism of his poetry. The normal judgment of Tennyson in the thirties and forties was based on assumptions, not about Tennyson himself, but about his audience, which were often demonstrably untrue. Victoria's reign was supposed to be a period of monumental complacency and moral stagnation; its capacity for self-congratulation, so it was said, was only equalled by its self-deception, and this corruption of the public mind spread itself into morals, into politics, into literature and art. This is the myth behind Lytton Strachey's *Eminent Victorians*, and it appears again in the nineteenth-century episodes in Virginia Woolf's *Orlando*. It is certainly the basis of Sir Harold Nicolson's *Tennyson*. The myth has two prominent archetypal figures, the Paterfamilias, and the Neurotic, the exceptional individual trembling like a leaf in the marmoreal corridors of the Victorian nightmare, gifted with a morbid insight, and, in the long run, either poisoned by his environment, or yielding to its shelter. Beddoes, Arnold, Tennyson, sometimes Newman or Browning, a curiously assorted set of creatures, are set apart from their age. No mention is made of those outwardly nonconformist figures, those agnostic giants, the Darwins, the Mills, the Sidgwicks, the Stephens, who were the creators of much of the new Victorian ethos. Nothing can be said about them, for their presence and their energy give the lie to the neat little model of the world in which Tennyson, for instance, stands as a kind of Victorian Lot's wife, for ever immobilised in gestures of despair or barren acquiescence.

Tennyson's generation was, in fact, at once more complex and more interesting in itself than the myths of its successors suggest. Outwardly the Victorian period presents a façade of solid community belief; inwardly it displays all the symptoms of a disintegrating culture. A disintegrating culture is not, though sometimes it is supposed to be, a declining culture. Things fall apart from age and wear, but sometimes also from the impact and pressure of internal and external forces, and the Victorian age shows both kinds of disintegration. It had its accepted forms, but the mere uniformity of codes of behaviour (agnostics were

as scrupulously upright and philanthropic as evangelicals) disguised and
aggravated a continuing shift of allegiances, a continuing growth of
new intellectual traditions, and the failure of old ones. Tennyson's own
circle of friends and acquaintances shows the situation in miniature.
The distance between the sober-minded, if not altogether orthodox
piety of F. D. Maurice, and the dilettante doubts and patriotic Protestantism of Edward Fitzgerald is very considerable. Besides these,
Tennyson included in his circle, amongst his newer friends, Clough,
Jowett, Patmore, Ward, and (on its outer edges) Henry Sidgwick.
These were the friends invited to stay, to suggest subjects to the Bard,
and to listen to new verses or old ones upstairs in the clouds of pipe-
smoke. They were his primary *audience*, and a more heterogeneous
group, or one less likely to drive Tennyson to the mouthing of false
attitudes cannot be imagined. For they shared nothing except an ill-
defined idealism, a sense that somewhere there were absolute values.
Clough does not seem even to have believed this, or not in the same
way, say, as Jowett did.

> So that I 'list not, hurrah for the glorious army of martyrs!
> *Sanguis martyrum semen Ecclesiae*; though it would seem this
> Church is indeed of the purely Invisible, Kingdom-come kind:
> Militant here on earth! Triumphant, of course, then elsewhere!
> Ah, good Heaven, but I would I were out far away from the
>   pother!

Clough and his family, a good solid middle-class Liverpool family,
illustrate almost perfectly the changing currents of the period. Everyone knows how Clough himself progressed from the solidly Protestant
piety of Arnold's Rugby to an astringent scepticism about the Rugby
doctrine of the Christian gentleman. He was in his time influenced
both by the Oxford Movement, and by the amiable modernism of
Jowett's Balliol, and he finally fell under the enchantment of that
strong and mystically minded personality Florence Nightingale whose
niece he married. He protected his sister Anne Jemima from the full
impact of his later scepticism; she found her shelter in Dr Arnold's
educational piety, and her vocation in the education of women. In
association with a group of Cambridge dons, whose massive integrity
made agnosticism *de rigueur* in 'the Establishment', she helped to found
one of the first women's colleges. The educational principles of Thomas
Arnold and those of Henry Sidgwick have very little in common:
Miss Clough combined them by holding prayers in the Principal's

room for the young ladies of Newnham.[3] Tennyson found both Clough and Sidgwick congenial minds, and Sidgwick's letter on *In Memoriam* is a classic of Victorian half-belief.[4] But he was equally at ease with the ultramontane, Ward, and with Coventry Patmore, whose Catholicism was so extreme as to be eccentric. It is impossible to imagine any other period in which the cultural breach between two educated persons of the same class and nation could be as wide as it was between Clough and Patmore, or Sidgwick and Ward, and the breach was not merely one of religious belief. It is painful to imagine Sidgwick's response to *The Angel in the House*, or Patmore's to *Amours de Voyage* for it would not be so much their beliefs as their sense of fitness which would be outraged.

The uneasiness of such times, the obstacles they place in the way of a poet cannot be too much emphasised. The sceptic of course comes off the worst. His dissatisfaction with traditional forms makes him unsettled and estranged from his fellows, and often he finds no peace in his scepticism: it is too new to be quite comfortable. Clough and Sidgwick are cases in point; Clough's dissatisfaction, like Arnold's, is well known, and if it did not, like Arnold's, wither his poetic talent, it twisted and soured its fruits. Sidgwick was not a poet, and he had the satisfaction of a steady purpose in life, but even he spent too much of his valuable energy trying to find valid evidences for the beliefs he had discarded. By contrast Patmore presents solidity and certainty. But the safety he achieved was purely personal: it touched none of the great Victorian problems; indeed he seems to make his religion a private world withdrawn from the great moral and social upheavals of his age. And his poetry suffers accordingly, for poetry is a common art.

It is because poetry is, fundamentally, a public, and not a private art that the absence of common traditions and forms of thought affects its development adversely. Matthew Arnold complained bitterly of the want of 'criticism' in his time: the want, that is, of a trained and sensitive tact brought to the judgment of literature, and the want, besides, of an accepted taste based on such a sensitive judgment. He wanted, in literature, a norm, a balance of feeling and judgment of a kind which, to his thinking, the French possessed and the English did not. But how was that norm, that balance of mind to which the trained taste would respond, to be established? Arnold himself complained that the Romantics wrote badly, by which he meant extravagantly, because everything was disintegrating around them; they were forced to create not only works of art, but also the criticism of art and ideas, the standards by which they could judge their own work; they could not rest in the accepted traditions and the common standards of a homogeneous culture. What was true of the Romantics was even truer of the Victorians. Every right-minded Victorian was engaged in making his own soul. He had to work hard at the highly individualistic task of absorbing the new science, the new philosophies, the new social conditions, and achieving, against the continued flux of things, an inward integrity. Every good Victorian was in one sense an eccentric: he was outside the central tradition because there was, in fact, no central tradition to be inside. Arnold pleads in vain for a central criticism, for authority; the tide of the times, and indeed his own preconceptions, made such a thing impossible.

Tennyson suffered more than anyone from this shift and flow of things. He was, as his glorification of the loyalty of Arthur's Knights shows, a man who would have responded eagerly to an acceptable authority. Yet he was open to every wind of the Victorian weather. He could not find an acceptable and authoritative tradition in which to shelter, and he found no comfort in outright scepticism. He suffered the difficulties in religion, and in intellectual and social development, which afflicted his generation, and he made an honest attempt to deal with matters of public moment, but like, everyone, else he could only offer private answers to public dilemmas. There was no commonly held principle to which he could direct the Victorian mind, and of which he could say 'This is the universal truth recognised by the wise of the ages', for the simple reason that he himself had qualms about the recognised principles to which many still clung. He could only offer his personal answer to difficulties. This means, of course, that he has certain advantages in writing poetry about doubt and weariness, about uncertainty, and difficulty, for these were common property; the Victorians shared emotions when they did not share ideas, and even so cold a poet as Arnold could create a masterpiece when, in *Dover Beach*, his personal distress coincided with the mood of his generation. Tennyson's poetical problems were most difficult when he wishes to present the principles in which he came to believe. For then there was no common ground, or very little, between him and his audience; he had to create such a ground, to explain, to define, to persuade, to recommend ideas, and to create symbols for them. Finally he had to impart to those symbols the imaginative power over an audience which normally comes from the mysteriousness of common associations.

The problem of expression perhaps arose from, and was certainly exacerbated in Victoria's day, by the almost complete absence of any accepted and vigorous poetic convention, and by the rapid development of the English language during this period. A comparison between, say, the descriptive passages of Mrs Radcliffe's novels and those of Ruskin's work, reveals that the formal logic which had controlled the syntax and movement of the eighteenth-century sentence has softened and melted before the fires of romantic sensibility; the structure of the sentence yields before the need to convey imaginative impressions rather than rational ideas. For Burke we have Carlyle, for Jane Austen, Meredith. And yet it was the syntax of the eighteenth century which was the support of the romantic, of Wordsworth's experiment with 'the language really used by men'. The idiom of his poetry really was the idiom of the prose of his period, a prose of statement, of abstract nouns and generalised adjectives:

> My seventeenth year was come;
> And, whether from this habit rooted now
> So deeply in my mind, or from excess `
> In the great social principle of life
> Coercing all things into sympathy,
> To unorganic natures were transferred
> My own enjoyments.

In his earliest attempts at poetry, before he struck out for himself, Wordsworth was assisted by the poetic conventions of his period, and the memory of those conventions persists in the careful and precise structure of his later work. It is possible, in studying his development and Coleridge's, to watch these pioneers remould and invigorate the spiritless traditions which they had inherited from the eighteenth century. From the *Ode to the Departing Year*, or *Descriptive Sketches*, to *Dejection: An Ode*, and the *Ode on the Intimations of Immortality* is a great distance, but it is a distance within recognisable stylistic limits. Even the famous 'conversational blank verse', the medium both of *Frost at Midnight* and *The Prelude*, has behind it the rhetorical structure of the Miltonic verse-paragraph, the use of which was discovered not by Wordsworth, but by Thomson and Cowper. What is true of Wordsworth and Coleridge is true of the younger generation, for like them, Byron, Shelley, and even Keats leaned heavily on the achievements of their immediate predecessors and their debt to Thomson (the Thomson not of *The Seasons*, but of *The Castle of*

Indolence), to Gray, and ultimately to Spenser, is as considerable and unrecognised as Wordsworth's to Milton and his eighteenth-century imitators. The conventions which they inherited were indeed enfeebled by long and insensitive use, they were debased and inhibiting, but they provided at least a minimum support, a foothold for the exploration of newer forms.

What is not realised is that when Tennyson began to write, the sources of his inspiration, his youthful models were exactly those which were available to the youthful Wordsworth. His mother read him Beattie; he read Thomson and Milton and Cowper. He read in fact what a boy of his generation would read, and had very much the literary background of a cultured character in Jane Austen. Modern writing, until he and his brothers went up to Cambridge, meant Byron and Sir Walter Scott. The Romantic style had not, in the twenties, established itself; where they were not ignored, Keats and Shelley were under violent attack, and even Wordsworth was not entirely regarded as of the poetic establishment. It was not until the late thirties and forties when Wordsworth was Poet Laureate and when, for instance, the death of Sir Timothy Shelley had made it possible for Mrs Shelley to publish her husband's authentic text, or later still, when Monckton Milnes published his *Life and Letters of John Keats*, that the reading public as a whole began to absorb the Romantic Mode. A few eccentrics, like Tennyson's Cambridge group, the youthful Browning, and the young Pre-Raphaelites, who found them in the penny trays of the booksellers, had read and enthused over the new poets. This has curious consequences. If Mr Eliot is right about the natural history of poetry, Tennyson and Browning should have been consolidators. Wordsworth had returned to the language of speech; the next generation of poets should have followed that new impetus by creating a new convention, a standard poetic convention based on Wordsworthian rhythm and language. Superficially it looks as if this is what happened. If we set *Michael* and *Morte d'Arthur* side by side, it is easy to remark a contrast between the language of daily life and the language of a conscious poet, and to see in Tennyson's work a withdrawal, both in subject and in medium, from the real world. But the matter is not as simple as this. Tennyson was undoubtedly influenced by Wordsworth, as indeed by other Romantic poets, but it is clear that he is not in the direct line of descent from him as, say, Pope was from Dryden. As we saw, the diction of his early poetry, with its insistent subordination of the rational sense to the total mood of the poem, and its sensitiveness to sound and movement was the instrument of a particular sensibility. Tennyson was not a follower, but himself as much a revolutionary as Wordsworth. He had to create, like him, a new poetic method for a new need, and like his, his diction was modified over sixty years of a varied experience.

The revolutionary nature of his poetry, of which he was not himself conscious, laid Tennyson open to certain dangers. There was nothing in the poetry of the period against which he could measure his achievement. When he was a young man, struggling for recognition, the critics saw the hope of the future in the tedious Shakespearean verse of Sir Henry Taylor; they admired Barry Cornwall, Miss Procter, Miss Elizabeth Barrett, and a whole tribe of album verse-makers less talented than these. There was no norm of judgment. The reviewers were not entirely unjust when they stigmatised Tennyson's first work as of 'the Cockney School'; for what they meant was that the young poet showed signs of a lush provincialism, a tendency to private whimsy, and the cultivation both of an eccentric sensibility and an eccentric use of language. And they were right: these faults reappear in various forms in a great deal of Tennyson's work; in the early poetry they appear as extravagance in feeling and diction. But the fault is not entirely Tennyson's. What the reviewers did not realise was that the tradition on which they based their own judgments, the Augustan tradition of the mean based on reason, was no longer available to younger poets. Sensibility had changed, the language was changing, the very forms of reason were no longer those which would be recognised by the poets of the great era. The new poet had to create his own discipline: to make and maintain his own tradition.

It is in the making of that tradition that some of the historical interest of Tennyson's work lies. Over nearly sixty years of a writing life he remains an experimentalist. He continually invents or modifies styles and techniques: not for the sake of technical achievement, though it is a factor in Tennyson's art that he enjoyed the actual manipulation of words and metres, but principally to articulate new ways of thinking and feeling, to turn a private intuition into a public philosophy. There is a central Tennysonian manner: in the blank verse of the *Idylls* Tennyson created a characteristic mode, a mode which influenced and dominated the style of minor poets both in his own generation and the next. But the central Tennysonian manner was not his only manner; the monumental marble of the *Idylls of the King* encloses only a part of his work, and even this is not entirely marmoreal. Much of the rest of his work is exploratory: the tone of his voice differs from period to period. Until *In Memoriam* the better part of his writing was lush and descriptive, consciously and deliberately poetic as in *The Gardener's Daughter*; it relied for its effects on sensuous associations, and is, within limits, the expression of a highly developed literary sensibility. The style of *In Memoriam* is nothing like so lush: it is poetry of a different kind from that of *The Palace of Art* or *The Lady of Shalott*. There is no enamel-work in it, it is reflective and argumentative, where it uses symbols it uses them in the context of analogical argument, and its choice of metaphor and analogy is more likely to lie in the range of the *gemütlich* than in that of the fantastic. There is another shift of style in the *Maud* volume, and still another in the group of poems discussed in the last chapter. These variations in manner, none of which necessarily precludes, or is uninfluenced by the others, were usually provoked by a variation in subject matter or, more importantly, in Tennyson's apprehension of it. The style of the first period, with its sensuous intensity and dream symbolism, reflected, as we saw, the mode in which the young Tennyson realised the world. This dream style, the drift and lull of sounds would be inappropriate both to the theme of *Maud* and to Tennyson's imagination of it. The combination of lyric and dramatic monologue, the easing of rhythms from formal song patterns to an almost conversational movement within those formal patterns gives *Maud* an aliveness, a reality which chimes with Tennyson's awareness of the individual in relationship with other men, but it does not smother his vivid expression of the private, exclusive consciousness of the estranged mind.

This continued creation and recreation of medium, the adaptation of style to vision, provides the background for a judgment of Tennyson's work. It forces us to regard him as a professional poet, that is, a poet who was interested in the techniques of poetry as well as in its content; professional in the sense in which Milton and Pope were professionals. And a judgment on technique is a valid judgment on his work. Auden's dictum that Tennyson had the finest ear of any English poet does not, I think, imply that there is something shameful about having a good ear, much less that Tennyson's metrical skill is mere virtuosity. It is one of Tennyson's achievements that he extended the range and the possibilities of English metrical systems, and poets can still learn a lot from his handling of sound and movement. But this does not mean that his technique was impeccable. On the contrary, the variety of his methods

made it more likely that he would misjudge the needs of his subject,
and the want of practice in a particular form led him into ineptitudes
just as it led Wordsworth into the clumsiness of the early Lyrical
Ballads. Wordsworth was clumsy, Tennyson over-musical or monotonous, and both show the faults of an unpractised hand. On the other
hand the freedom of continued experiment imparts that flexibility and
variety to his writing which Mr Eliot insists on as his peculiar merit.
It is these qualities which make the easy, the generalised judgment
dangerous. Not all Tennyson's early, moody poetry is good, not all
his later moral poetry is bad. The poetry of mood can fall into its characteristic excess, into cloying richness, or stifling but unconvincing
atmospherics:

> But sometimes in the falling day
>   An image seem'd to pass the door,
> To look into her eyes and say,
>   'But thou shalt be alone no more.'
> And flaming downward over all
>   From heat to heat the day decreased,
> And slowly rounded to the east
> The one black shadow from the wall.

It can degenerate into melodramatic trickery:

> I rose up in the silent night:
> I made my dagger sharp and bright.
>   The wind is raving in turret and tree.
> As half-asleep his breath he drew,
> Three times I stabb'd him thro' and thro'.
>   O the Earl was fair to see!

His moral poetry cannot be dismissed on the ground that it is not *his
genre*; still less on the facile assumption that all morality is ruinous to
art. There may indeed be no place in the visual arts or in music for
instruction, but there is a legitimate genre of instructive verse, to which
belong, for instance, the *Essay on Man*, the *Ode to Duty*, and Ulysses'
speech on Order in *Troilus and Cressida*. The judgment of Tennyson
turns, given the present assumptions about his art, on whether he does
or does not succeed in this genre.

It was of course in moral poetry that his difficulties were most acute,
and his handling of his technical problems least secure. For, by a
paradox, instructional poetry rarely instructs; it articulates the poet's
convictions, or his moral intuitions, within the framework of accepted

and often traditional doctrines. The poet can utilise familiar systems, they are a common ground between him and his reader. But no such traditional system of morality was available to Tennyson: he was not able to realise his own moral and spiritual intuitions in terms of the religious and ethical doctrines familiar in his own time. Where he had a common ground with his generation and shared a common knowledge with them, Tennyson's instructional verse was confident and clear, as we see, for instance, in the lectures and the arguments about women's rights in *The Princess*:

> This world was once a fluid haze of light,
> Till toward the centre set the starry tides,
> And eddied into suns, that wheeling cast
> The planets: then the monster, then the man;
> Tattoo'd or woaded, winter-clad in skins,
> Raw from the prime, and crushing down his mate;
> As yet we find in barbarous isles, and here
> Among the lowest . . . .

*   *   *

> Here might they learn whatever men were taught:
> Let them not fear: some said their heads were less:
> Some men's were small; not they the least of men;
> For often fineness compensated size;
> Besides the brain was like the hand, and grew
> With using; thence the man's, if more was more;
> He took advantage of his strength to be
> First in the field: some ages had been lost;
> But woman ripen'd earlier, and her life
> Was longer; and albeit their glorious names
> Were fewer, scatter'd stars, yet since in truth
> The highest is the measure of the man,
> And not the Kaffir, Hottentot, Malay,
> Nor those horn-handed breakers of the glebe,
> But Homer, Plato, Verulam; even so
> With woman: and in arts of government
> Elizabeth and others; arts of war
> The peasant Joan and others; arts of grace
> Sappho and others vied with any man.

Psyche's argument is supported by some of Tennyson's constant themes, an account according to the so-called 'nebular hypothesis' of the origin and development of the world, the idea of progress, and

the firm conviction that 'the highest is the measure of the man'. He
had already expressed these in the ringing tones of *Locksley Hall*:

> But I count the gray barbarian lower than the Christian child.

> I, to herd with narrow foreheads, vacant of our glorious gains,
> Like a beast with lower pleasures, like a beast with lower pains!

> Mated with a squalid savage—what to me were sun or clime?
> I the heir of all the ages, in the foremost files of time—

> I that rather held it better men should perish one by one,
> Than that earth should stand at gaze like Joshua's moon in Ajalon!

> Not in vain the distance beacons. Forward, forward let us range,
> Let the great world spin forever down the ringing grooves of
>   change.

> Thro' the shadow of the globe we sweep into the younger day:
> Better fifty years of Europe than a cycle of Cathay.

These views can be regarded as in some sense moral, for they are
certainly concerned with the place of man (and woman) in society, and
in the physical universe. They are not, of course, non-controversial:
the nebular hypothesis, for instance, was one of the earliest causes of the
standing controversy between religion and science. But the idea of
progress, of the world evolving from a cloud of light, and the brain of
man growing by use through the ages was familiar to the reading
public of the forties, so that it was not unreasonable to present the less
familiar topic of female equality and female rights in these terms. The
poetry is not perhaps great, but it is firm and pleasing. Where Tennyson's
moral attitude is in line with that of his contemporaries, he displays the
same quiet virtues:

> We might discuss the Northern sin
> Which made a selfish war begin;
>   Dispute the claims, arrange the chances;
> Emperor, Ottoman, which shall win:

> Or whether war's avenging rod
> Shall lash all Europe into blood;
>   Till you should turn to dearer matters,
> Dear to the man that is dear to God;

> How best to help the slender store,
> How mend the dwellings, of the poor;
> How gain in life, as life advances,
> Valour and charity more and more.

There is no need in such passages to enter into an elaborate explanation, or defence of valour and charity, though it does sometimes seem as if criticism of this kind of poetry arises from the dislike of the virtues which the Victorians took for granted.

Tennyson's major fault in exhortatory poetry is one of technique; he is inclined to over-ornamentation. Instructional verse, perhaps from the familiarity of the subject, or the need to persuade, perhaps simply from the fact that it belongs to the Augustan tradition, retains the convention of periphrasis. There is a legitimate use of this device, but Tennyson often misuses it, and elaborates his sentiments beyond their capacity.

> Pray for my soul. More things are wrought by prayer
> Than this world dreams of.

So far so good: even if the sentiment is unacceptable the expression is terse and plain; even the slightly conscious word 'wrought' is better for its purpose than its synonyms, done, made, created, worked. But the passage goes on:

> Wherefore, let thy voice
> Rise like a fountain for me night and day.
> For what are men better than sheep or goats
> That nourish a blind life within the brain,
> If, knowing God, they lift not hands of prayer
> Both for themselves and those who call them friend?
> For so the whole round earth is every way
> Bound by gold chains about the feet of God.

Something, certainly, is added to Arthur's statement by this, and there is a vividness in the presentation of animal sentience, the 'blind life within the brain', with its contrast between blindness and life, frustration and power, which quickens our awareness of the consciousness of man. But most of the passage is nothing but an elaboration of the first statement, a rococo superstructure on the original theme. The decorative gold-leaf of Tennyson's expression is thickest in the final image:

> The whole round earth is every way
> Bound by gold chains about the feet of God.

The whole passage evokes the visual memory, not of Victoriana but of elaborate seventeenth-century title pages, and the emblematic designs for masques. There is nothing of course essentially wrong with this kind of decorated art. The *Morte d'Arthur* was written in a consciously archaic and artificial style, and Arthur's speech represents a certain kind of rhetorical achievement. The elaboration, the vivid image serve to make the passage memorable, and to be remembered is one of the virtues of instructional verse. But sooner or later someone is sure to ask whether the gold chain really adds anything to our sense of the value and the necessity of prayer, whether it does not direct our attention away from the sentiment to the decoration. This stylised image breaks away from the main structure, and appears like the carved bits of baroque altars lying about antique shops and ateliers, a curio, an *objet d'art*, rather than a functional part of the argument. This tendency of Tennyson's art (he lends himself very much to the aphoristic quotation) does not matter so much in his earlier work. Later it was to be dangerous to him.

Successful didactic poetry is normally concerned with a subject matter which is both familiar to the audience and easily reducible to intellectual formulae. It is easy to translate sentiments about moral behaviour into poetry, into a certain kind of poetry: the achievement is rather rhetorical than poetic. The more difficult task is to translate direct moral experience into common terms. Oddly enough it is when Tennyson is concerned with his own experience, or with convictions realised through experience, that he is least secure in his handling of his material. Here we must distinguish; the record of his search for the moral meaning of great experience in *In Memoriam* presented difficulties in expression which are quite different from those which arose in his expression of the settled philosophy of *The Ancient Sage*. In *In Memoriam* Tennyson's discovery of moral and spiritual purpose is communicated to the reader as a shared experience, and in the long run perhaps this is the best way to express moral conviction. But Tennyson's own anger in *Locksley Hall Sixty Years After*, his personal spirituality in *The Ancient Sage* are recognised by the reader, not felt or shared. This failure to communicate has, like Tennyson's other failures, a technical cause. Technique must be understood here as something more than the mere manipulation of language and metre. The inarticulateness of Tennyson's later poetry arises from his want of a certain kind of intellectual skill, his inability to understand his own experience, to formulate it to himself before expressing it to others. One of the troubles lay in what is perhaps his major virtue as a poet; his intelligence was of an intuitive and synthesising kind, it was not analytical. Even supposing that it had been, the condition of the language in the Victorian period did not favour the composition of the precise intellectual poetry which both the subject and the purpose of *The Ancient Sage* and the other poems of this group demand. Swinburne made devastating fun of the verbal confusion of *The Higher Pantheism*:

> One, who is not, we see; but one, whom we see not, is;
> Surely, this is not that; but that is assuredly this.

> What, and wherefore, and whence: for under is over and under;
> If thunder could be without lightning, lightning could be
>   without thunder.

> Doubt is faith in the main, but faith, on the whole, is doubt;
> We cannot believe by proof; but could we believe without?

The parody makes a legitimate point. Swinburne did not however, realise that in *The Higher Pantheism* Tennyson was attempting an exactness of meaning of which the curious imprecision of Victorian writing had robbed the language. His subject stems from an experience of the real which is, or was believed to be, trans-sensuous, and which indeed appears inconsistent with the evidence of the senses. He did not try to describe what he felt although that would be comparatively easy. In *In Memoriam*, in passages of the *Idylls of the King*, and even in *The Ancient Sage* he had already achieved an adequate and revealing expression of the subjective aspects of religious experience, of what it feels like to enter into states of trance or exultation. In *The Higher Pantheism* and elsewhere he wished to objectify that experience, to present it as part of an interpretation of reality, an interpretation which the experience is believed to validate, and which carried certain consequences in the field of ethics. But it was precisely in matters of this kind that there was no common ground between Tennyson and his age. The Victorians were susceptible to 'uplift' and, beneath a sober front, highly imaginative; they responded to weirdness and to the preternatural with a kind of delicious spiritual titillation, shown in their fondness for the ghost story and the pseudo-mediaeval. But, perhaps because of this, they were deeply suspicious of the mystical. The kind of thing Tennyson described was beyond their normal experience, and, until the end of the century, not within the range of their normal theological and philosophical vocabulary. A comfortable middle-class and nationalist

Protestantism, a spikily rational scientific scepticism—neither of these could in the least accommodate the absorption of personality into 'his great World-self and all in all'. Tennyson seems to have been well aware of this. *The Higher Pantheism* and *The Ancient Sage* have the form of an argument, or a lesson; they are attempts to explain and define. As so often in such cases the explanation proceeds by negatives:

> And when thou sendest thy free soul thro' heaven,
> Nor understandest bound nor boundlessness,
> Thou seest the Nameless of the hundred names.

In these negatives Tennyson attempted to emphasise the trans-sensuous quality of religious experience and the non-material nature of the Nameless. Normal experience does not touch on these realms of being and therefore normal experience cannot comprehend or give warrant for them:

> Thou canst not prove the Nameless, O my son,

At the same time Tennyson wished to emphasise that the normal experience of the visible world is the channel through which we come to know the Nameless, and it is this position, perfectly familiar to older traditions, but not to the Victorians, which led him into tedious paradox.

All this may be philosophically sound, but for Tennyson it is poetically disastrous. For in the negative paradox of these poems he attempts to move from the imaginative and sensuous world into that of the conceptual, and he has not the equipment for it. There was no technical vocabulary for his doctrine: he had to invent it—as he does, for instance, in *De Profundis*. *De Profundis*, although much admired by Jowett, is an intolerably bad poem, but not because there is anything wrong with the sentiment; it is, after all, a strange thing to reflect that an hour, a week, a month ago, this particular infant was not. The evil is that Tennyson has confused the mysterious but undoubtedly material arrival of his elder son with the mysteriousness of immaterial being and brooded on it so long that both spiritual reality and actual birth have disappeared into a mist of mysteriousness:

> Out of the deep, my child, out of the deep,
> From that great deep, before our world begins,
> Whereon the Spirit of God moves as he will—
> Out of the deep, my child, out of the deep,
> From that true world within the world we see,

> Whereof our world is but the bounding shore—
> Out of the deep, Spirit, out of the deep,
> With this ninth moon, that sends the hidden sun
> Down yon dark sea, thou comest, darling boy.

It is very difficult, in this wilderness of seas, and shores, and moons, to hang on to the plain fact that Hallam Tennyson, like anyone else, was born of a woman's womb. But the fault in the passage is not only that Tennyson has, as it were, floated away from a physical reality, it is that he is out of touch with any reality. 'The great deep' in the *Idylls of the King* is indeed symbolic, but as a symbol its vividness is derived in part from its existence in a non-symbolic context. The deep here is the sea beyond Lyonnesse of the Arthurian tales, the real sea dashing against the Cornish rocks, and against the bleak Lincolnshire coast of Tennyson's boyhood. The mysteriousness which it symbolises is also felt in experience. But in *De Profundis* the word 'deep' suggests none of this, it has no lien on a concrete palpable world: what is more, it is not conceptual in significance, not the verbal sign for one of a class of deeps. It is simply a counter or label for an important element in Tennyson's system. He has named something or other 'the deep' and he repeats the word over and over again like an enchanter's spell in which it is vital that the words should be emptied of common meaning. It is as if he expected us to realise the significance of what he is saying by making a ritual of a word. Then, to make matters worse, he elaborates on the word *deep* in a way which adds something to his meaning, but which does not help us to apprehend anything about the deep which would justify its use as a symbol:

> Out of the deep, my child, out of the deep,
> From that true world within the world we see,
> Whereof our world is but the bounding shore.

Any attention to a real 'deep', lake, or sea, or deep hole in the earth, makes nonsense of this sentence. The word has in fact been stretched and stretched beyond its original content like the rubber of a balloon blown up almost to bursting point.

This inflation of language is the characteristic fault of Tennyson's later poetry. He acquired a whole vocabulary, a set of counters which for him stand for complex realities, but which for the reader have no value at all, words and phrases like *deep, Nameless, noble, forms of faith, Highest in the Highest,* and it seems as if he thought the mere repetition

of them would communicate his meaning. This habit of style is the
end product of the mannerism we have already discussed: the use of the
striking periphrasis, image, or aphorism, which is detachable from the
main body of the work, and which seems a kind of stucco decoration on
experience. To some extent periphrasis helps to convey Tennyson's
meaning:

> That which knows
> And is not known, but felt through what we feel
> Within ourselves is highest.

This is at least a means of defining an object of knowledge by its effects
on us. Even 'the Nameless of the hundred Names' has some value in
suggesting identity. But there comes a point in these poems when the
reader is aware that Tennyson is concerned more with the striking
phrases than with clarity: he has forgotten that language has a function.
What shall we understand by this, for instance?

> the pain
> Of this divisible-indivisible world
> Among the numerable-innumerable
> Sun, sun and sun, thro' finite-infinite space
> In finite-infinite Time—

The irony of this is that it has clearly begun as an attempt to translate
into poetry some of the difficult awareness of the depths of space, but
the striking paradox is too obviously enjoyed by the poet, he cannot
resist repeating the effect. The need to explain and define, combined
with the enjoyment of elaboration, has developed into a garrulousness
which defeats both enjoyment and understanding.

What is so odd about Tennyson's adoption of this oracular but
unenlightening manner is that he was capable of a kind of writing in
which the images used both have a power over the imagination and yet
are the means of carrying forward an argument. As we saw in earlier
chapters, he was experimenting with a half-analogical, half-impression-
istic imagery as early as *Isabel*, and some of the finest passages of *In
Memoriam* are the expressions both of mood and of reflection:

> Now dance the lights on lawn and lea,
>   The flocks are whiter down the vale,
>   And milkier every milky sail
> On winding stream or distant sea;

Where now the seamew pipes, or dives
  In yonder greening gleam, and fly
  The happy birds, that change their sky
To build and brood; that live their lives

From land to land; and in my breast
  Spring wakens too; and my regret
  Becomes an April violet,
And buds and blossoms like the rest.

Every detail of this passage belongs to the description of Spring and helps to create the mood of the season, but equally every detail helps to point the analogy between the state of the season and the new view of his experience in Tennyson's mind—the wider, brighter horizons, the birds that change their sky as he himself returns from the exile of continual grief, the rebirth of the April violet which is like the rebirth of hope in his mind. How far he could develop this analogical method of writing can be seen in *The Voice and the Peak*. In this poem the reader's attention is directed not so much to the qualities of a particular scene as to the familiar feelings of awe, to the sense of something beyond the world of sense, but glimpsed through it and in it, which for the Victorian was roused by mountain peaks, stars, and falling water:

The voice and the Peak
  Far over summit and lawn,
The lone glow and long roar
  Green-rushing from the rosy thrones of dawn!

All night have I heard the voice
  Rave over the rocky bar,
But thou wert silent in heaven,
  Above thee glided the star.

Tennyson is not so much concerned with the mountain as with a total experience, the mountain in the physical world, the sense of awe in the watcher. He strives to draw the two realities together by isolating and emphasising those elements of mountain scenery which lend themselves to associations of awe:

Thou wert silent in heaven,
  Above thee glided the star.

And by the use of a certain dissonance in vowel sounds, a dissonance which is not unpleasant in itself, he suggests the hollow noise of wind and falling water at a distance, sounds which excite a sense of the alien:

> The lone glow and long roar
>
> Rave over the rocky bar

As the poem develops it is clear that the Peak comes to stand for the total experience of reality, and finally the Peak and its voice for symbols of the relation between the permanent and the transient. Or to speak more accurately, Tennyson attempts to present his awareness of these relationships through the analogy of a known relationship, that of the Peak and the waterfall. The Peak, that is, stands for a conception in Tennyson's mind, and his argument is worked out by reference to it. But this concept is based on an interpretation of experience in which the mountain itself played a part. This lien on physical reality has a salutary effect on the poetry. The careful statement of emotional associations with which it opens establishes the Peak as a reality to which the imagination responds: it is not, like the deep of *De Profundis*, a magician's meaningless word. There is here a real sense of the 'finite-infinite', there is the Peak that 'standest high above all', from which the waters flow down with a thousand voices like the voices of time, the Peak which seems to be the very image of eternity: and there is the geological peak, which is no more permanent than anything else. Tennyson does not need to be explicit and impressively paradoxical about this relationship. The imagery establishes it for him:

> 'The deep has power on the height,
>   And the height has power on the deep;
> They are raised for ever and ever,
>   And sink again to sleep.'
>
> Not raised for ever and ever,
>   But when their cycle is o'er,
> The valley, the voice, the peak, the star
>   Pass, and are found no more.'

It is man's awareness of these physical things which gives them their mysterious power and their symbolic value:

> The Peak is high and flush'd
>   At his highest with sunrise fire;
> The Peak is high, and the stars are high,
>   And the thought of a man is higher.

In returning to the finite character of his symbol Tennyson completes his statement about the relationship between the permanent and the transient. Only the mind of man can comprehend and transcend the enormous division between infinity and the finite. His theme is much the same as it was in *De Profundis*, but it is a good deal more lucid when apprehended through the image of the mountain than in the earlier poem's conflict of abstractions.

The success of *The Voice and the Peak* illustrates the thesis of this chapter very well indeed. For in this poem Tennyson is able, for once, to use images from the common stock, images which were neither exclusively Victorian, like the subject pictures in *In Memoriam*, nor so intolerably hackneyed as to be emptied of meaning. Victorian sensibility had been trained to respond to mountains, to regard them as the proper objects of awe. If the age had read nothing else, it had read *Childe Harold* and Mrs Radcliffe; the more cultured of its members, at this late period, had also read Rousseau, Wordsworth, Coleridge and Shelley. Everyone made his private visits to the Alps, and stayed, like Walpole, Byron, Ruskin, and the whole family of the Dorrits, at the hospice of St Bernard. The educated Victorian was also familiar with, even if he disliked, the idea of a never-ceasing change in the universe:

> Not raised for ever and ever,
> > But when their cycle is o'er,
> The valley, the voice, the peak, the star
> > Pass, and are found no more.

Tennyson was lucky. His own sensibility was not normally responsive to mountains, but to flat wastes and seas, so that when his imagination was seized by the mountain he could write of it with freshness and confidence, yet, because of the familiarity of the image, he had no need to enter into tedious explanations, or to spend his energies on the recreation of private emotion.

But the vision of reality in *The Voice and the Peak* is Tennysonian rather than Victorian. Tennyson's awareness of the natural world as a fleeting dream, or as the symbol of the infinity from which it arises is equally alien to the sturdy Protestantism, and the sturdier materialism of his age. The coincidence of his insights with common symbols was accidental, and on the whole the Victorian public misunderstood him. This does not mean of course that Tennyson himself never had a belief in common with any of his fellows. The schizophrenia of

Victorian culture was not a simple matter of the artist contracting out
of the common life; the common life itself is riddled with contradictions. The Dorrit family visit the hospice of St Bernard in accordance
with fashion and make the appropriate gestures of tourist reverence, but
in reality neither monks nor mountain moved them or their creator. To
the Romantic living in the exclusive but homogeneous culture of
nascent European liberalism mountains were genuine powers,
symbols which overturned the imagination as 'with a might of waters'.
The Victorians had a convention of falling into appropriate attitudes
about mountains, but it was a convention which was unrelated to their
real pursuits and interests; it was a cultural frill. In the same way the
Pre-Raphaelites fell into attitudes about the ritual of a religion whose
creed and discipline they rejected. The angels of Burne-Jones are
emasculate not because Burne-Jones had never looked at the human
body (though that is true too) but because he did not believe in angels,
and certainly not in Principalities and Powers or Ministers of flaming
fire. In the same way when Tennyson speaks of cycles, in which he did
believe, he can rely on the education of his readers to supply the notion
of geological change, but he cannot rely, as a mediaeval poet could
when speaking of Fortune's Wheel, on his audience's possessing as a
part of their common mind a sense of the inevitability of the rise and
fall of things. Some would be debarred by the assumptions of Christian
eschatology from sharing Tennyson's meaning: Judgment Day does
not permit of cycles. Others, full of the sense of progress, would find no
room for a sense of the inevitable collapse. The fact is that the Victorian
mind was furnished not with common beliefs but with odds and ends,
the left-overs and experiments of incongruous systems. Its archetypal
figure is the character in *Alice* who could believe several impossible
things before breakfast, but most Victorians could do more, they could
confuse together mutually exclusive philosophies and religions.

During the Renascence this meeting of old and new ways of thinking
enriched poetry. Milton, for instance, was able to cast his Protestant
theology in a humanist mould, and none of us, in spite of Dr Johnson,
really objects to the conjunction of nymphs and apostles. But the
conjunction of Christian and pagan symbols in Victorian poetry is
another thing again. Milton could expect that the stronger Christian
culture of his audience would exclude some of the associations of pagan
names and symbols: to call Jehovah Jove is not, for example, to ascribe
some of Jove's more amorous exploits to the Lord of Hosts. But
Swinburne's poetry is based on the perfectly valid assumption that in

his period the two systems of association, pagan and Christian, lie open to each other; the mind does not fail to recognise, or recoil from the association of Venus and the Virgin Mary, Christ and Sappho; on the contrary it receives an extra titillation from them, the thrill of blasphemy unaccompanied by revulsion, which it was Swinburne's intention to evoke. He exploits, and very cleverly exploits, both the remaining strength of Victorian faith, and its growing weakness. He is of course an extreme example, but his age with a wonderful energy was busy arranging, just as he did, the marriage of all kinds of incongruities—Arnoldian headmasters in the fake Gothic architecture of the new public schools, Pre-Raphaelite ladies in drawing-rooms full of Japanese prints, mediaeval relics and collections of *objets d'art*, as in *The Princess* or the Great Exhibition, in settings full of the energies and the artefacts of the steam age. Having no central allegiance the Victorian had no sense of what to exclude—he had, in short, no taste. Swinburne presents us with the poetic apotheosis of bad taste, but for any other poet, for a more serious poet, the position was not less difficult for being largely unrealised.

We need not then attempt to explain or justify Tennyson's failures in terms of too close an alignment with a stodgy public, or again as the result of a fastidious withdrawal from the real problems of his age. The disintegration of a culture under the pressure both of intellectual and social change affected both Tennyson and his readers, and it robbed both of standards of judgment by which to measure their achievement. And yet the measure of Tennyson's importance is increased by the difficulties of his background. He did not succumb to temptation as Arnold and Swinburne, in their different ways, succumbed. Against the shift and instability of the period he built a central poetic tradition which served his successors as a support. Dr Leavis quite rightly shows that Yeats emancipated himself from the Tennysonian convention, but the fact remains that the convention was there for Yeats to use and develop until he was mature enough to discard it. It is after all only small poets who allow themselves to be imprisoned by the style and the sensibility of their predecessors, and Yeats was not a small poet. But even the great need support when they begin: the Tennysonian tradition supported not only Yeats but Eliot, whose poetry with its exploitation of associations, its cadences like a tired voice falling to silence, its movement from significant complexes of images to paradoxical balances of words and verbal definitions, is more Tennysonian than perhaps Eliot himself realises. It is the measure of a poet that he expands the possibilities of the language. That Tennyson did so while creating and maintaining a poetic tradition which the first mass audience in the world could accept, and in which it found comfort was in itself, a considerable achievement. That he did so in a cultural situation unpropitious to literature, suggests an unusual greatness.

List of Abbreviations Used

AT	Charles Tennyson: *Alfred Tennyson*, London, 1949.
CEPT	*Critical Essays on the Poetry of Tennyson*, ed. John Killham, London, 1960.
Memoir	Hallam Tennyson: *Alfred Lord Tennyson: A Memoir*, 2 vols., London, 1897.
STE	Charles Tennyson: *Six Tennyson Essays*, London, 1954.

E and S	English Association *Essays and Studies*.
MLN	*Modern Language Notes*.
PMLA	*Publications of the Modern Languages Association of America*.
PQ	*The Philological Quarterly*.
RES	*The Review of English Studies*.
UTQ	*University of Toronto Quarterly*.

NOTES AND REFERENCES

Unless otherwise stated the city of publication is London

Chapter I: The Status of Tennyson in Criticism

1. W. H. Auden: *Tennyson: An Introduction and a Selection*, 1946, p. x.
2. *Tennyson* (The Leslie Stephen Lecture), 1909.
3. H. D. Rawnsley: *Memories of the Tennysons*, Glasgow, 1900, p. 159.
4. 'The Dilemma of Tennyson', *CEPT*, p. 162.
5. Ibid. p. 156.
6. Ibid. p. 159.
7. W. H. Auden: op. cit. p. xv.
8. See G. Robert Stange: 'Tennyson's Garden of Art', *CEPT*, pp. 99-112.
9. See *Médaillons et Portraits:* 'Tennyson vu d'ici', also '*Mariana:* traduit de l'anglais de Tennyson'.
10. See, for example, John Heath Stubbs: *The Darkling Plain*, 1950.
11. In the earlier version of *Œnone* the conflict between Pallas Athene and Hera turns, explicitly, on the nature of power. Pallas does not offer moral advice but a power greater than the crude materialism of Hera's promise:

> Self-reverence, self-knowledge, self-control
> Are the three hinges of the gates of life,
> *And open into power, every way*
> Without horizon, bound or shadow or cloud.

The Early Poems of Alfred Lord Tennyson, ed. J. C. Collins, 1900, pp. 81-83.
12. See E. J. Chiasson: 'Tennyson's *Ulysses*—A Re-interpretation', *CEPT*, pp. 164-173.
13. See E. F. Shannon: 'The Critical Reception of Tennyson's *Maud*', *PMLA*, LXVIII, 1953.

Chapter II: Tennyson's Sensibility

1. The common ancestor of Alfred Tennyson and the Earl of Chatham was a sixteenth-century gentleman whose two sons, William and Thomas, both founded dynasties. Tennyson's great-grandfather, George Clayton, was the grandson of George and Lady Jane Pitt of Strathfieldsaye who were descended from William. Chatham was descended from Thomas. See *Memoir*, I, p. xxiv, and Sir Tresham Lever: *The House of Pitt*, 1947.
2. Op. cit. *The Nineteenth Century*, XXXIII, pp. 164-188.
3. Joan Evans: *Time and Chance*, 1943.
4. *Unpublished Early Poems*, ed. C. B. L. Tennyson, 1930, p. 12.

5. See *Memoir*, I, p. 320.
6. Sir James Knowles, op. cit.
7. 'On Sublimity', *Poems by Two Brothers* (facsimile edition), 1893.
8. *The Alien Vision of Victorian Poetry*, Princeton, 1952.
9. For Tennyson's early reading see T. R. Lounsbury's analysis of the quotations in *Poems by Two Brothers: The Life and Times of Tennyson*, 1915, pp. 47–53.
10. *The Devil and the Lady*, ed. C. B. L. Tennyson, 1930, p. 41.

Chapter III: 'Tennyson, we cannot live in Art'

1. The Society was founded in 1820 by a group of young men at St John's College. Members were elected to it and to qualify for election had to have more than ordinary talents as well as a distinct and original personality. F. D. Maurice joined it, and remodelled it, and under his influence it reached its peak during the period from 1824–30. It continued to exist right through the nineteenth and into the twentieth century and numbered most of the leading Cambridge men of that time. Accounts of it can be found in Mrs Brookfield's *The Cambridge Apostles*, 1906, Mrs Sidgwick's *Memoir* of her husband and Sir Roy Harrod's *Life of Lord Keynes*, 1951, as well as in the various accounts of Tennyson's Cambridge period.
2. F. D. Maurice was the son of a Unitarian Minister and he went up to Cambridge to read law. John Sterling introduced him to the Society in 1823 and he took it over. Maurice later went to Oxford where he took Holy Orders. His later history is the history of an unsettling but persistent influence, indeed persistent even today, on the theological and social thinking of the Anglican Church. With Ludlow and Charles Kingsley, he was one of the founders of the Christian Socialist movement.
3. John Sterling was the son of Edward Sterling, the original 'Thunderer' of *The Times* newspaper, and himself a journalist. He became a clergyman for a time but his faith appears to have been unstable. He had great enthusiasm, talent, and charm of personality but, because he was constantly ill with the consumption from which he died, he never fulfilled his promise. See Thomas Carlyle: *The Life of John Sterling*, 1893.
4. See *Memoir*, I, pp. 51–54. Carlyle, op. cit. Pt I, Chaps. ix and x.
5. Arthur Henry Hallam, the eldest son of the historian Henry Hallam, was a young man of great charm and brilliance, and a leader of his set both at Eton where he was a friend of Gladstone's, and at Cambridge where he went in 1828. His father set him to study law with a Mr Walters of Lincoln's Inn, when he came down from Cambridge, but it is clear from his juvenilia that his talents were literary and philosophical, not legal or political. His death in 1833 was held to be a blow to the hopes of his generation.
6. See T. R. Lounsbury: *The Life and Times of Tennyson*, 1915, pp. 151–152.
7. *Memoir*, I, p. 120. R. C. Trench was a High Churchman who became Archbishop of Dublin, and a member of the Committee which produced the Revised Version. He was also a distinguished philologist, and largely responsible for the pioneer work on the *Oxford English Dictionary*.
8. *Unpublished Early Poems*, ed. C. B. L. Tennyson, 1931.
9. *Œnone* (1832 version), *Early Poems*, ed. J. C. Collins, 1900, p. 82.
10. Ibid. p. 81.
11. *Unpublished Early Poems*, ed. cit. p. 45.
12. In 1830 Tennyson and Arthur Hallam travelled to the Pyrenees with messages for the Spanish Revolutionaries (*AT*, p. 95). The landscape both of *Œnone* and of *Mariana in the South* is described from Tennyson's memory of the scenery of this southern journey.

13. G. Robert Stange: 'Tennyson's Garden of Art', *CEPT*, pp. 99–112.
14. *Early Poems*, ed. J. C. Collins, 1900, p. 92.
15. Ibid. pp. 82–83.
16. *Memoir*, p. 118.
17. Ibid. p. 119.

Chapter IV: In Memoriam A. H. H.

1. *Memoir*, I, p. 109.
2. *AT*, p. 146.
3. These poems appear both in the Heath Commonplace Book and in the Trinity Notebooks (see Appendix A). In the Trinity Notebooks they appear side by side with poems on which Tennyson was working in the summer of 1833, before Hallam's death. *Morte d'Arthur* and *The Two Voices* (called *Thoughts of a Suicide*) are mentioned in a letter to Spedding which Hallam Tennyson dates in 1834 (*Memoir*, I, pp. 141–143). There is another letter to Kemble (ibid. p. 131) dated 1833 in which Tennyson asks for *Morte d'Arthur*, but here he may be enquiring for Malory.
4. This is from the short version of the poem in the Heath Commonplace Book. See M. J. Ellman, 'Tennyson's Revision of *In Memoriam*, Section 85', *MLN*, LXV, 1950.
5. The Commonplace Book also contains a version of *Tithonus* which was never published. Tennyson remodelled it in 1859, and the present version was published in the *Cornhill Magazine* for February 1859. See M. J. Donahue; 'Tennyson's *Hail Briton* and *Tithon* in the Heath Manuscript', *PMLA*, LXIV, 1949.
6. *Tennyson*, Second Edition, reprinted 1949, p. 125.
7. Ibid. p. 125.
8. Ibid. p. 126.
9. *AT*, p. 181.
10. 'In Memoriam', *CEPT*, p. 212.
11. *Enoch Arden and In Memoriam*, ed. Hallam Lord Tennyson (The Eversley Edition), 1909, pp. 203–204.
12. Ibid. p. 204.
13. Ibid. p. 204.
14. See n. 4. Hallam Tennyson mentions this poem as among the first written of the elegies (*Memoir*, I, 109).
15. Hallam Tennyson says the poem was written in Barmouth and includes among the letters to Emily Sellwood one from Barmouth which he dates in 1839. (*Memoir*, I, p. 173). Tennyson did not visit Barmouth again until 1857.
16. See R. H. Shepherd: 'The Genesis of Tennyson's *In Memoriam*', *Walford's Antiquarian Magazine*, 1887, p. 407. Shepherd describes the proof copy. I am unable to trace any copy of this trial edition in England.
17. See Bibliography.
18. *Memoir*, I, p. 107.
19. See Appendix.
20. *Memoir*, I, Chap. IX.
21. See Appendix.
22. See Appendix.
23. See Wilfred Ward: *Aubrey de Vere: A Memoir*, 1904.
24. See R. H. Shepherd, op. cit.
25. *Enoch Arden and In Memoriam*, ed. cit. p. 204.

26. Ibid. p. 187; Hallam Tennyson: *Materials for a Biography of Alfred Tennyson* (privately printed), p. 127; and *Memoir*, I, p. 109. These three accounts differ from one another and no one of them coincides with any of the MSS I have seen.
27. *Memoir*, I, p. 162.
28. See Appendix.
29. James Knowles: 'Aspects of Tennyson II. A Personal Reminiscence', *The Nineteenth Century*, XXIII, p. 182.
30. Karl Ernst Von Baer (1792–1876) was a pioneer in the study of the embryology of vertebrates. Certain lines both in the published and the unpublished versions of *The Two Voices* suggest that Tennyson was familiar with the idea that the embryo passes through certain stages:

> Before the little ducts began
> To feed thy bones with lime—

This kind of question can of course only be settled when we know more of Tennyson's reading.
31. See Charles Darwin: *Autobiography*, 1958.
32. *Memoir*, I, p. 44.
33. Sir Charles Lyell: *The Principles of Geology*, 1832, I, p. 292.
34. Ibid. I, p. 70. The quotation is from Hutton's *Theory of the Earth*, 1788, 1795.
35. Ibid. II, p. 163.
36. Ibid. II, p. 147.
37. Ibid. I, pp. 552–553.
38. See Dr John Brown: 'Arthur Henry Hallam', *Tennyson and His Friends*, ed. Hallam Tennyson, 1911, pp. 449–450 and 453–454. This essay incorporates Henry Hallam's memoir of his son. Arthur Hallam's translation of the *Vita Nuova* will be found in his *Writings*, ed. T. V. Motter, New York, 1953.
39. *Memoir*, I, p. 304.

Chapter V: Out of the Wood

1. See *Memoir*, I, Chap. IV. *AT*, Chaps. 15 and 16.
2. Joyce Green: 'Tennyson's development during the "Ten Year's Silence" ', *PMLA*, LXVI, 1951.
3. This appears in the Heath Commonplace Book. See Chap. IV, n. 5.
4. The setting of *The Princess* was Park House, near Maidstone, the family home of Edmund Lushington who married Tennyson's sister Cecilia.
5. Maurice had been concerned with the project for Queen's College since 1843. John Killham (*Tennyson and 'The Princess'*, 1958) discounts the theory that Tennyson's interest in female education was influenced by Maurice, and suggests that it arose from Apostolic discussion. But Maurice *was* an Apostle.
6. *Memoir*, I, p. 254.
7. Ibid, I, p. 239.

Chapter VI: The Laureate's Vocation

1. See E. F. Shannon: *Tennyson and the Reviewers*, Cambridge, Mass., 1952.
2. See Noel Annan: 'The Intellectual Aristocracy', *Studies in Social History*, ed. J. H. Plumb, 1955.
3. The recordings which Tennyson made, in his old age, of his readings of *The Charge of the Light Brigade*, and *Ode on the Death of the Duke of Wellington*, reveal, through the crackling, the strong Lincolnshire colouring of his voice.

His reading was obviously incantatory: the records, imperfect as they are, make us realise that the strength and fullness of his lines are scarcely conveyed by the standard 'poetry voice' of modern readers.

4. *AT*, p. 491.
5. See E. F. Shannon: 'The Critical Reception of Tennyson's *Maud*', *PMLA*, LXVIII, 1953.
6. '*Locksley Hall* and the Jubilee', *The Nineteenth Century*, XXI, p. 19.
7. One of the major difficulties in dealing with the relations between social and literary history is, bluntly, that the literary historian is hampered by an inevitable ignorance in adjudicating the claims of rival hypotheses in social history. Students of the literature of the nineteenth century tend to accept as axiomatic the view of the Industrial Revolution associated with the Hammonds. That associated with Ashton and Clapham is more optimistic, and is the view referred to in the text.
8. *AT*, p. 100.
9. "The lesson taught by American Secession joined with the strict balance-sheet methods of leading Victorian minds to check dreams of dominion over regions not easily accessible to British ships. '*No news would be received with greater pleasure*', wrote the Foreign Secretary from London at the end of 1865, '*than that Canada had declared herself independent or had annexed herself to the United States.*'" *The Cambridge History of the British Empire*, 1940, II, p. 548.
10. *Memoir*, II, p. 109.
11. See Charles Tennyson: 'Tennyson's Politics', *STE*.
12. Ibid. See also *AT*, Chap. 25.
13. *AT*, p. 480.
14. See n. 7.
15. See Humphrey House: *The Dickens World*, 1942, pp. 28–29.
16. *Past and Present*, Bk. IV, Chap. I.
17. *The French Revolution*, Vol. I, Bk. VII, Chap. IV.
18. *Theological Essays*, 1957, p. 37.
19. 'The Character of the Warrior', *Sermons on the Sabbath Day*, 1853, pp. 90–91.
20. In Tennyson's lifetime the study of comparative religion and of ancient religious systems became a science on its own, but in his youth the dominant work had the character of fantasy. See Jacob Bryant: *A New System or an Analysis of Ancient Mythology*, 1774–76, and G. S. Faber: *The Origins of Pagan Idolatry*, 1823. Arthur is identified with other heroes as the hero of a sun cult, and all, for some reason, are connected with the story of the Flood and of Noah. The lunatic speculations of the mythological theorists receive some attention in E. B. Hungerford's *The Shores of Darkness*.
21. *Sermons on the Sabbath Day*, ed. cit. pp. 17–18.

Chapter VII: The Laureate's Art

1. *AT*, p. 491.
2. *Memoir*, I, pp. 469–470.
3. See Mrs Cecil Woodham Smith: *The Reason Why*, 1953.
4. See *Memoir*, II, Chap. V.
5. See Chap. VI, n. 20. Both Bryant and Faber identify Arthur with tribal-hero gods who represent the deification of natural forces.
6. See Sir James Knowles: 'Tennyson's Arthurian Poems', *Tennyson and His Friends*, ed. Hallam Tennyson, 1911.
7. See E. D. H. Johnson: 'The Lily and the Rose: Symbolic Meaning in Tennyson's *Maud*', *PMLA*, LXIV, 1949.

Chapter VIII: The Ancient Sage

1. *AT*, p. 528.
2. Ibid., pp. 380–381.
3. See Chap. II.
4. *Theological Essays*, 1957, p. 60.
5. Ibid. pp. 61–62.
6. Ibid. p. 67.
7. This point of view is developed in *The Kingdom of Christ*, 1843, and in *The Religions of the World*, 1847.
8. See J. F. Maurice: *The Life of F. D. Maurice*, 1884.
9. See 'On Eternal Life and Eternal Death' and the 'Note on the Athanasian Creed', *Theological Essays*, ed. cit.

Chapter IX: Evaluation

1. 'What is Minor Poetry?' *On Poetry and Poets*, 1957.
2. 'In Memoriam', *Essays Ancient and Modern*.
3. See Blanche Athena Clough: *A Memoir of Anne Jemima Clough*, 1897.
4. *Memoir*, I, p. 304.

APPENDIX A

The Manuscripts of 'In Memoriam'

TENNYSON believed both that a poet's life should be studied in and through his works, and that the poet himself should have the final decision on the accepted, the canonical, version of those works. Variants were his affair, no one else's. These views caused him to arrange for a kind of posthumous control over his manuscripts. 'My Father', Hallam Tennyson writes in a letter to the Master of Trinity,

> 'owing to his hatred of the publication of his "various readings" (which he thought confused the final version of the texts) wished that *no* copy of it, or of any part of it should be taken and that nothing in it which has not been published should ever be published, and, subject to that condition, it is now given into your custody, and that of your successors in the Mastership, to be kept in perpetuity in the Library of Trinity College.'

'It' is the manuscript, or rather, *a* manuscript of *In Memoriam*, and the condition presents us with an increasingly irritating problem.

The Trinity manuscript is variously described by Hallam Tennyson, and by Lady Simeon, who once owned it, as 'the first jottings', 'the first drafts' of *In Memoriam* and as the papers left in Tennyson's lodgings in Hampstead in 1850. It was originally scraps of paper, or so Lady Simeon said. Sometime in 1859 or 1860 Tennyson was in the library at Swainston with Sir John Simeon and asked him to give him down a particular book from a shelf. As Sir John pulled it out as he pulled out from behind it,

> 'a little roll of what could hardly be called *papers* but scraps of paper, of all sizes and shapes, soiled and torn, which in falling were scattered about the floor. . . . They were covered with your father's writing, who laughed and said "I promised to give you a bit of manuscript one day—so now I have brought you this." As soon as possible they were taken to Bedford, the first book binder of that time. . . . By him the scraps were, with the utmost care, pains and difficulty, joined and pared and shaped and pasted into the long narrow book they are now in which was so beautifully bound and put in an outer case.'

It was arranged between the Tennysons and the Simeons that when Lady Simeon died this volume would be returned to Hallam Tennyson and that, because of his father's wish, he should pass it on to the Library of Trinity College, Cambridge. This manuscript presents any number of problems. Bedford was, certainly, a wonderful bookbinder but the condition of the manuscript now in Trinity College Library does not suggest that it was at any stage of its existence 'torn and soiled sheets' of all shapes and sizes. It is a long book in a leather binding, and consists of fifty-two leaves, some of which have been torn or cut. All the leaves are the same size and shape, and some have been left blank. It contains about seventy lyrics for *In Memoriam*, and a version of *On a Mourner*. One or two of the lyrics differ radically from the final version printed, and some were not printed with the poem. Once or twice the manuscript gives two versions of the same poem. The lyrics are numbered, but not in the sequence of the printed poem (for example, the present 23 is labelled 2 in the manuscript). The missing lyrics all belong to the first or the last sequences of the poem, and the manuscript does not contain versions either of the Epilogue or the Prologue, or what is more surprising of certain famous and crucial lyrics in the Somersby and last Christmas sequences, "By night we lingered on the lawn', 'Ring out wild bells', and 'It is the day when he was born". The whole manuscript is annotated in pencil, in a different hand, with guides to punctuation and queries about meaning and syntax. These notes were probably made by James Spedding.

One thing is absolutely certain about this manuscript. It is not the 'first jottings' of *In Memoriam*. Trinity College Library also possesses certain other manuscripts, mostly notebooks which Tennyson was using in the mid-thirties. There are four of these, some of them are dated or dateable either by Tennyson's own inscription or by that of the bookseller, and all contain poems which Tennyson is known to have written between 1833 and 1835. *Morte d'Arthur* and *Thoughts of a Suicide* (that is, *The Two Voices*) were in circulation amongst Tennyson's friends by the beginning of 1835, and the Trinity notebooks contain versions for every, or nearly every stage of their composition. They also contain rough drafts of some of the earliest lyrics of *In Memoriam*, and these poems appear, in fair copy, in James Heath's Commonplace Book in the Fitzwilliam Museum. James Heath was for many years a friend of Tennyson and his Commonplace Book contains poems by all the poets in Tennyson's own set, Arthur Hallam, Tennyson's brothers, and the other Apostles. The Trinity notebooks contain drafts of (*a*) 'Fair Ship that from the Italian Shore', (*b*) 'Thou comest much wept for', (*c*) "Tis well, 'tis something', (*d*) 'When Lazarus left his charnel cave', (*e*) 'This truth came borne with bier and pall', and (*f*) 'The Time draws near the Birth of Christ'. The first three of these are numbered in roman numerals and appear as a sequence. The Heath Commonplace Book has all these poems, except (*f*), and two others, 'With trembling fingers did we weave', and 'The Danube to the Severn gave'. 'Fair Ship that from the Italian Shore' is dated October 6th 1833 and both it, and the other two ship poems, are, I think, written in Tennyson's own hand. These groups of poems represent the Ship sequence, and the first Christmas poems, sequences which were the germ of *In Memoriam*, and if any manuscript represents 'the first jottings' of the poem it must be the Trinity Notebooks, not the manuscript of *In Memoriam* which Trinity received from Hallam Tennyson and Lady Simeon.

The problems of the Trinity manuscript have, recently, been complicated by the emergence of another manuscript of *In Memoriam*. In 1959, a hundred and fifty years after Tennyson's birth, the Usher Art Gallery in Lincoln staged an Exhibition of Tennysoniana. It was an exhibition which, afterwards, became the permanent Tennyson collection at present housed in the Gallery, and included, among other papers, a very fine manuscript of *In Memoriam* lent to the Gallery by the present Lord Tennyson. Sir Charles Tennyson describes this manuscript, in his catalogue of the collection, as almost certainly the butcher's book which Coventry Patmore rescued from the food cupboard in Tennyson's Hampstead lodgings. This is a claim which Lady Simeon also made for the Trinity manuscript, and her claim had not, till now, been challenged. The Lincoln manuscript is, undoubtedly, a 'butcher's book', that is, it is a long ledger bound with a leather spine and heavy board covers of the kind used by Victorian butchers for their accounts. On the verso of the fly-leaf there is a curious inscription enclosed in one of the endless drawings of churches with which Tennyson adorned his manuscripts. It says 'November 3, 4, 5, 1842'. On the verso of the next leaf the book is inscribed 'Hallam and Lionel Tennyson'. It contains about a hundred and five lyrics for *In Memoriam*, and a version of the Epilogue (The Epithalamium for Edward Lushington and Cecilia Tennyson). Some of these lyrics differ radically from the versions printed, and many have variant readings. Certain of the lyrics in the Trinity manuscript are not in the Lincoln manuscript, notably 'When rosy plumelets tuft the larch', and it lacks a number of lyrics in the final sequences of the poem. Again, it does not contain any version of 'Ring out wild bells'. None of the lyrics are numbered though they do follow a sequence similar both to that of the published version, and of the Trinity manuscript. And in both manuscripts a good deal of space, sometimes whole pages, sometimes a sequence of leaves, is left between the poems. The Lincoln manuscript is, however, less heavily corrected than the Trinity manuscript.

The question which at once arises is, of course, what is the relationship between these two manuscripts? What stages in the poem's development do they represent? First, it is quite clear that neither of them represents a final version of the poem. Both T. J. Wise and Richard Hearne Shepherd say that the proof copy of *In Memoriam*, the trial edition which Tennyson circulated among his friends, contained 119 lyrics. Neither of the manuscripts has that many lyrics in it and in both some, at least, of the poems are not written down in their final version. Neither of them contains the Prologue which was, probably, written in 1850. (The manuscripts of this poem are in the Library of Harvard College.) And we may reasonably suppose that there are other manuscripts at least of parts of *In Memoriam* which have not yet come to light. But though we are not yet in possession of all the evidence we may, I think, come to certain tentative conclusions. The Trinity manuscript may be one of two things: it may just possibly be the remnant of the text which Tennyson sent to the printer, or it may be an early attempt to put the 'Elegies' into a coherent order. The position of the Lincoln manuscript is, I think, clearer. It is almost certainly the butcher's book which Tennyson's friends describe in their reminiscences of the poet in the eighteen-forties.

Lady Simeon says that the Trinity manuscript was originally torn scraps of paper. Now it was Tennyson's custom to send the printer pages torn from his notebooks to use as copy. The state of the manuscript presented to Sir John Simeon certainly suggests that it may have been used in this way, and that the missing lyrics were lost in the progress from printer back to poet. The lyrics are in fact numbered and, for the most part, the numbering virtually coincides with that of the final version of the poem, a fact which would seem to indicate that the intervening poems were lost. Unfortunately, there are some significant irregularities in the numbering of the lyrics which make it difficult to maintain this hypothesis. The lyric which is twenty-third in our version of the poem is labelled No. 2 in them, 24 is labelled 4, 26 is labelled 5, and 38 is labelled 6.* These numberings

* These numberings are in Arabic numerals.

are marked in ink, the numberings which correspond to the published versions are marked in pencil, a fact which gives rise to the suspicion that they were added after the poem was printed. This alternative placing of poems, especially of the early poems, strengthens the other possibility, that is, that the Trinity manuscript shows Tennyson's first arrangement of his collection of elegies. And if this is so we can suggest a date for the manuscript. It contains one poem of the group associated with the removal from Somersby, No. cii, 'We leave the well beloved place', but none of the other poems in this sequence. It does not, however, contain the exquisite lyric 'Sweet after Showers, ambrosial air' No. lxxxvi, which we know was written during a visit to Barmouth in 1839. This makes it seem likely that the poems were gathered together into this manuscript sometime between 1837 when Tennyson left Somersby, and 1839 when he visited Barmouth. This is by no means certain: Tennyson may have begun his work of gathering the 'Elegies' together before his family left Somersby, and there is, in any case, a difficulty about the later date. The Trinity manuscript does include 'Do we indeed desire the dead' (li) which Edward Lushington says Tennyson read to him at Christmas in 1841 and described as just written. This is by no means conclusive. It is possible, for the ink in which this poem is written is darker than that used in the rest of the manuscript, that li was added to the manuscript at a later date. The other poem which Tennyson read to Lushington at this time (vi) is not in the Trinity manuscript, and there is some reason to suppose, in the case of the Epithalamium, that the time at which Tennyson read his verses to Lushington was not necessarily the time at which they were composed. For Lushington says that Tennyson's first reference to the Epithalamium was in 1845, and this poem has, in consequence, always been dated in that year. But Cecilia Tennyson was married in 1842, and the poem appears in an early draft in the Lincoln manuscript. Now there is no doubt or difficulty about the date of the Lincoln manuscript. It is labelled November 1842 in Tennyson's own hand. Tennyson probably worked on it for a year or two, but I think we may reasonably suppose that it represents work on the poems between 1842 and the time at which, in the mid-forties, he is described as at work on the 'Elegies'.

Beyond this we cannot, I think, go. But it would seem that we can trace at least three and possibly four stages in the genesis of the poem. The stage immediately after Arthur's death when the lyrics were accumulating in Tennyson's notebooks, a stage between the departure from Somersby and the marriage of Cecilia Tennyson when Tennyson was arranging his material, a stage represented by the Trinity manuscript; and a later stage from 1842 when it is clear from the Lincoln manuscript, that Tennyson was not merely arranging but writing for a completed poem, and the final stages for which we have, as yet, no manuscript evidence. It is obvious that if we could once discover all the manuscripts, and establish their order, we should know a great deal about the genesis of *In Memoriam*. But even the present evidence indicates that the one thing *In Memoriam* is not is a spontaneous, emotional and undisciplined cry of woe.

APPENDIX B

Select Bibliography
Unless otherwise stated the city of publication is London

BIBLIOGRAPHICAL AND TEXTUAL STUDIES

M. J. Donahue: 'Tennyson's *Hail Briton* and *Tithon* in the Heath Manuscript', *PMLA*, LXIV, 1949.

M. J. Ellmann: 'Tennyson: Revision of *In Memoriam*, Section lxxxv', *MLN*, LXV, 1950.

E. F. Shannon, Jr and W. H. Bond: 'LiteraryManuscripts of Alfred Tennyson in The Harvard College Library', *Harvard Library Bulletin*, Vol. X, No. 2, 1956.

R. H. S(hepherd): *The Bibliography of Tennyson.* A Bibliographical List of the Published and Privately Printed Writings of Lord Tennyson, 1896.

R. H. S(hepherd): *Tennysoniana*, 1879.

Sir Charles Tennyson: 'Tennyson Papers', *Cornhill Magazine*, CLIII, 1936.

Sir Charles Tennyson: 'Tennyson's Unpublished Poems', *The Nineteenth Century*, March-June 1931.

T. J. W(ise): *A Bibliography of the Writings of Alfred Lord Tennyson*, 2 vols, 1908 (privately printed.)

MANUSCRIPTS

1. *Manuscripts in the Library of Trinity College, Cambridge*

A. A collection of four manuscript notebooks:

i. *Notebook in imitation leather covers.* Bookseller's mark: Rees Davies/Bookseller/ Lowgate/Hull. Dated in Tennyson's hand. 1833–35. Contains versions of *The Two Voices*, 'With trembling fingers', *Morte d'Arthur*, 'Love Thou Thy Land', 'Fair Ship', Thou comest, much wept for', ' 'Tis well, 'tis something', two versions of 'When Lazarus left his Charnel Cave', 'This Truth came borne with bier and pall', *The Gardener's Daughter* and other poems.

ii. *Another Notebook in red imitation leather covers.* Labelled III. Watermark: J. Green and Son 1832. Contains, *Thoughts of a Suicide, Sir Lancelot*, parts of *The Gardener's Daughter.*

iii. *Notebook in faded orange imitation leather covers.* Labelled XXII. Contains versions of *Tithon, The Voyage,* 'O that 'twere possible'.

iv. *Notebook in less-faded imitation leather covers.* Labelled XXX. Boards marked, Alfred Tennyson, Louth, Lincolnshire, Anno Domini 1833. Contains *St. Simeon Stylites, Ulysses,* and fragments of *The Two Voices.*

B. *In Memoriam.* Fifty-two long narrow sheets, bound by Bedford. Inscribed on the fly-leaf to Lady Simeon. Contains about 70 Lyrics of *In Memoriam* including some not printed in final version of poem, but printed by Hallam Tennyson in the notes to the Eversley Edition. Annotated throughout in pencil, perhaps by James Spedding. A version of *On a Mourner.*

2. *In the Usher Art Gallery, Lincoln*

In Memoriam. Manuscript of the poem written in a tall narrow ledger. Bound in boards with a leather spine. Verso of fly-leaf inscribed Alfred Tennyson, November 3, 4, 5, 1842. On the verso of next page inscribed Hallam and Lionel Tennyson. The property of the present Lord Tennyson. Contains about 106 sections of the Poem and a version of The Epilogue.

3. *In the Fitzwilliam Museum, Cambridge*

The Heath Commonplace Book. A pocket commonplace book, quarto size, with Locke's Index, issued by Taylor and Hessey of Fleet St., London, about 230 pages. Inscribed J. M. Heath, 24th September, 1832. Contains MS. copies of poems by Tennyson, his brothers, Arthur Hallam and other Apostles. Includes Lyrics of *In Memoriam,* ix, xvii, xviii, lxxxv, xxx, xxxi, xix (in that order) *Tithon, The Gardener's Daughter, Ulysses, Morte d'Arthur, St. Agnes Eve, St. Simeon Stylites, Galahad, The Two Voices,* 'O that 'twere possible' and other poems.

WORKS OF TENNYSON

Works: Eversley Edition, Ed. Hallam Tennyson, 9 vols, 1907–8.
The Poetical Works including the Plays. Oxford Standard Authors, 1953.
Poems by Two Brothers, Ed. Hallam Tennyson (Facsimile Edition), 1893.
Poems, Chiefly Lyrical, 1830.
The Early Poems of Tennyson, Ed. J. C. Collins, 1900.
The Devil and the Lady, Ed. C. B. L. Tennyson, 1930.
Unpublished Early Poems, Ed. C. B. L. Tennyson, 1931.
A Selection from the Poems, Ed. W. H. Auden, 1946.

BIOGRAPHY

T. R. Lounsbury: *The Life and Times of Tennyson from 1809 to 1850,* Ed. W. L. Cross, New Haven, 1915.
H. Nicolson: *Tennyson: Aspects of his Life, Character and Poetry,* 1923.
Charles Tennyson: *Alfred Tennyson,* 1949.
Hallam Tennyson: *Materials for a Biography of Lord Tennyson* (privately printed, N.D.).
Hallam Tennyson: *Alfred, Lord Tennyson: A Memoir,* 2 vols, 1897.
Hallam Tennyson: *Tennyson and his Friends,* 1911.

CRITICAL AND OTHER STUDIES OF TENNYSON AND HIS INFLUENCE

P. F. Baum: *Tennyson Sixty Years After*, Chapel Hill, 1948.

A. C. Bradley: *A Commentary on Tennyson's 'In Memoriam'*, 1902.

A. C. Bradley: 'The Reaction Against Tennyson', *A Miscellany*, 1929.

Cleanth Brooks: 'The Motivation of Tennyson's Weeper', *The Well Wrought Urn*, New York, 1947.

J. H. Buckley: *Tennyson, A Reappraisal*, 1960.

T. S. Eliot: 'In Memoriam', *Essays Ancient and Modern* (see also John Killham, *Critical Essays of the Poetry of Tennyson*, 1960).

Hugh I'A. Fausset: *Tennyson: A Modern Portrait*, 1923.

W. E. Gladstone: '*Locksley Hall* and the Jubilee'. *The Nineteenth Century*, XXI, 1887.

Joyce Green: 'Tennyson's development during the "Ten Years Silence" (1832–42)'. *PMLA*, LXVI, 1951.

Graham Hough: 'Natural Theology in *In Memoriam*', *RES*, XXIII, 1947.

Graham Hough: 'Tears, Idle Tears', *Hopkins Review*, IV, 1951.

Humphrey House: 'Tennyson and the Spirit of the Age', *All in Due Time*, 1955.

Humphrey House: 'In Memoriam', ibid.

E. D. H. Johnson: *The Alien Vision of Victorian Poetry*, Princeton, 1952; 'The Lily and the Rose: Symbolic Meaning in Tennyson's *Maud*', *PMLA*, LXIV, 1949.

R. C. Jones: *The Growth of the Idylls*, 1895.

W. P. Ker: *Tennyson*: The Leslie Stephen Lecture for 1909, 1909.

John Killham: *Tennyson and 'The Princess'*, 1958.

John Killham: *Critical Essays of the Poetry of Tennyson*, 1960.

F. R. Leavis: *New Bearings in English Poetry*, 1950.

Stéphane Mallarmé: 'Tennyson vu d'ici' *Quelques Médaillons et Portraits en pied. Oeuvres Complètes*, Bibliothèque de la Pléiade, 1945.

Eleanor B. Mattes: '*In Memoriam*': *The Way of a Soul*, New York, 1951.

W. D. Paden: *Tennyson in Egypt*, Lawrence Kansas, 1942.

G. R. Potter: 'Tennyson and the Biological Theory of Mutability in the Species', *PQ*, XVI.

F. E. L. Priestley: 'Tennyson's Idylls', *UTQ*, XIX, 1949.

W. R. Rutland: 'Tennyson and the Theory of Evolution', *E and S*, XXVI, 1940.

E. F. Shannon: *Tennyson and the Reviewers* (1827–51), Cambridge, Mass., 1952.

E. F. Shannon: 'The Critical Reception of Tennyson's *Maud*', *PMLA*, LXVIII, 1953.

Sir Charles Tennyson: *Six Tennyson Essays*, 1954.

Basil Willey: *Nineteenth Century Studies*, 1949.

BACKGROUND

A

T. H. Carlyle: *Collected Works*, Ed. H. D. Traile, 1896–99.

R. Chambers: *Vestiges of the Natural History of Creation*, 1844.

Charles Darwin: *On the Origin of Species*, 1859.

Charles Darwin: *Autobiography*, 1958.

Arthur Henry Hallam: *Writings*, Ed. T. V. Motter, New York, 1953.

Sir Charles Lyell: *Principles of Geology*, 1830–33.

F. D. Maurice: *The Kingdom of Christ*, 1838, Modern Edition, 1958.

F. D. Maurice: *Theological Essays*, 1853, Modern Edition, 1957.

F. D. Maurice: *Christmas Day and Other Sermons*, 1843.

F. D. Maurice: *Sermons on the Sabbath Day*, 1853.

B

Mrs W. H. Brookfield: *The Cambridge Apostles*, 1906.
G. S. Faber: *Jowett*, 1957.
J. F. Maurice: *The Life of F. D. Maurice*, 1884.
W. R. Nicholl and T. J. Wise: *Literary Anecdotes of the Nineteenth Century*, 1895–6.
J. C. Reid: *The Mind and Art of Coventry Patmore*, 1957.
A. and E. M. S(idgwick): *Henry Sidgwick: A Memoir*, 1906.
J. Symons: *Carlyle: the Life and Ideas of a Prophet*, 1952.
A. N. Terhune: *The Life of Edward Fitzgerald*, New Haven, 1947.
Wilfred Ward: *Aubrey de Vere. A Memoir*, 1904.

C

Noel Annan: 'The Intellectual Aristocracy', *Studies in Social History*, Ed. J. H. Plumb, 1955.
Joseph Baker, Ed.: *The Reinterpretation of Victorian Literature*, Princeton, 1950.
Asa Briggs: *The Age of Improvement*, 1959.
J. H. Buckley: *The Victorian Temper*, 1952.
The Cambridge History of the British Empire, Vol. II, *The Growth of the New Empire 1783–1870*, 1940.
J. H. Clapham: *An Economic History of Modern Britain 1815–1915*, 1930–38.
F. E. Faverty *et al.*: *The Victorian Poets: A guide to research*, Cambridge, Mass., 1956.
M. Goodhart, Ed.: *Nineteenth Century Opinion*, 1951.
E. Halévy: *A History of the English People*, 1924–1940.
C. Singer: *A History of Scientific Ideas to 1900*, 1959.
Mrs Cecil Woodham Smith: *The Reason Why*, 1953.
E. L. Woodward: *The Age of Reform*, 1938.
G. M. Young: *Victorian England*, 1936.

INDEX I

A

Ainger, Canon Alfred, 72
Albert, Prince, 148, 152
Aldworth, 20, 151, 220
Allegory and symbol, Tennyson's use of, 34, 42–46, 52, 59–60, 64, 68–77, 121, 214–217, 267
'Apostles', 50–52, 62, 65, 66, 77, 128, 166, 231
Arabian Nights, The, 28
Arnold, Matthew, 1, 153, 195, 209, 248, 250–251, 269
Arnold, Dr Thomas, 249, 269
Arthur, King, 12, 25–26, 122, 134, 139, 158, 184–188, 190, 193, 208, 214, 228 (see also *Idylls of the King* and *Morte d'Arthur*, Index II)
Athenaeum, The, 50
Auden, W. H., 1, 5, 7–8, 24, 255
Augustine, St, 230
Austen, Jane, 150, 252, 253; *Mansfield Park*, 190
Australasia, 163–164

B

Barmouth, 89
Barrett, Elizabeth, 148, 254
Baudelaire, Charles, 6; *Fleurs du Mal*, 11
Baum, P. F.: *Tennyson Sixty Years After*, 4 n.
Bayons Manor, 79
Beattie, James, 253
Beddoes, Thomas, 248
Blackwood's Magazine, 51

Bourne, Aunt, 104–105
Bradley, A. C., 2, 3, 80, 88, 98–99
Bridgwater Treatise, 102
Bright, John, 181
Bristol Riots, 160
British Academy, 2
Browning, Robert, 248, 253; *A Death in the Desert*, 224; *Karshish*, 93
Buckley, J. H.: *Tennyson, A Reappraisal*, 4 n.
Buffon, Comte Georges, 102
Burke, Edmund, 167, 170, 177, 252
Burne-Jones, Sir Edward, 268
Burns, Robert, 46, 194
'Butcher's Book', 90–91
Byron, George Gordon, Lord, 34, 169, 192, 252, 253, 267; *Childe Harold*, 267

C

Cambridge, 7, 34, 49–52, 55, 78, 86–87, 102, 103, 150, 235, 253; Conversazione Society, *see* 'Apostles'; King's College, 236; Newnham, 249–250; Trinity College, 91 (*see also* Trinity notebooks)
Canada, 162–164
Carlyle, Thomas, 129, 174–178, 185–187, 252; *Heroes and Hero Worship*, 186; *Past and Present*, 175
Chambers, Robert: *Vestiges of Creation*, 102, 104, 116
Chartists, 127, 128, 135
Christian Socialism, 177
Churchill, Sir Winston, 191

INDEX II

Tennyson's position as the official
Victorian Bard and his popularity with
his contemporaries did his posthumous
reputation no good. The Laurel Crown
identifies him with the myth of 'Victorian-
ism'. Besides, he was a romantic poet,
introverted and solitary by temperament,
and moodily musical in his poetic talent:
his place as the Laureate must, a later
generation decided, have been a bought
place, bought at the price of his poetic
integrity.

Miss Pitt suggests that this is a picture
out of focus. Tennyson was a successful
Laureate precisely because he was a
Romantic poet, sensitive to the terror of
change and formlessness which lay behind
the façade of Victorian respectability. The
Laureate passion for social, even for domestic order, and the sense of a moral and
prophetic mission were not, in Tennyson,
a denial of the mystical intuitiveness of
his youth. On the contrary, they represent
the attempt, though not always the successful attempt, to communicate to his
own generation the sense of order in chaos
which was the fruit of his own experience
in the death of Arthur Hallam. Tennyson
discovered the shape of emotional experience *through experience,* and this brooding
over his own intuitions, the brooding of
them into shape, is the secret of his method
as a poet.

[*continued on the back flap*